LEONIDAS AND THE KINGS
—— OF ——
SPARTA

Illustration 1. Artemis Orthia (from lead figurines in the Spartan Museum) (Pamela M. Bradford)

LEONIDAS AND THE KINGS
—— OF ——
SPARTA

Mightiest Warriors,
Fairest Kingdom

Alfred S. Bradford

Illustrated by
Pamela M. Bradford

PRAEGER

AN IMPRINT OF ABC-CLIO, LLC
Santa Barbara, California • Denver, Colorado • Oxford, England

Library of Congress Cataloging-in-Publication Data

Bradford, Alfred S.
    Leonidas and the kings of Sparta : mightiest warriors, fairest kingdom / Alfred S. Bradford.
        p. cm.
    Includes bibliographical references and index.
    ISBN 978–0–313–38598–8 (cloth : alk. paper) — ISBN 978–0–313–38599–5 (ebook) 1. Sparta (Extinct city)—Kings and rulers. 2. Sparta (Extinct city)—History, Military. 3. Leonidas, King of Sparta, d. 480 B.C.   I. Title.
DF261.S8B7   2011
938′.9—dc23   2011027594

ISBN: 978–0–313–38598–8
EISBN: 978–0–313–38599–5

15 14 13 12   2 3 4 5

This book is also available on the World Wide Web as an eBook.
Visit www.abc-clio.com for details.

Praeger
An Imprint of ABC-CLIO, LLC

ABC-CLIO, LLC
130 Cremona Drive, P.O. Box 1911
Santa Barbara, California 93116-1911

This book is printed on acid-free paper ∞

Manufactured in the United States of America

To my daughter Alexandra

Contents

Illustrations, Maps, and Tables

Illustrations

Maps

Tables

Preface

In Sparta one day Aristotle and I were having a glass of wine.

"Stephan'," Aristotle said to me, "do you know . . . what is *haros*?"

We were at a table in the courtyard of a restaurant called *en Hatipi*. Michael, the owner, and his friend, "Nicholas of Sparta and Toronto" were sitting with us. Michael poured some more wine as I replied,

"No . . . " I thought Aristotle had said *hieros*. " . . . saint?"

"No, *bat*. They say when you die the bat comes and gets you, but never in the mountains, not in the big mountains, here the *haros* can not get you."

As we were sitting beneath Taÿgetus—the highest mountain range in southern Greece—this information was both pertinent and appropriate.

(Later I looked up the word, *haros*, or, to be exact, *charos; charos* is not *bat* but *Charon*, the ancient ferry man of souls transformed into the angel of death.)

Michael told us of a man who sought immortality in the mountains and disappeared from human view. "Nicholas of Sparta and Toronto" added,

"Spartans today say that the Taÿgetus mountain range is male and the Parnon range . . . "

He gestured in the other direction.

" . . . is female, because Taÿgetus is rugged and hard while Parnon is mild and friendly."

Aristotle passed me the end of the loaf of bread and said, "Eat it, Stephan'. It will make you love your mother-in-law."

We all drank a toast to her and then to the mountains and then to Sparta, and to Laconia—the territory of Sparta—and to the ancient Spartans and finally one more to King Leonidas.

Aristotle was my driver and he—like many Greek men—had been born with a double-dose of personality, so that he usually dominated whatever group he was with, but not in this place. In this place the dominant personality was Taÿgetus.

Aristotle raised his glass, "To the king . . . Taÿgetus."

As I sipped my wine—made by a friend of Michael's—I reflected upon my travels up and down the valley of the Eurotas River, the ancient "hollow Lacedaemon," home of the Spartans, set between the impenetrable barrier of the Taÿgetus mountain range and the "mild" Parnon range, easily crossed and hard to defend.

I proposed a toast, "To the kings of Sparta. For six hundred years they led the Spartans in battle. For six hundred years they kept the loyalty of the people of Laconia. For six hundred years they risked their lives to defend their realm."

And so we drank a last toast to a day when we would all meet again at Michael's restaurant below the peaks of Taÿgetus to celebrate the publication of this book—*Leonidas and the Kings of Sparta*.

Introduction

The little town of Sparta (population today some 25,000 people) was chosen as the location for the world premiere of the movie *300*. In the movie, Leonidas, the king of Sparta, is the lone hero who inspires the Spartans—and other Greeks—to fight the Persian invaders. The movie was so popular that it influenced Greek public opinion about the American war in Iraq—"Once," Greeks said, "we were the men who defended the West against the East. Once we had heroes like Leonidas." In fact, in this regard, the movie had it right. Leonidas was, indeed, the driving force behind Greek resistance, he did lead his elite guard of three hundred to Thermopylae, and he did decide to stay there and die for the good of Sparta and Greece.

Leonidas ("Son of a Lion") and his fellow king Leotychidas ("Luck of a Lion")—Sparta had two kings and two royal families—were the commanders-in-chief of all Greek forces fighting the Persians on land and sea. The Spartan kings were the only commanders acceptable to all the Greek allies, both because no other Greek state was as powerful as Sparta, but also because no other Greek leader had the prestige of a Spartan king.

They were the aristocrats of the aristocrats: members of Sparta's two greatest families, the Agiads and the Eurypontids, who were believed to be the descendants of the most powerful, most famous, and most revered of all Greek heroes, Heracles, the son of Zeus. And, of course, they were descendants of Zeus, too, and thus they were related to his other sons, Castor and Pollux, the twins. The twins, one mortal, one divine, as the Spartans believed, watched over the kings and guided and protected them on the battlefield: the twins' symbols—two caps and two stars—became the symbols of the two kings, and the kings were believed to be closer to the gods than were any other living mortals. To oppose the kings' lawful commands was sacrilege.

The kings were expected to use their special, semidivine insight, their experience, and their common sense to analyze omens, portents, and prodigies, the flights of birds, the behavior of animals, earthquakes, and thunder, dreams, oracles, a sneeze, or the shape of the sacrificial animal's liver. When seers rushed to King Leotychidas to report a terrible prodigy—a serpent coiled around the key of the temple gate—Leotychidas said, "That's not a prodigy. A prodigy would be . . . the key coiled around the snake."

The kings' most important sacred duty was to determine the will of the gods and, in particular, the will of the king of the gods, Zeus, their ultimate progenitor, before they led the army out of Sparta and out of Laconia. The kings conducted sacrifices in Sparta to Zeus the Leader and to Athena and the other gods associated with Zeus. They observed the soothsayer as he conducted the sacrifice and examined the liver, its general shape, its texture, and its lobes; then they would determine if the omens were favorable. If they were, the kings instructed a Spartan known as the "Fire-Bearer" to light a torch at the altar and lead the army to the border of Laconia; at the border the kings again would conduct sacrifices to Zeus and Athena. If they determined that the omens were still favorable, then, and only then, would they lead their army across the border.

The kings stood between their people and the gods—to recognize and avert, or circumvent, divine displeasure and to curry divine favor. If the resident god of a river forbad them to cross, could they go around without risking divine retribution? If the enemy declared a certain month sacred, only to prevent an attack by the Spartans, could the Spartans ignore the declaration? If they were shaken by an earthquake while they were on campaign, was the earthquake a warning to the Spartans or an ill omen for their enemies?

On the day the kings expected to fight, if they had detected no cautionary signs, they initiated the religious ceremonies preparatory to a battle—they sacrificed to the Muses (to invite them to witness the courage of the Spartans and to inspire poets to write about their heroic deeds); and they sacrificed a goat, not to examine its liver, but simply to offer it to the gods as a treat. After they had completed these preliminaries, they ordered the Spartans to form their phalanx, and, at the first sight of the enemy phalanx, they instructed their men to put wreaths on their heads (as portents of victory), and they told the flute-players to play the royal battle song, "The Song of Castor," and they sang it, too.

The kings were the first on the battlefield and they were the last to leave; they fought in the front of the phalanx with an elite bodyguard of three hundred men, the best of the Spartans. Once, a Spartan athlete refused a bribe to throw an event, and when he won the prize of victory—a simple wreath—his opponent jeered at him, "So, Spartan, what profit have you gotten from your victory?" He replied, "I have won the right to fight in front of my king in battle." No other honor among the Spartans compared to the honor of displaying their courage before their kings and no disgrace was so great as living when the king died on the battlefield. The bodyguard was there to give their lives to preserve the life of the king.

The kings' bodyguards swore an oath to fight to the death, never to desert their kings, or their unit, nor to leave anyone on the battlefield unburied, and all swore to remain on the battlefield until led away by their kings. Their legendary courage on the battlefield was because, a king explained, "We have learned not to be afraid of our kings, but to revere them."

The kings were the high priests of Zeus and they presided at all sacrifices offered on behalf of the state. They were presented with the hides of the sacrificial animals. They received one piglet from every litter of pigs. They had the place of honor at all city feasts and they received a double portion of food.

The kings were the judges of last resort.

They had their private estates and their royal estates and they had parcels of land in the territory of every village in Laconia, an enormous holding, but one which—when challenged to tell exactly how much property he really did have—a king described as, "Just enough."

These parcels of land did provide them with income, but they also provided them with an interest in the lands of all the free Laconians, whose loyalty the kings depended upon.

When the kings arrived at dinner—they dined together with the Spartan men every evening—all the men rose to their feet.

When a king died, the cavalry carried the news throughout the whole of Laconia. If the king had died abroad, his body was packed in a barrel of honey and brought back to Sparta for special funeral rites.

From the earliest kings, who established Spartan power, to the last kings, who, for a time, revived Spartan power, the kings exemplified the best of the Spartan ideal.

"Here's to our king," the Spartans sang, "beloved of Zeus. He led us to victory."

Names and Terms

The name of the city (polis) was Sparta; the name means "sown" or "seeded" and it appears in the *Iliad*. Sparta the polis was located in the Eurotas River valley, which was known as the "Hollow;" the area encompassing the farms of the Spartans, and the most fertile area of Laconia, was called Lacedaemon or "Hollow Lacedaemon." The Eurotas River—*eurotas* means "flows well"—never dried up. Lacedaemon was part of the larger geographical entity, Laconia. (Laconia is to Sparta what Attica is to Athens, Boeotia to Thebes, and the Argolid to Argos.)

The Spartans called themselves "Lacedaemonians" and the term was extended to include everyone, Spartan or not, who was eligible to fight in the phalanx with them, including Spartan residents who were not full citizens and also free Laconians. The name of their state was "The Lacedaemonians" and when they put up a memorial to those brave men who were killed at Thermopylae they called them the "Lacedaemonians." Among the Lacedaemonians were those who had gone through the complete training required for citizenship, could vote in the assembly, were eligible to hold office in Sparta, and were members of the evening messes. These were called the "Spartiates." In this book I call "the Lacedaemonians" "the Spartans," since we use that expression much as the Spartans used the expression "the Lacedaemonians" and I will use "Spartiates" to designate the full citizens who had all rights and privileges.

The villagers were called the *perioeci*, a word which means "those whose households (*oikoi*) are around (*peri*)" and which is usually translated with the awkward expression, the "dwellers around," but we will call them the "Laconian neighbors." The Laconian neighbors, as "Lacedaemonians," gave their loyalty to the kings.

ELIS

ARGOLID

ARCADIA

Pamisos River

MESSENIA

T
a
y
g
e
t
o
s

M
o
u
n
t
a
i
n
s

Eurotas River

*La ce-
dae mon*

P
a
r
n
o
n

M
o
u
n
t
a
i
n
s

LACONIA

Messenian
Gulf

Acritas
Promontory

Laconian
Gulf

Taenarum
Promontory

Malea
Promontory

CYTHERA

Map 1. The Southern Peloponnesus (Alfred S. Bradford)

Map 2. Southern Greece (Alfred S. Bradford)

Map 3. Greece and the Aegean (Alfred S. Bradford)

MACEDONIA

Mt. Olympus

Mt. Athos

CHALCIDICE

THESSALY

Artemisium

Eretria

Thermopylae
Delphi

EUBOEA

Thebes

BOEOTIA

Marathon

Megara

Athens

Corinth

Carystos

Argos

Salamis

Aegina

Sparta

Cythera

MEDITERRANEAN SEA

Map 4. The Greek Peninsula (Alfred S. Bradford)

—— PART I ——
THE DORIAN WARS

Table 1. The Kings of the Dorian Wars

Heracles
Hyllos
Cleodaeos
Aristomachos
Aristodemos

Eurysthenes   Procles

Eurypontid Royal House	Agiad Royal House
Procles (930–)	Eurysthenes
[Soos] (–895)	Agis I (930–900)
Eurypon (895–865)	Echestratos (900–870)
Prytanis (865–835)	Labotas (870–840)
Polydectes (835–805)	Doryssos (840–815)
Eunomos (805–775)	Agesilaos I (815–785)
Charillos(775–750)	Archelaos (785–760)
Nicandros (750–720)	Teleclos (760–740)

Kings highlighted in bold. This book follows the dating scheme of W. G. Forrest, *A History of Sparta*, London, 1968. The dates can only be speculative and approximate guesses.

Illustration 2. Heracles (from a Spartan coin) (Pamela M. Bradford)

1

By Bus to the "Hollow"

I was going to Sparta by bus . . . my first trip there . . . 1979. As I boarded the bus in Athens, I noticed, first of all, that the driver had a television screen adjusted so he would be able to watch it as he drove. Oh well. I took a window seat and settled in, but soon a passenger, who had paused briefly beside me and mumbled something unintelligible, came back with the conductor, the conductor gestured for my ticket, pointed out a number on it, pointed to the number on the seat I was in—not the same number—and conducted me to my proper seat. The Greek passengers laughed at me. Every Greek knows, and foreigners don't, that bus seats are reserved. When the bus pulled out the conductor punched the tickets, did his paperwork—a task beneath the dignity of the driver—and distributed little plastic bags to the ladies, so they could discreetly throw up. Ladies in buses, boats, trains, and cars prove their delicacy by vomiting. From time to time the conductor would collect a bag and toss it out the door.

Not far below Athens we crossed from one geologic zone to another, and then, a few miles farther on, near the isthmian town of Megara, we entered a third. The Greek penisula was produced by the collisions of three major tectonic plates—the African plate is moving counterclockwise against the southern edge of the Eurasian plate (from which arise the Alps) and simultaneously is forcing its way northeast under it. The Arabian plate is pulling away from Africa and moving northward, colliding with, and pushing, the Anatolian platelet west—so that, in effect, the Aegean region is being shoved southwest and at the same time is being lifted and twisted by the meeting of the Eurasian and African plates. In plain English Greece is just one big jumbled mess.

South of Megara we crossed to the Peloponnesus. In ancient times this spot was marked by a pillar inscribed "Ionia here, not peloponnesus" on the north side and on the south side, "Peloponnesus here, not ionia." The word "Peloponnesus" means "Pelops' island." The designation "island" was then only figuratively true, although then, and even now, the inhabitants of the Peloponnesus—the Peloponnesians—were considered a separate people with a distinct personality . . . in a country chock full of people with distinct personalities. Today, thanks to the Corinth Canal, the Peloponnesus has become, in fact, an island.

South of the Corinth Canal is the city of Corinth. In ancient times Corinth was famous for its prostitutes and the visit of St. Paul. It is a city in a particularly active section of a particularly active earthquake zone. Tremors you can't even feel cause file drawers to slide open as if by magic; slightly stronger tremors, you feel as an uncertainty in walking, quite ambiguous if you have just knocked back a couple of ouzos at the local taverna; but, if you are unlucky, you wake in the middle of the night—a train (or, a couple of millennia ago, Poseidon's chariot and his team of horses) is rushing through the earth beneath your bed, shaking the room: walls crack, plaster falls, the building heaves.

Past Corinth, as a friendly gesture to the American passenger, the driver played an American song on his tape deck—"Does Your Chewing Gum Lose Its Flavor on the Bedpost Overnight?" And then the highway passed into a new geologic zone before we turned east through Argos to Nauplion across another zonal boundary. I spent two nights in Nauplion, during which time I drank retsina from a bottle sealed with a metal cap, climbed the thousand steps of Palamidi, ate gyros, and discovered, as an innocent bystander waiting his turn at the front desk, that prostitutes expect to get a lower room rate than tourists, and, if they don't, they use forceful language filled with modern Greek words I could only guess at. The next day I resumed my travel back across the boundary of the geologic zone into a new zone on my way to Sparta.

The bus wound its way up a mountain and then down into a postage-stamp-sized plain and then up we rose again, winding around the grey stone mountains, their slopes in late April covered with wild flowers and scraggly trees, mountains with—I would say—"majestic, snow-capped peaks," but which geologists describe as "limestone and marble fragments stacked over metamorphosed clay and basalt." (Basalt is volcanic and heavy; limestone and granite are—comparatively—light, and thus float to the top.) I had a moment to reflect upon this truth before we wound up another mountain, whipped around a curve past an over-turned truck, its wheels still spinning, and then down into a tiny green plain through a dusty little town, on past the ancient poleis along a fifty-mile stretch of road—Lerna . . . Cenchreae . . . Hysiae . . . Tegea . . . Manthyria . . . Eutaea . . . Aegys . . . Carystus . . . Sellasia. . . . Truly, the Greeks who farmed these tiny plains ate, not all they wanted, but all they had.

We passed the ruins of Tegea (an early rival of Sparta) and the mountain where the god Pan was spotted by the Athenian runner on his way to Sparta with the news that the Persians had landed at Marathon. The runner ran the distance from Athens to Sparta (about 150 miles) in two days. A car can drive from Athens to Sparta in two-and-a-half hours. An army can complete a leisurely march from Sparta to Athens in six days.

"Sparta's too close," an Athenian said, when he saw the first map ever in his life, "Move it farther away!"

We pass into a new geologic zone (the Gavrovo zone) encompassing all the southeast corner of the Peloponnesus, and, at last, into Laconia; Laconia in area is about 1400 square miles (3600 square kilometers) or approximately one-fifth of the Peloponnesus. Rain is not abundant, but the Eurotas River never runs dry. After the tiny valleys we had traversed, the plain of the Eurotas River looked immense. Eleven miles long, six miles wide, "Hollow Lacedaemon" is one of the most beautiful spots on the face of the earth and has been considered an amenable place to live for over eight thousand years. It has a long dry summer (made drier by the Taÿgetus range) and a mild, moist winter. A pastoral people could graze the slopes of Taÿgetus in the summer and the valley in the winter. "Up in May, down in October," modern Spartans say. Fields of flowers, citrus groves, olive, cypress . . . and flocks of sheep . . . passed by the windows of the bus. The fields and the mountain slopes were green.

"Spring!" the ancient Spartan song goes. "Green is the wheat and there's nothing to eat."

Sparta today is a small town of 25,000 people, without spectacular ruins, much as the Athenian historian Thucydides, described the Sparta of 2400 years ago.

"If the city of Sparta was suddenly deserted, but the shrines and the building foundations were left, people who came here many years later would not believe that the Spartans had been so powerful as has been reported, although they directly controlled two-fifths of the Peloponnesus, they were the leaders of the rest, and they had many other allies besides, because they did not found and settle a polis with temples and extraordinary buildings, but they live in villages according to the old ways of the Greeks and so the ruins would appear poor."

Evenings I would sit on the balcony of my hotel room, which looked towards the Taÿgetus Mountains. The famed, "good-flowing" Eurotas River had disappointed me, an American familiar with the Missouri and the Mississippi, and had seemed to be a stream rather than a river, and sometimes, in the heat of the summer, not much more than a creek. On the other hand, the Taÿgetus Mountains were more impressive than I had expected. They were snow-capped in May—I have seen snow on them in June and a shepherd told me that the snow sometimes lingers into July. I watched the sun go down behind the mountains and the swifts and swallows flit through the roof antennas of other buildings while I ate bread and cheese and olives, drank a glass of retsina, and wondered if there were any better place in the world to eat supper than beneath the Taÿgetus mountains on a pleasant day in the month of May. If only I had, somehow, been able to sit at a table with the Spartans of long ago and listen to their conversation.

Another evening I sat in the dusk on the acropolis of Sparta. The word *acropolis* is misleading—Sparta had no impressive outcropping of rock, no natural refuge, like the acropolis of Athens or the Acrocorinthus. Its security depended upon the Spartans controlling the whole of the large, fertile plain of Laconia and all the mountain passes of Taÿgetus and Parnon. The Spartans themselves defended the one pass across Taÿgetus but they depended upon the loyalty of the Laconian villagers—the other Lacedaemonians—to defend the Parnon range and the rest of Laconia.

2

"Tell the Spartans . . ."

2006. I met my driver, Aristoteles Tollis, at the front desk of the Hotel Leda after breakfast. Aristoteles was having a conference with the desk clerk and two young men about where to take the American tourist and what to see. One of the young men asked me, "Do you speak ancient Greek?" and he recited the epitaph (memorized by generations of Greek school boys) for the Three Hundred—*a angelon Lakedaimoniois.*

Go tell the Spartans, you who pass us by,
That here, obedient to their laws, we lie.

We drove over to the office of the ephor of Sparta and Laconia, K. Vasilogamvrou, a young woman whose task it is to manage the antiquities of Laconia, investigate, and try to prevent, looting (for sale in the black market), maintain the historic sites, promote tourism, publish monographs, and encourage academic activities, in part, by receiving visiting scholars like me. Mrs. V. was friendly, courteous, and helpful.

We discussed the modern city. In a paroxysm of ancient patriotism, the founders of the modern city had build it exactly on the site of the ancient city—a precious notion which has about put an end to the archaeology of ancient Sparta—archaeologists can't run an exploratory trench through the middle of the city—and it has also made new construction nearly impossible. You (a Spartan of today) start digging and unearth some antique object and then you wait for the archaeologist to certify the site for further work . . . or not. As the wait can stretch out to a year, you are better off just throwing the object away or selling it to a tourist.

Mrs. V. was suggesting places I should see when she got a phone call. Someone had unearthed what looked like it could be a Mycenaean site and she had to rush before the looters heard of it. Twenty-seven years before, my conversation with the ephor of that time—Elene Kourinou—had been interrupted in exactly the same way—looters at a Mycenaean site. Apologies, goodbye, good luck.

She has a tough job made tougher by understaffing and inadequate funding.

"Athens gets all the money," Aristoteles said, "We are all still paying for the Olympics, and yet all Athenians want to move to the country."

I could understand why Athenians would want to live in Laconia. We drove south between the Parnon range (highest peak 6350 feet), which forms the eastern promontory, Malea, and the Taÿgetus mountain range, which forms the central peninsula of the Peloponnesus, the Mani, and has the highest peak (7897 feet) in the Peloponnesus. On this morning the Mediterranean climate was at its best: sun and blue sky and moderate temperatures, the valley green and fragrant between the mountains rising on both sides. I consulted my geologic guide and said,

"Hey, Aristoteles, did you know that the valley of the Eurotas is a *neogene graben?*"

"*Graben*? What is a *graben*?"

"No idea, but let's see: *neogene* comes from Greek, *neo* new and *gene* extended family or kinship group, while *graben* appears to be German and related to English *grave* so perhaps it is something dug, such as a ditch or a trench. So, I guess, the valley of the Eurotas is a 'new kind of trench.' "

Digging deeper into the book, however, reveals that *neogene* means a "recent geologic age" (*recent*—that is, twenty-five million to two million years ago) during which the continents drifted to their present locations, the mountains were formed, and the Mediterranean filled with water. So the Eurotas valley is a trench—geologists call it a "depression"—created as the Parnon and the Taÿgetus ranges pull away from each other and thrust upwards while, simultaneously, the land between them sinks.

The Eurotas River rises to the north in a district in Arcadia, flows down through the mountains, debouches into the Spartan plain about three miles north of the city, and continues through "Hollow Lacedaemon" to the sea. We followed the river through the olive groves of Sparta and past the village of Amyclae where the temple of Apollo and the shrine of Hyacinthos are located. Hyacinthos was worshipped as a deity of death and rebirth long before the Spartan polis was formed, perhaps before Greeks inhabited Laconia at all. The Spartans worshipped Apollo Hyacinthios at a throne depicting the ascent into heaven of Hyacinthos and his maiden sister Polyboea ("a girl worth many cattle").

In the month (*Hyacinthios*) when the hyacinth blooms, the Spartans celebrated the *Hyacinthia*, a festival to honor—according to their story—the beautiful young man who won the deadly love of Apollo. Alas—*ai ai* in Greek—Apollo was so smitten with love that he lost interest in everything else except impressing the boy with feats of godly strength. He threw the heavy iron discus farther than any mortal could throw it, and the boy ran after it, to mark it and bring it back, but the discus ricocheted from the hard earth—some say that the jealous West Wind blew it off course—struck the boy in the head, and killed him. His blood flowed into the earth and from his blood there grew a white flower; on the flower Apollo wrote AI AI with the boy's blood.

We drove through citrus groves and vineyards. Laconian wines are not famous now nor were they ever, unless being famously bad is fame. Even mixed according to ancient custom, one part wine to three parts cold water, they were not pleasing to the palate; but Spartans were not supposed to drink for pleasure. They had to be able to make their way home in the dark after dinner without a torch or suffer the consequences: loss of citizenship.

About three-and-a-half miles south of Sparta we passed an ancient quarry of grey marble and then we veered west away from the Eurotas River to the port city Gytheion and beyond, into the deep Mani, where the sea spray cracks the rocks, winter snows close roads, every mountain looks different, you can smell the sea, no matter where you are, and the only crop that can be grown for profit is the olive. We saw prickly pear, a few goats, cows, and beehives. Of course, there is fishing, and, in ancient times, quarries of red and white marble. The Mani has too little rain for grapes and wine ... and life in the Mani is hard, but the Maniotes love their rugged land: as the poet says of another rugged land,

There is no wide plain for horses to run nor any meadow. It is a place to nourish goats— and more lovely to me than any land that rears horses....

We stopped abruptly to talk with an elderly lady dressed in black. She had a ready smile and in a couple of minutes she told us her life story—her husband had died "two years ago next Sunday," she had two children, her daughter helped her husband on his fishing boat, her son had a little moving business, she was fine, and she was walking to town.

We took a break in the picturesque village of Gerolimenas—the whole of Laconia, and the Mani in particular, is spectacularly photogenic—and I stood by the little harbor and faced west, where, to my left, the tip of the mountain range ran into the sea and to my right as far as I could see, was a fault scarp (ten–twelve feet high) of an earthquake that shook the Mani some thousands of years before Sparta was settled. One quarry, at the very tip of the peninsula, is not far from the cave where Heracles was said to have descended into the underworld to fetch back Cerberus, the three-headed hound of hell.

The next morning, after what seemed to me to be a violent confrontation between Aristoteles and a half dozen Spartan cab drivers but which turned out to be a discussion about the best routes, we started up Taÿgetus. Taÿgetus, because of the composition of its rock, resists erosion and is a formidable barrier of steep slopes, deep gorges, and lofty peaks, which bear snow sometimes into the summer. In ancient times its slopes were heavily forested up to the tree line. Except for one tortuous pass, it forms an impassible wall between Laconia and the district to the west, Messenia. Laconia gets half the rainfall Messenia does, because this mountain barrier blocks rain from the west. The distance by road up and over, from one side of the mountain range to the other, from Sparta in Laconia to Kalamata in Messenia, is thirty-six miles.

Twenty-seven years earlier I had gone by bus. We wound up and around curves with spectacular views . . . or dangerous drop-offs, depending on your degree of confidence in the driver. The trees grew sparse and my nose tickled with the altitude and then we came to an unexpected turnaround. The bus stopped and everyone took their luggage and got off. No explanation at all. "*La-te, la-te*," a little old lady in black said to me and pulled my arm. She pointed at my backpack so I took it and I followed her off the bus. We had reached the demarcation between Laconia and Messenia and a Laconian bus dared not cross it, so all the passengers had to transfer to a Messenian bus . . . and pay another fare. I don't know how many times I was saved by ladies in black—then the only respectable Greek women who could talk to strange men. Now, twenty-seven years later, I was traveling in style . . . or, at least, in a yellow Athens taxi.

At the base of Taÿgetus we crossed the fault scarp left by the Great Earthquake of 464 BCE. We stopped to examine the rocks, fractured, twisted and broken. The slopes of Taÿgetus were bathed in sunshine and the highest peaks were wrapped in cloud. The whole ride took about two hours—you could almost drive to Athens in the time it takes you to go from Sparta to the Messenian city of Kalamata.

"Now," I told Aristoteles, "the Spartan army is marching up Taÿgetus to conquer a little Messenian border town and begin the conquest of the whole of Messenia."

How long would it take an army to climb up to the border village and surprise it at dawn with its gates open? The trail, as it would have been then, is about fifteen to twenty miles. Twenty miles on the level can be covered by an army, packs and all, in some eight hours—if the soldiers are in condition. The Spartans would have been carrying some sixty pounds of arms and armor up a steep and arduous route. Even so they could have left Sparta in the afternoon and arrived at the Messenian town about dawn.

We drove into mist and then out again. The day became cool and breezy. The tints of green and the shape and color of the rocks shifted. We could see fracture lines; rock falls are common. We drove through a tunnel, past gorges, with almost no traffic, no people. Aristoteles suddenly stopped and backed up to a spigot gushing water.

"Here," he said, "we drink Taÿgetus."

The water was cool and fresh. And then we wound down Taÿgetus and before us was the plain of Messenia—"Messenia, good to sow and good to plow"—larger and more fertile than the plain of the Eurotas and just the sort of place to be coveted by a powerful neighbor.

We descended to Kalamata. In 1986 Kalamata was shaken by an earthquake of a magnitude estimated at 5.8. The earthquake destroyed a large part of the city and caused a section of the riverbed of the Pamisos River to drop half a meter. (By contrast, the Great Earthquake which struck Sparta is estimated to have generated fifty times that amount of energy.) The city was a cacophony of beeps and shouts, it had too many cars and too little parking, the air was humid and heavy and hot, it smelled of diesel, and the coffee and pastry were overpriced. We could not wait to get on the road and go back up the mountain.

At *En Hatipi* that evening I was explaining to Aristoteles and Michael the ancient Sparta custom called the *xenelasia*—the "driving out of strangers"— when the king or the ephors would decide that there were too many outsiders in town and they would order them all to depart.

"Villagers today see the world as 'us' and 'strangers.' They are different, . . ." Michael said.

The monumental scale of Taÿgetus, its looming presence, its changing appearance, its palpable personality, can lead to strange thoughts.

"They don't come to the city—they don't want to talk with you. Some, they think the mountain will perhaps take them inside, hold them, and make them without death."

After dinner I went for a stroll along *Lycurgos Street*, turned north and walked six blocks, crossing *Brasidas, Dioscuri, Thermopylae, Heraclidae, The Three Hundred*, and *Alcman* Street. After visiting the ancient theater I returned by walking east across *Lysander, Agis,* and *Leonidas* up to *The Three Hundred* and *Constantine Palaeologus* and back to *Lycurgos*. I walked from one end of Sparta to the other in half an hour.

Shop signs on the main street announce that the shops are owned by "Agis" and "Agesilaos" (names of famous Spartan kings) and the owners assured me that they were, indeed, descended from the kings of old. The Spartans, they said, fled up the slopes of Taÿgetus to get away from the Goths in CE 396 and they stayed in the mountains for fourteen centuries until the last invaders, the Turks, went home; then they ventured again into the Eurotas valley and refounded Sparta.

Our last day-excursion was to Monemvasia ("the Gilbraltar of Greece"). We drove beside, and, eventually, through, the Parnon range ("the Queen"), through prosperous orchards. We saw olive, orange, lemon, grape. . . . Laconia was justly praised to its king,

"Menelaus, you are the master of an ample plain, in which the fragrant sedge grows in your meadows and wheat, the white and the red, and barley, too, grows everywhere."

We stopped for a coffee.

"Greeks drink their coffee slowly, slowly, or your stomach will hurt."

I took a little sip.

"Okay, drink your coffee, we have to go."

He delivered me to the causeway into Monemvasia and I wandered the narrow streets for a few hours. Whatever moves in Monemvasia, moves through muscle power. I sat beside the blue sea and under the brilliant blue sky, which set the buildings in sharp clarity, and I thought about muscle power. All the work in the territory under Spartan control, all farm labor, all tasks in the city, building and fetching, hauling and carrying, cooking and serving, all were done by the state-owned slaves, the helots, and all their work was done with muscle power.

I strolled back over the causeway to join Aristoteles at the coffee shop and we drove back to Sparta by a different route, stopping now and then to ask directions and have a conversation. Just so an ancient traveler would stop to ask the way to Sparta or how to get to the next village—and pause to hear the other's story and to tell his own.

Laconia is not a large district. From Sparta to the port of Gytheion is some twenty-five to thirty miles, depending upon your route, and would be a good day's stroll. For people used to walking, Sparta to Gytheion and back again on the same day is perfectly possible. From Gytheion to the tip of Taenarum, and the shrine there, is some thirty to forty miles and, given the terrain, would be a full day's hike. From Sparta to the last significant village on the eastern peninsula (Malea) is about sixty miles. From Sparta to the northern border of Laconia is about twenty miles. From Sparta east to the Aegean coast is about forty miles as the crow flies—but there is no direct or easy route. From Sparta a good walker could probably reach any spot in Laconia in one long day on foot, certainly in two, and a horseman could carry news to any place in Laconia within one day.

The sun rose over the mountains at 6.30 A.M. On our last day we went to the Menelaion, possibly the site of the residence of the Mycenaean rulers—it offers, as do so many Mycenaean sites, a panoramic view of the surrounding territory, "hollow Lacedaemon." From here the last Mycenaean rulers watched the invaders—the future Spartans—ravage and pillage their land.

We also visited the shrine of Artemis Orthia—an odd shrine in that it is located in a low and marshy place rather than on a height (and, therefore, closer to the gods above). Orthia appears to have been an independent goddess who was later identified with Artemis as Artemis Orthia. Her cult statue was a small wooden image with a thirst for human blood, and her cult, perhaps the oldest cult unique to the Spartans, was associated with them and celebrated in a unique way.

The festival featured a procession of youths disguised as women, girls disguised as men, fabulous creatures, and an air of licentiousness. (Representations of these figures are found as dedications in the sanctuary of Artemis Orthia.) Here teenage Spartan boys ran a gauntlet for a prize of cheese—they rushed the altar and tried to grab pieces of cheese while older boys whipped them and tried to drive them away. The boy who got the largest chunk won. A priestess held the wooden cult statue of Artemis Orthia. If the goddess was pleased with the spectacle her statue remained light and easy to hold, but, if she wanted more blood, her statue became heavy, it sank, and the guards knew that they must bear down with the whips. The sturdy boy who could absorb the most punishment had a good chance of winning, but so did the sly boy who waited for someone else to be the center of attention before he slipped to the altar and grabbed the cheese. In Roman times this spectacle drew so many tourists that the Spartans put up bleachers. One visitor said that he saw a boy die under the lashing.

This is Laconia, the land of the Spartans, the valley of the Eurotas nestled between the Taÿgetus and Parnon mountain ranges, "hollow Lacedaemon."

3

The Sons of Heracles

If we could dine at Sparta, 2500 years ago, we would be greeted by the oldest member of the syssition *(the mess); he would point to the entrance and say, "Through that no word goes out." We would prefer to sit at the table of one of the kings—they had tents to themselves—where we might have a roast of venison from the day's hunt, rather than just the Spartan staple, the Black Broth (pig's blood, vinegar, and salt). A foreign ruler tasted it, spit it out, and exclaimed, "It's horrible!" The cook told him, "Well, if you want it to taste good, you have to exercise in the Spartan gym and then take a swim in the Eurotas River."*

As we sip the inferior Laconian wine with these dark-haired, long-bearded men—their upper lips were shaven—dressed in the simplest garb, we might want to ask a king, as a "stranger" had, why do Spartan men avoid glamorous clothes and personal adornment and yet spend so much time on their hair. And the king might answer, "Hair is cheap." Finally, we would have our chance to ask, "Who are you Spartans, where did you come from, how did you settle here in Laconia, why do you have two kings, and why do you live the way you do," and they would tell us the story of heroes of long ago, of Perseus and Heracles and Heracles's children, of dynastic disputes, murders, and meals of human flesh, of the loves of Zeus, king of the gods, and the jealousy of his queen and sister, Hera. They would tell us . . .

Once upon a time . . .

. . . a prophecy was given to the king of Argos—his name was Acrísius—that his daughter, Danäe, would have a son who would kill Acrisius. Acrisius shut Danäe up in a tower and refused ever to let her leave. Every day she climbed the stairs to the top of the tower where she wept under the open sky. And there, on the top of the tower, the king of the gods, Zeus, saw her, fell in love with her, and poured down on her in a shower of gold. King Acrisius was furious when he learned that his daughter was pregnant, and when she had a son—Perseus—he locked them in a chest and had it thrown into the sea. The sea, however, at the behest of Zeus, carried the chest safely to the shore of an island where Perseus grew to young manhood.

Perseus had many adventures: he killed the three-headed gorgon and decapitated Medusa—one look from her was enough to turn a man to stone—and he rescued the princess Andromeda from a ferocious sea monster—but, after a life of adventure, he decided to return to his grandfather's city, Argos. When Acrisius heard that Perseus was coming, he was afraid and he fled from the city. Perseus went after him, not to punish him, but to assure his grandfather that he felt no ill-will and that he intended him no harm. As far as he was concerned, the prophecy could go unfulfilled. His grandfather was so relieved, and so happy to see his grandson, a hero and the son of Zeus, that he sponsored games to celebrate their happy reunion. Alas, when Perseus took his turn with the discus, the discus slipped from his hand . . . and struck and killed his grandfather.

The prophecy was fulfilled and Perseus inherited the throne of Argos, but he couldn't bear to assume an inheritance stained with familial blood, and he exchanged his kingdom for the kingdom of Tiryns. He ruled Tiryns for a while and then he founded Mycenae ("rich in gold" and the future seat of power of Agamemnon, the overlord of all Greece in the *Iliad*). Perseus's descendants were kings throughout Greece, but his greatest descendant was his granddaughter's son, Heracles. Heracles never became king, though Zeus planned it and wished it.

(Heracles's story is going to require another dip of the cup into the mixing bowl of wine and cool water drawn from Taÿgetus.)

When Heracles's mother was in her ninth month and about to give birth to him, Zeus boasted to the gods, who were gathered together at a feast, that a child of his blood would be born on that day and that this child would be king and the ruler of all men. Zeus's wife, Hera, was infuriated—once again Zeus had had an affair with a mortal woman and now he was throwing it in her face—but she concealed her anger and she teased Zeus: Was he sure? Perhaps he was not so powerful as he thought. Fate might decree differently. Was he really so determined to make his blood descendant king of the Greeks, no matter what?

Zeus became too angry to think things through and he swore a binding oath—on the waters of the river Styx—that the child of his blood born on that day would be king and the ruler of all men. Once he had sworn this oath and could not take it back nor change its wording, Hera fetched the goddess of childbirth, rushed to Argos, and, there, in the seventh month compelled the birth of Eurystheus who was of the blood of Zeus (because he was the great grandson of Perseus). Eurytheus, then, and not Heracles, was born on that day, and so by the oath of Zeus Eurystheus was destined to rule, while the favored child, Heracles, whom Zeus had intended would become king, became the despised—and feared—subject of Eurystheus. Eurystheus set the twelve labors of Heracles . . . and everywhere Greeks have settled, the stories of Heracles's twelve labors are told.

Eurystheus was afraid to give the orders personally to Heracles. And do you know the name of the man he sent to issue the orders?

His name was "Crapper."

Heracles was—and remains—the greatest hero of all of Greece, but, when he died, Eurystheus and his sons drove Heracles's son Hyllus and his grandsons from the kingdom of Argos, pursued them to Attica, and forced them to fight a battle. "The fool," as Homer would say, "because he did not know . . ." that he and all his sons would be killed in that battle. Hyllus, after his victory, thought that now he could reclaim his rightful inheritance, the inheritance both from his father and from his ancestor Perseus, both sons of Zeus, but he was so confident of the justice of his claim that he agreed to fight a champion of the opposition in single combat to the death, the winner to be the ruler of Greece. Hyllus lost.

His surviving sons took refuge with the king of the Dorians. (Doris is a tiny kingdom in central Greece to the north of Delphi.) The sons—grandsons of Heracles—were known as the *Heraclids*, the "sons of Heracles," -id being the suffix denoting "son of" or "descendant of."

We dip our cups again—but do not ask for seconds of the soup—and hear about the oracle at Delphi and the prophecy of "three harvests."

From their new home in Doris the Heraclids sent an envoy to Delphi to inquire if they would ever recover the kingdom that was rightfully theirs. The envoy brought back a prophecy that *after three harvests* they would return and win what was rightfully theirs. Therefore, in accordance with the oracle, three years later they renewed the invasion . . . and they were defeated. Only then did they realize that "three harvests" meant, not harvests of *grain*, but harvests of *men*, or three generations, and so they settled on the land that Aegimius, king of the Dorians, granted them, they enjoyed equal terms with Aegimius's own sons and with his people, the Dorians, and they bided their time, generation after generation.

Meanwhile . . .

After the death of Hyllus and the retreat of the Heraclids to Doris, another dynasty seized the throne of Argos. This dynasty, the second great dynasty of Greece, was founded by Pelops (the Pelops after whom "Pelops's island" was named). Pelops was the son of Tantalus, who was as great a villain as there ever was in Greece, as villainous as Heracles was heroic. Tantalus was on intimate terms with the gods until the night he served them a roast . . . roast Pelops, that is . . . just to see if they could tell that they were eating human flesh. The goddess Demeter ate some of the shoulder. For this crime, and others just as bad—he tried to rape Hera—Tantalus was condemned to eternal punishment in the underworld, forever reaching in vain for fruit to eat, forever bending in vain for water to drink . . . to be—in a word—tantalized.

Pelops was restored to life, his masticated shoulder was replaced with ivory, and he went on to marry a princess whose hand he won by murdering her father. Pelops had two sons, Atreus and Thyestes, who were rivals for the throne which had fallen vacant upon the death of Eurystheus. Atreus won the argument by kill- ing, cooking, and feeding Thyestes two of his three sons—the crime was so grisly that the sun recoiled in horror. Atreus became king and in due course was succeeded by his son, Agamemnon, while his other son, Menelaus, became king of Sparta.

Agamemnon and Menelaus married sisters, Clytemnestra and Helen, the daughters of Tyndareos (the king of Sparta, grandson of Perseus, and friend of Heracles), though Helen, in reality, was the daughter of Zeus. Helen's beauty attracted suitors from all over the Greek world; the suitors wanted her, but they also knew that her beauty could be trouble, so they all swore an oath to support whoever won her hand, if at any time he suffered because of Helen's fatal attraction. And, indeed, Menelaus did suffer because the goddess Aphrodite caused Helen to fall in love with the Trojan prince, Paris, and run away with him, thus precipitating the Trojan War, the deaths of many heroes, and the destruction of Troy.

Menelaus and Helen returned safely to Sparta and oversaw the marriage of their daughter Hermione to the son of Agamemnon, Orestes. Orestes and Hermione had a son, Tisamenos, and Tisamenos was king during the "third harvest" after the first failure of the Heraclids to return to the Peloponnesus.

The Return . . .

The time for the fulfillment of the prophecy had come.

(Greek chronographers figured out that the conquest, or occupation, of Laconia had occurred one-and-a-half centuries after the fall of Troy, or, as we would say, the latter part of the eleventh century [1050–1000 BCE])

The descendants of Heracles—the Heraclids Temenos, Cresphontes, and Aristodemos (with the two descendants of the Dorian king, Dymas and Pamphylos)—had marshaled their forces for the invasion, but, just before they crossed to the Peloponnesus, Aristodemos was killed by a lightning strike and his twin sons, Eurysthenes and Procles, took his place. They crossed the Gulf of Corinth on rafts at its narrowest point, fought Tisamenos, and defeated and killed him in a ferocious battle. Dymas and Pamphylos were also killed in the battle.

The victorious Heraclids drew lots for the most fertile regions of the Peloponnesus—the Argolid, Laconia, and Messenia. Temenos received the Argolid, the twins received Laconia, and Cresphontes (by cheating, it was alleged later) received Messenia.

This is the story the Spartans might have told us.

— 4 —

The First Kings of Sparta

Today some historians maintain that the legendary account of the fall of Mycenae and the resettlement of southern Greece by an invasion of Dorians is a coherent and credible account, which in detail might be wrong, but in outline—a troubled society falling to a foreign, albeit Greek, invader—is no less than the truth. After all, in classical times Dorians were living where the Mycenaeans had once lived and, if they did not invade, where did they come from?

The archaeological record, while not unambiguous, does support this view: Mycenaean civilization was under attack, the major centers were burned and destroyed, fragments of writing refer to "a call up of the chariot corps" and the dispatch of "watchers to the coast" and perhaps human sacrifice, and a defensive wall was built across the isthmus. On the other hand, the destruction seems not to have occurred all at once, as it would have in a massive invasion, but to have been spaced over a century, and, moreover, the whole of the Eastern Mediterranean was under attack, not just Greece. Invaders overthrew and resettled the powerful kingdom of the Hittites in Anatolia and attacked Egypt by land and sea. These invaders, whom the Egyptians called the "Sea-Peoples," were certainly not "Dorians."

Skeptics postulate that the Dorians had always been in the Peloponnesus, but as an underclass which rose up when the Mycenaeans fell apart under the stress of foreign invasion and civil war. Or (as other scholars postulate) they may have taken advantage of the destruction of the Mycenaeans to migrate from the north and occupy a devastated land. The Dorians were, after all, a pastoral people, tied to their flocks, and divided into bands limited in mobility and size by the resources available to them.

"Pastoral," however, can be a misleading term: it evokes words like *idyllic* and *peaceful*, when, rather, it should evoke words like *blood feud, lion hunts, border wars, rustling*, and *woman stealing*.

The Dorians were used to protecting their herds from man and beast. They knew mountainous terrain and they could move in the foothills where the Mycenaean chariots could not reach them and from the foothills they could raid incessantly and keep the Mycenaeans from harvesting their crops. Nor were they helpless against the chariots, even in the plain; just so, in the *Iliad* a hero on foot strikes a charioteer in the head with a rock and jeers as he tumbles to the ground,

"Ah me! You are an agile man, I see—you dive so easily. You could dive in the fish-filled ocean and provide quite a feast, so easily do you dive to the ground from your chariot."

The band that occupied Laconia (according to the legend) was led by twin kings whose descendants formed the two royal families of Sparta—the Agiads and the Eurypontids. Although they were twins, they differed in every regard and they never agreed on anything . . . except to occupy Laconia.

The early kings are little more than names to us, but the names speak of war and ambition—"Strong Everywhere" (Eurysthenes), his son "Leader" (Agis—the namesake of the Agiad royal family), and their successors "Holds the Army," "Shepherd of the Folk," "Spear-Shaker," "Leader of the Folk," "First of the Folk," and "Famous Afar." ("Folk"—*laos* in Greek—denotes the men under arms.) The kings of the other royal house, descendants of the other twin, "First in Fame" (Prokles), are somewhat less militantly named, "Charge," "Heard Afar" (Eurypon—that is, his war cry was heard afar—he was the namesake of the Eurypontid royal family) and their successors, "President," "Deep Understanding," "Law and Order," "Dear to the People," and "Victorious Warrior."

The kings followed a consistent strategy, to occupy and control the central region of Laconia, that is, hollow Lacedaemon, to seal off all passes into Laconia, and to extend their control south throughout the whole of Laconia. Early in the attempts to secure the northern passes, King Soos and his army were trapped in a rugged, waterless place. He offered to leave the disputed land and never return, and he swore sacred oaths that he would do so after the whole Spartan army had taken a drink from a nearby spring. Then he proposed to his warriors—they were all aristocrats,

"If any one of you will refrain from drinking, I will transfer the kingship to you."

But they all drank and, after every one in the Sparta army had taken a drink, and in the presence of the enemy, the king came forward, knelt down by the spring, and splashed his face with water, but he did not swallow any, and so, without fulfilling the terms of the oath which would bind him, he led his army away from that land and later returned to conquer it.

In the early 900s the Spartans expelled the population of Cynuria, a district between Sparta and its major rival Argos, which was using it to launch raids into Spartan territory. The Spartan kings resettled Cynuria with men who were loyal to them and who would defend it from the Argives. These men, and others scattered in villages throughout Laconia, were the "neighbors" (*perioeci*). The kings gave land to the Laconian neighbors and local freedom in exchange for their loyalty and a limited military obligation—primarily to defend their own territory, and the passes leading to Sparta, against raiders. The Laconian neighbors also provided artisans and merchants.

By the middle of the eighth century the kings had secured the two passes to the north between Arcadia and Laconia, they had occupied the Cynurian land on the east coast between the Argolid and Laconia (although they continued to conduct operations against Argos and would continue to do so for the rest of Spartan history), the two kings Charillos and Archelaos had attacked and enslaved the population of Aegys (which they suspected of plotting with the Arcadians), and they had initiated a system of control and domination over the people of Laconia. The Spartans were always at war. The images of their gods, King Charillos explained, ". . . are armed so that we can not accuse them of cowardice, as we do men, and also so our young men would not pray to unarmed gods."

The kings considered the Laconian neighbors' territory theirs to administer, to settle with outsiders, and to set aside for shrines. They did not treat the other inhabitants of Laconia so generously. They reduced the conquered population to the status of state-slaves called *helots*. The Spartans offered two explanations for the word *helot*—one, the word means "captives," which the helots certainly were, or, two, the Spartans had reduced the population of the first conquered town, Helos, to the status of bound laborers, and the particular name of that group, *helots*, was extended to all captives reduced to that status. The Spartans had complete and absolute power over them, and they came to depend upon them for all labor.

The greatest accomplishment of the kings during this early period was the organization of the Spartan polis. They brought together five villages of aristocrats and their followers, including some of the aristocratic survivors of the defeated Mycenaeans. They united the tribes, kinship groups, and households around a central location and they built shrines to the gods there—the Spartans worshipped all of the traditional gods, though sometimes in a unique and peculiar way—and the kings called the aristocratic leaders to meet there to settle disputes and to conduct business.

The kings claimed direct descent from Heracles, the son of Zeus, and the Spartan aristocrats—for that matter, all Greek aristocrats—traced their ancestry back to the gods. They believed that by virtue of their divine blood they had a right, and a duty, to rule; they were the first to risk their lives to defend their polis, their land, their crops, and their flocks. When they fought, they fought as individual champions, trained at their own expense, armed, and armored, like the heroes of the *Iliad*, but, unlike the heroes of the *Iliad*, they learned to cooperate with each other and to accept that they were part of a larger entity, the polis. The two kings ruled in cooperation with a council of older aristocrats called the *gerousia*. The rivalry between the kings gave the aristocrats the opportunity to make their voice heard. The kings created one of the first poleis in Greece.

Under the leadership of King Teleclos ("Famous Afar"—760–740 BCE) the Spartans finished the conquest and organization of the villages of the Laconian neighbors, they drove the last of the Mycenaeans from Laconia and, after a long war with Amyclae—a memorial was still to be seen in the second century CE—they reached a compromise by which the Spartans would accept the Amyclaeans on equal terms and would honor Amyclaean sacred places, festivals, and deities, while, for their part, the Amyclaeans agreed to subordinate themselves to the two Spartan kings.

The Amyclaean leader who accepted these terms was warned, "You will be a sheep among wolves," and so he became known by the nickname, "Sheep-n-Wolf" (Oeolycos). His descendants formed one of the great aristocratic clans of Sparta.

Their organization of the polis, and the arrangement with Laconian neighbor villages, gave the Spartans enormous power, enough to control the whole of Laconia, secure the passes to the north, and confront Argos on equal terms, as the Argive king and aristocracy failed to unite the Argolid the way the Spartan kings had united Laconia.

The kings were the preeminent war leaders, but they also were concerned with the amity and unity of the Spartan aristocratic families and the different generations. King Teleclos defended the custom of younger men standing up in the presence of older men by saying—"They honor their own fathers more when they honor those who are not their fathers." When a Spartan complained to the king that his own father was speaking ill of him, Teleclos told him, "If it was not something that needed to be said he would not have said it."

The single area of dispute which the kings had not resolved was the control of a shrine of Artemis called Limnatis used by both Laconians and Messenians and claimed by both. In the reigns of Teleclos and the Eurypontid king Nicandros ("Victorious Warrior"), Messenian men assaulted some young, unmarried Spartan women participating in a festival at the shrine. When King Teleclos tried to defend the women, the Messenians murdered him. The women killed themselves because of the shame and the Spartans determined to seize the shrine, a nearby Messenian town, and then the whole of Messenia.

—— PART II ——
THE MESSENIAN WARS

Table 2. The Kings of the Messenian Wars

Eurypontid Royal House

Nicandros
|
Theopompos
|
Anaxandridas
|
Archidamos I
|
Anaxilas

Agiad Royal House

Teleclos
|
Alcamenes
|
Polydoros
|
Eurycrates
|
Anaxandros

Eurypontid Royal House	Agiad Royal House
Nicandros (750–720)	Teleclos (760–740)
Theopompos (720–675)	Alcamenes (740–700)
Anaxandridas (675–660)	Polydoros (700–665)
Archidamos I (660–645)	Eurycrates (665–640)
Anaxilas (645–625)	Anaxandros (640–615)

Kings highlighted in bold.

Illustration 3.   Apollo of Amyclae (from a Spartan coin) (Pamela M. Bradford)

5

Over the Mountains

A Spartan who climbed to the top of the pass over the Taÿgetus mountains would see the whole of the Messenian plain spread out below him, broad, green, and so beautiful that it was called "Blessed." Small wonder if he wished it were his, especially as the Messenians did not seem to be formidable foes. The Messenians, as far as we can tell from the material remains (stone implements and no ironware, scant bronze, and little pottery) were still living in the Stone Age. Their land was their wealth. They had not coalesced into a single polis nor did they give obedience to one king or worship at a central shrine, although the aristocrats did identify themselves as "Messenians," when they competed in the games at Olympia. (A list of the victors of the games was kept from the very first contest in the year 776 BCE and the first victors were Messenians.)

Olympia had become a major religious center by the end of the eighth century and its games, held every four years in honor of Olympian Zeus, drew competitors, spectators, and celebrants from all over the Peloponnesus. The footrace, the *stadion* (equivalent to a two-hundred-yard dash), was the major event, but Greek aristocrats came here to meet and mingle . . . and to impress each other. Here the Spartan kings and aristocrats lay claim to the leadership of the Peloponnesus by their displays of power and wealth. They brought their own bronze smiths and supplies of bronze, they set up their own smithies, and they dedicated the bronze tripods cast on the spot—bronze tripods had a particular force in religious observation and practice in this era in Greece. They competed with, and surpassed, their chief rival, the Argives, in the lavishness of their dedications.

The Spartans intended to conquer Messenia and displace the Messenian aristocrats. They had their ancient claim that the Messenians had won their land through fraud and they had an immediate cause, the rape of the Spartan girls and the murder of their king by men from the village of Ampheia. The Messenians offered to submit their grievance to arbiters, but the Spartans refused, because the

Messenians insisted that the arbiters come from their ally, Argos. Nonetheless, the Spartans hesitated to act so long as the Messenians could depend upon the Argives. Then, opportunely, Argos was drawn into a war—the Lelantine War—between the two greatest seagoing powers of that time, Chalcis and Eretria (poleis on the island of Euboea).

The Lelantine War was fought over a plain, known as the "Lelantine Plain," which lay between the two cities. Chalcis was famous for its spearmen and the two opponents—aristocrats with ideals straight out of the *Iliad*—agreed not to use long range weapons against each other; they enlisted allies from all of Greece, and they fought upon the plain with thrusting spears and swords. Their war lasted about as long as the Trojan War and it had profound effects on the balance of power in Greece. Corinth replaced Chalcis and Eretria in the western Greek world and dominated the west with colonies and trade. The oracle at Delphi predicted correctly that Chalcis would win and, thereby, enhanced its own prestige. Argos supported Eretria.

As Argos became too involved in the Lelantine War to help the Messenians, the Spartan kings, Alcamenes (the son of Teleclos) and Theopompos (son of Nicandros), decided to begin their subjugation of Messenia with a surprise attack on Ampheia. As far as they could they made their preparations in secret and they imposed an oath on the Spartan aristocrats that neither the length of the war, if it was not decided in a short time, not any reverses, even if there were great ones in the war, would turn them away before "they had conquered with the spear and possessed the Messenian land." Once they had taken this oath, King Alcamenes led them out at night against Ampheia. He had a personal grudge against the Ampheians, because they had murdered his father Teleclos.

Ampheia was a small Messenian town near the Laconian border. It lay on a high crest with permanently flowing springs of water and was a convenient place from which to prosecute the whole war, but it was also difficult of access and easy to defend . . . so long as its guards were alert. The Spartans, therefore, made their approach in the dark. They each bore some sixty pounds of arms and armor, they arrived just before dawn, and they waited. The gates opened and they charged, knocked aside the guards, and seized the town. (This first attack, ancient chronographers calculated, occurred in the second year of the ninth Olympiad, "when Xenodocos a Messenian won the *stadion*," or, as we reckon it, 743 BCE.)

This war was fought between the aristocrats of Sparta and the aristocrats of Messenia. Messenia, like all Greek societies of this period, was divided into two classes, the few aristocrats and the many who were not aristocrats. The non-aristocratic class was tied to the land and to the aristocracy in one way or another. In different regions of Greece they had different names, but their condition was the same: subservient if not servile. The Spartans planned to conquer Messenia by harassing the Messenian aristocracy, until they fought a battle, and then to break them, kill as many as they could, and drive the rest from their villages and, eventually, from all of Messenia. A Spartan victory, which drove the

Messenian aristocracy into exile, would leave the rest of the Messenians to serve their new Spartan masters.

Even after the Spartans seized Ampheia, the Messenians could not believe that the Spartans intended to wage war on them. They asked the Spartan king, as he was leading the army into Messenia,

"Are you really going to lead your army against your brothers?"

"No," he said, "I'm just going to walk through their territory to the land that is vacant."

For three years the Spartans harassed the Messenians. They conducted raids throughout Messenia, drove off the herds and flocks, carted away grain and fruit, and carried off whatever could be carried off, but they did not chop down trees or burn down buildings, because they intended to occupy this land and they already thought of it as their own. They succeeded in their initial plan: they forced the Messenian aristocrats to abandon their villages and concentrate in the northern part of the Messenian plain called Stenycleros (the name means "narrow lot"). The Spartan raids also forced the Messenians to work together and to subordinate themselves to a king. The Spartans hoped, next, to force the Messenians to fight a battle, but after one cavalry skirmish, the Messenians withdrew into a fort and refused to come out and fight.

The Spartans were discouraged and they returned home, where the older men reviled them, called them cowards, and reminded them of the oaths they had sworn, so that a year later the two kings, Theopompos the son of Nicandros and Polydoros the son of Alcamenes (who had died during the war), led another expedition. And this time, when they offered battle, the Messenians did come out to fight. The stakes were clear: for the Spartans, conquest, for the Messenians, survival.

We do not know any of the details of the fighting in this battle, but we do know that battle in this period was particularly brutal.

Two disorganized lines approach each other, the polished bronze armor glittering in the sun, and men throw their spears or throw the rocks they pick up on the battlefield. A great roar arises—the screams of the wounded and the war cries of the men who struck them down. Helmets and shields ring under the impact of stones. Deep notes reverberate as spears glance off the rims of the shields or the armor. The two armies meet. They smash their shields against each other's shields: the shields, spears, and the bronze-armor of the warriors themselves clash. Men suffer horrible wounds. The earth runs with their blood. Ankle bones and tendons are shattered—a wounded man falls to the ground, helpless, while the enemy close around him and jab him in the belly with their spears. His intestines pulse out on the ground.

Another man is hit below the nipple, and the spear pierces his lung, but he clings to life until an enemy stabs him in the belly with a sword. A spear, hurled through the air, strikes a man on the nose beside his eye—the point smashes through the bone into the back of his mouth, cuts off his tongue, and protrudes from the back of his head.

The shield and body armor protected the torso, but left the legs and the face partially exposed. A common place to be wounded was through the helmet's eye slits . . . struck under the eyebrow in the socket of the eye. The spear pierces the eye socket and sticks out the back of his head while the force of the blow causes the eyeball to pop out of its socket.

Skulls are smashed. Another man is struck in the mouth. The spear point passes through his skull, under the brain, breaks the bones, shatters his teeth and fills his eyes with blood—blood gushes from his nostrils and his gaping mouth. Belly wounds are common, if the shield is knocked to one side and the breastplate is too short or not strong enough. A spear thrust between the navel and testicles was said to inflict the most painful wound a man could suffer.

No wonder that some soldiers tried to surrender, to be held as hostages until they could be ransomed by a parent or friend, but surrender was risky, because the prisoner was completely at the mercy of the captor and some captors had no mercy. One cut off his prisoner's hands and head and kicked the body so it rolled like a boulder. Both sides tried to recover their fallen comrades, because the enemy did not necessarily respect the dead and might decide to take a head as a trophy and feed the body to the dogs.

Such was the nature of battle in the time of the Spartan invasion of Messenia.

In this first battle between the Spartans and the Messenians, the Spartans tightened their ranks and fought in a disciplined manner, and the Messenians charged individually and recklessly. King Theopompos on the right wing tried to close with the Messenian king and fight him hand to hand but was driven back. King Polydoros on the left wing finally forced the Messenians opposite him to retreat but darkness prevented any pursuit. Though both sides suffered heavy casualties, both sides refused to concede defeat, but neither side had the will to resume the battle the next day. In the end both sides collected their dead under a mutual truce and the Spartans withdrew.

The Spartans had not won the battle, but they did not have to win the battles to win the war. They only had to make life insupportable for the Messenian aristocrats, and they were succeeding. The Messenians were worn down by the fighting. They were low on supplies and could hardly support themselves and their garrisons in the different villages in Stenycleros. They were losing their slaves and serfs to the Spartans, and they were stricken by plague and famine. Consequently, they decided to abandon their villages in the plain, settle on Mount Ithome, and there make their last stand.

The Messenians sent to Delphi to ask for advice and received this oracle:

> A virgin girl to the powers below,
> chosen by lot from the blood of the noblest clan,
> in a nighttime killing, sacrifice her.
> Or if you would sacrifice from another house,
> sacrifice if he gives willingly for the killing.

The Messenians chose one girl, but her father ran away to Sparta with her. They chose another girl, but her fiancé claimed that they had had intercourse and she was pregnant . . . and so not a "virgin girl." Her father was so furious at the slur that he killed her himself and cut her open to show that her womb was empty. Thus the father proved that his daughter was a "virgin girl" and in the process she was killed, but had she been "sacrificed?" Since no one else was willing to give up a daughter, the Messenians decided that this death fulfilled the oracle.

The Spartans knew about the oracle and, when they heard that it had been fulfilled, they were discouraged. They let five years pass before they decided to risk another battle with their whole army against the Messenians in Ithome. Once again the two armies fought, champion against champion, from morning to evening. The Messenian king, who had reigned for the thirteen years of this war, was fatally wounded. The Spartans and the Messenians fought over his wounded body, but the Messenians managed to drag him back to their side, where he died.

The Messenians now had to choose a new king and, after a heated argument, they chose the man who had killed and butchered his own daughter. In the fifth year of this new king's reign, both sides, exhausted by the long war, agreed to fight one more battle to decide the war. The Spartans and the Messenians again fought through the course of a whole day, fought with slingers and archers, heavy infantry and light infantry, in lines of battle and individual combats. Both sides suffered heavy losses, but in the end the Messenians held the field and the Spartans retreated. Most of the Spartans were discouraged and ready to quit, but King Theopompos decided to appeal one last time to Apollo at Delphi and Apollo's sacred priestess, the Pythia, gave him this response:

> Apollo bids you not only to carry on the battle with your hands,
> but the people hold the Messenian land by guile.
> With those same crafts it will be captured as it began.

The oracle convinced the kings to continue the war, even though they had now been fighting for twenty years. The Pythia also gave a response to the Messenians:

> To those who first set up tripods around the altar
> of Zeus of Ithome, to the number of twice five tens,
> the power grants glory in war and the Messenian land.
> So Zeus ordains. Fraud set you up before
> and now punishment is after, you will not cheat god.
> Do what must be done. Some will be destroyed and others not.

A Spartan named Oibalos learned of the oracle. Oibalos was not a member of one of the more distinguished families in Sparta nor had he accomplished anything particularly notable in his life, but he was a sharp thinker. He fashioned a hundred tripods of clay, hid them in a bag, took up some nets and, as far as anyone knew, left Sparta to go hunting. The Messenians suspected nothing and he was able to enter Ithome in the evening mixed in with the farm workers. When night came, he set up the tripods to the god and then returned to Sparta and told the Spartans that he had fulfilled the oracle.

Now omens revealed the impending doom of the Messenians. The bronze Artemis dropped her shield. The dogs gathered together every night and howled, and finally the whole pack ran off to the Spartan camp. The Messenian king told the Messenians that he had a prophetic dream and then he committed suicide. After the king's death the Messenians hung on for five months, but as the year drew to a close, they abandoned Ithome. They had been at war for twenty years in all, as Tyrtaeus, the Spartan general and poet who lived two generations after the war, writes:

Here's to our king, who has pleased the gods, our Theopompos. He it was under whom we conquered broad Messenia, Messenia, good to plow and good to sow, over which we fought for nineteen years, those warriors, fathers of our fathers—they put courage in their hearts and never faltered—and in the twentieth year the enemy left the rich land and fled from the massive peaks of Ithome.

(The twentieth year, according to ancient chronographers, was the first year of the fourteenth Olympiad, that is, 724 BCE.)

Tyrtaeus describes the harsh conditions the Spartans imposed upon the Messenian helots.

> Like asses worn with great and painful burdens,
> bearing for their masters under bitter necessity,
> half of every fruit as much as the land bears.
> Crying aloud for their masters, yes, their wives and themselves,
> Whenever the destructive fate of death came on someone.

The change to new masters did not necessarily worsen the condition of the agricultural workers in Messenia, but their situation was clear: they were protected by no law, or custom, and they could be killed with impunity. As a Spartan told an impudent helot—the story is supposed to illustrate Spartan self-control— "If I were not angry I would kill you."

The Spartans by their conquest had doubled the amount of fertile land they possessed, but they had to control a large subject population—the helots—and they also had made inveterate enemies of the exiled Messenian aristocrats, who settled throughout the Peloponnesus and passed on their enmity to their sons and grandsons.

The Lelantine War and the conquest of Messenia were the prelude to the great, two-hundred-year struggle between Sparta and Argos for the control of the Peloponnesus.

— 6 —

Shoulder to Shoulder

The Spartan conquerors of Messenia led an almost idyllic life. They had a surplus of wealth. They lived in one of the most beautiful places on the face of the earth, the Eurotas Valley. During the day they competed with their fellow aristocrats in athletic events, the javelin- and discus-throw, wrestling, and the "hundred yard" dash, they went hunting in the foothills of Taÿgetus, they toured their estates, and then they gathered together in the evening to drink some wine, eat an ample, but measured, meal of bread, olives, cheese, grapes, and blood soup, and, as the sun dropped behind the high, snow-capped peaks of the Taÿgetus mountain range, they conversed.

The one threat to their easy life was the discord created by a group of nobly-born Spartans whose very existence seemed to be an impossibility. These children of the nobles had been born during the Messenian War when the Spartan men had sworn an oath not to return to Sparta until they had conquered Messenia—twenty years—and yet, nonetheless, their noble wives had continued to give birth to children. Who could the fathers of these children be? . . . Certainly not forsworn Spartan aristocrats. . . . Or helot-lovers taken by lonely wives. . . . Or anyone else. These children could not be excluded from a share in power—they were the children of aristocratic mothers—and they could not be included—they were as illegitimate as they could be—and so they were designated *Partheniai*, the "virgin births," and, when they grew up, they were sent to found a colony in Italy—Taras (or, as the Romans knew it, Tarentum). Taras became one of the most prosperous and successful colonies in the Greek West.

Sparta was a cosmopolitan city open to the world, "a land pleasing to the Muses," and the homeland of the lyric poet Alcman, who called Sparta "the mother of the Arts." (Alcman was so influential that his dialect, the Doric dialect, became the dialect of choral lyric throughout Greece.) Spartans exported Laconian vases throughout the whole of the Mediterranean and they imported luxuries from

Lydia and Egypt, so that aristocratic ladies—known throughout Greece for their beauty—could dress in the latest fashions. In Sparta aristocratic women were free to appear in public and free to dance in the chorus where all could see their beauty and grace.

"I sing at the light of Agido, like the sun which Agido calls to rise. But our famed choral leader will not allow me to praise her or blame her before she herself is celebrated in my song. For she seems to me to be most like a stallion, seen only in our winged dreams, standing in pasture, firm-set with ringing hooves."

At dinner the Spartan men would discuss the singing, the dances, and the dancers—and the old stories behind the songs. How, once upon a time, before the Dorians returned, Hippocoon was king of Sparta. He drove his brother, Tyndareos, from the throne, but, in the fighting, Hippocoon—arrogant fool that he was—killed a friend of Heracles and Heracles came to Sparta to avenge his friend's death. He seized Sparta, killed Hippocoon, and brought Tyndareos back. (Tyndareos was the father of the Dioscuri, Castor and Pollux, the protectors of the Heraclid kings.)

Now Hippocoon had ten sons: Looter, Shouter, Fighter, Lucky, Stag, Galloper, Ox, Mighty, Brave, and Big. The sons proposed marriage to the daughters of the Old Man of the Sea and they fought the sons of Tyndareos. Alcman wrote:

It is not part of human destiny to woo the goddess of love or the daughters of the Old Man of the Sea. Fate, oldest of the gods, weaves our destiny. Cut down in the might of their youth, by arrow and millstone, they went down into Hades, that evil that each had planned for others and then had suffered themselves. Punishment comes from the gods. He is blessed who passes through his woven day without lamentation, happy in his heart.

The sons of the men who had conquered Messenia must have believed that they, indeed, were blessed by fate, but their sons, in the beginning of the seventh century, saw it all come apart, not by their own faults, but by the ingenuity of an Argive king who transformed Greek society (much against his will). He was the last king of the royal Argive line. His name was Pheidon ("Faithful") and he invented the hoplite phalanx.

King Pheidon understood that if he could create a disciplined formation of heavily armed and armored men he could defeat any old-style aristocratic army. He decided to draft and train men, nonaristocrats, who had become prosperous in the new Greek economies, based on the introduction of coinage and the possibility of making a fortune through export and import. These men were craftsmen, merchants who furnished the luxuries for the aristocracy, and small landowners who were prosperous enough to buy a team of oxen to plow their fields. Pheidon compelled these men to buy the equipment (in Greek, the *hopla*, the "stuff") to arm themselves with the panoply ("all the stuff")—helmet, breastplate, greaves, a thrusting spear, and the most important piece of equipment, the shield (specifically, the *hoplon*). The *hoplon*, the circular shield (weighing between twelve and fifteen pounds), protected its bearer from chin to knee. The whole panoply weighed fifty to sixty pounds (on a man 5′2″ to 5′4″). A man so accoutered—the *hoplite*—was a one-man tank.

Pheidon's innovation, however, was not to put men in armor—hoplites would not have been out of place in the battle line of the *Iliad*—but to put a large number of ordinary men in armor and to train them to fight in a *phalanx*. In the phalanx the men formed eight (or more) lines and each man crowded in next to the man to his right so that his right side would be protected by his neighbor's shield. Thus every man in the formation was protected and, as long as the phalanx did not break, the soldiers were almost invulnerable ... except for the rightmost man. If he was flanked by the enemy phalanx, he was dead, so he guided the formation to the right to edge past the enemy phalanx to avoid being flanked.

A Spartan general described what happens when an army of aristocrats fighting in the old way meets "men who stand their ground. The aristocrats are not up to it. Since they are not in formation they are not ashamed to give ground; retreat and attack are both equally honorable to them and their manhood is never tested (for each individual always has a good excuse for saving himself)."

The limits of the phalanx were obvious—it was designed to fight a battle, not to conduct a siege and not to occupy a territory. Opposing phalanxes were like opponents in a duel, fighting to resolve a specific grievance, rather than enemies determined to conquer or annihilate the other. The objective of phalanx warfare was to dominate the enemy's territory long enough to control his crops, and by controlling that territory, to force the enemy to accept peace terms set by the victor.

Pheidon used the phalanx to win victory after victory and make Argos the dominant power in the Peloponnesus. Pheidon's success persuaded the Messenian exiles that the time was right to liberate their ancestral homeland.

7

"Never Retreat"

The Messenian exiles chose Aristomenes to be their leader and their king. Aristomenes was a natural-born leader, charismatic, aggressive, and courageous. (He became the national hero of the Messenians.) He led the exiles, the grandsons of the defeated aristocrats of the First Messenian War, into Messenia. Their invasion caused the helots to rebel. The invasion and rebellion began the Second Messenian War in the thirty-ninth year after the end of the first war and in the fourth year of the twenty-third Olympiad [685 BCE] when the kings in Sparta were Anaxandros, the grandson of Polydoros, and Anaxilas, the great grandson of Theopompos. The war lasted for twenty years and brought the Spartans to the brink of defeat.

In the first year after the revolt, at a place called Derae, the Messenians fought the Spartans to a draw. The year after the battle at Derae, the Messenians with their allies, the Arcadians and the Argives, fought the Spartans at a place called the Tomb of the Boar (in Stenycleros). The Messenians defeated the Spartans. Subsequently, Aristomenes raided the borders of Laconia and the Messenians composed a song about him:

> To the middle of the plain below,
> and to the mountain peak
> Aristomenes chased the Spartan foe.

The Spartan aristocrats had suffered so many casualties that they lost heart and even considered giving up Messenia, but the kings emulated Pheidon, enrolled men from the nonaristocratic class, perhaps even some helots, to replace the aristocrats, created a Spartan hoplite army, and continued the war. Aristomenes attacked towns in Laconia and drove off cattle. He kidnapped maidens who were dancing in honor of Artemis at one town, but when he attempted to carry off maidens from the sanctuary of Demeter at another town, the women beat him with their burning torches and captured him. The Spartans threw him, and fifty of his comrades, into the Keadas, a chasm into which the Spartans threw condemned criminals. For a time the Spartans congratulated themselves that the rebellion was over, but Aristomenes survived the fall and lay there for three days in despair until he saw a fox feeding on the dead and he realized that the fox must know a way in and out. He caught the fox by the tail and crawled after it, as it tried to escape, until it brought him to its hole to the outside. He resumed the kingship and continued his raids.

In this crisis a Spartan general named Tyrtaeus composed and sang such inspiring and patriotic songs that he persuaded—and shamed—the Spartans to fight on.

"To die for your country is good, . . . to be among the first to fight for your native land. For a man to desert his city and prosperous fields and become a beggar, to have to wander, homeless, with his mother, his white-haired father, his children, and his lawful wife, of all things, this is most wretched. All to whom he comes, to beg for food and shelter, will despise a man like that, who has shamed his ancestors, who has shown his noble appearance to be a lie, who has fled because of his own dishonor and cowardice.

"Now if so little be thought of a beggar, if he gains so little honor, respect, or pity, let us resolve to fight for this land and give our lives. Let us die for our children."

Tyrtaeus addressed the new hoplite army.

"Spartans, show no fear of a multitude of men. Do not flinch. Let every man hold his shield straight forward and make life his enemy and the black spirits of death as desired as the rays of the sun.

"Close with the enemy. Set foot by foot, shield on shield, helmet on helmet. Fight hand to hand with your long spear.

"Let us place our trust in the immortal gods and go forward, obedient and faithful to our sacred king. And all of us soon will level our spears as we stand among the spears our comrades have leveled. How dreadful the noise will be as each line drives their shields up against the shields of the enemy, how awful the screams as soldiers rush upon each other and pierce an enemy's chest with the spear. And we will not retreat because of the rocks, because we are hit by the giant rocks. No, our helmets will protect us from the thrusts of war and we will not give way."

Tyrtaeus's songs reveal the tactical transformation in which individual exploits are less important than collective discipline and cohesion.

"Young men, be loyal to one another when you fight. Do not be the first who flees like a coward, do not be afraid, be brave and stiffen the heart in your breast. Do not love life too much when you meet the enemy, but think of the older men, whose knees are no longer strong.

"Do not retreat and let them fall to the ground, for when the older men, gray-haired already and white, lie mixed with those who have fallen in front, lying there in front of the younger men, gasping out their courage in the dust, and clutching their bloody intestines in their hands—this is dishonor, an ugly sight, a disgrace for eyes to see, especially the naked flesh. But all this is good when a man is young, when he has the noble blood of lovely youth. While he lives, all the men admire him, and all the women love him, and when he lies dead on the battlefield, then is he truly beautiful.

"So let us bite our lips with our teeth and stand with both our feet implanted in the earth."

Tyrtaeus appealed directly to the aristocrats' sense of their innate nobility and their heritage.

"Show courage. You are descendants of unconquered Heracles and Zeus has not yet turned away from us. Do not fear a multitude of men, do not be afraid. Let each man rush to hold his shield in the line and make his life an enemy and the darkness of death as desired as the golden rays of the sun."

Tyrtaeus also appealed to—and gave a new definition to—the nonaristocrats. How should the aristocrats think of them—men who did not train for athletic events, who were not wealthy landowners, who did not practice speaking or dancing or singing? How should they think of themselves? Tyrtaeus introduced a new concept of innate nobility, manhood, and citizenship.

"I would not waste a word upon a man even if he won first prize in track or outwrestled the champ or had the strength and stature of a cyclops, or ran more swiftly than the wind, or had more money than Midas or bluer blood than a king, or had the sweetest voice of any man on earth, or showed me every virtue, every one but courage, for a man should not be considered brave until he has dared to look upon the deadly contest, until he has charged the enemy and struck at him—this is what it means to be a man, this is the greatest prize on earth, and the grandest that a young man can carry off. This it is that profits your fellow citizens and your city.

"He that falls in front and loses his cherished life for the glory of his people, his land, and his father, struck again and again through the breastplate and the shield he held before his chest and through his chest, this man is lamented by the young and old alike and the city weeps for him with bitter regret. His grave and his children stand out among men and the children of his children and their descendants too. Never will his noble fame be lost nor his name forgotten. Though he lies buried in the ground he becomes immortal, if he shows his courage, before savage war destroys him, if he stands fast and fights for his land and his children.

"And if he escapes the talons of death which are clutching at his life and, in victory, wins renown and glory with his spear, everyone, both young and old, will honor him. He will enter Hades after a blessed life. And as he ages he will stand out among the people, every one of whom will respect and honor him. All of them, the young, and those of the same age as he, and even the older men will give up their seats to him. These are the heights of glory each man should resolve to attain. He should never retreat from battle."

Tyrtaeus asserted that combat had ennobled the Spartan hoplites.

By the third year of the war, the Argives had become involved in the northern Peloponnesus and other Peloponnesian powers had withdrawn from the struggle to confront the Argives, and so the Messenians were alone when they fought the Spartans at the place called the Great Trench. There for the first time the new Spartan phalanx fought a battle . . . and it proved itself. The Spartans killed so many of the Messenians that the Messenians despaired of survival. Without their allies they could never match the Spartans in manpower or defeat the new Spartan army in battle. Aristomenes persuaded the Messenians to leave the central plain and to settle in a mountain stronghold. There the Messenians held out for eleven years.

Pheidon tried to rescue his Messenian allies by engaging the Spartans in a battle, Argive phalanx against Spartan phalanx at the battle of Hysiae in 668 BCE. The Spartans were defeated, but, nonetheless, they did not lift their siege of the Messenians, and Pheidon could not follow up his victory because he had to go to the rescue of his aristocratic allies in Corinth. Three years later the Messenians capitulated.

The Spartans, despite their victory, or because of their victory, were thrown into turmoil. The creation of hoplites and the new phalanx had unforeseen social consequences. Every polis in Greece developed a hoplite phalanx and the hoplites—the new class created by the phalanx—clashed with the aristocracy, because the aristocrats wanted to dismiss the hoplites when the war was over. The hoplites, however, had the power to demand political concessions and to receive them, or else.

Some aristocratic governments found an acceptable compromise, but in those poleis where the aristocrats would not compromise, the hoplites used force to put a champion (usually a favorite—and aristocratic—general) in power. Such a man was called a *tyrant*. (The tyrant was a ruler outside the constitution who held his position through force.) In Corinth the tyrant expelled or murdered the aristocrats. In Sicyon (a city in the northern Peloponnesus) the new tyrant promoted his own tribe to power and renamed it the "Rulers;" he renamed the three aristocratic Dorian tribes, "Pigs," "Donkeys," and "Swine." In Athens a century of anarchy, attempted reform, and double-crosses led eventually to tyranny. In the end the tyrants were no more interested in sharing power with the hoplite class than the aristocracy had been, and the hoplites overthrew them, and in most poleis instituted hoplite democracies.

The hoplite reform transformed Greek social and political life. The hoplite class assumed the outlook of the aristocracy on athletics, the ethos of war, and the definition of a good citizen. As men met in the wrestling ground and exercised there for beauty, sport, and war, they formed a bond with each other and they created a way of life—the only way of life—that enabled them to remain physically conditioned for that one campaign and that one battle, in which in twenty minutes they would live or die.

Pheidon, in an ironic twist familiar to all who study history, was killed trying to prevent the new hoplite class in Corinth from overthrowing his friends (the

Bacchiad aristocracy). Pheidon was the last king in Argos. The new hoplite democracies stopped further Argive expansion.

The Spartan kings had had to fill the depleted ranks of the aristocrats with non-aristocrats. Their desperate measures won the war but the consequences threw Sparta into crisis. Aristocrat and hoplite clashed. The aristocrats believed that they were the "best" people, descended from the gods, born (and raised) to rule. The hoplites considered that they had done exactly what Tyrtaeus had asked of them—they had "rushed to hold their shields in the line and make their life an enemy and the darkness of death as desired as the golden rays of the sun." They had heeded his exhortation, they had fought to put down the rebellion, and they demanded their share of land and some participation in the government of Sparta. The aristocracy did not recognize the changed circumstances—that their security, their way of life, and their very freedom, depended upon the new army—and they wanted to maintain their exclusive rights to the land.

The situation could have degenerated into violence very quickly, as similar situations in the rest of Greece had, but Sparta was different; it had kings. The kings had just led the hoplite army to victory, they had enormous prestige, and they stood somewhat outside of society and somewhat apart from the aristocracy, so that they could see both sides of the question. Moreover, the kings had their own agenda—to preserve their own prerogatives, to ensure their position for the future, to ensure the strength and security of Sparta irrespective of any class, and, therefore, to ensure that they retained the loyalty of the instrument of their power, the hoplite army.

In the end the kings were convinced that compromise was absolutely essential and they turned to a man named "Wolf"—Lycurgos.

— 8 —

Deeds of the Wolf

If we could return to our table in the syssitia of the Spartans . . . By now we are no longer repulsed by the black broth or the sour wine, and we can concentrate on the conversation and ask questions. Who was this "wolf" Lycurgos? What does his name mean anyway? Wolf-Worker? Wolf-Hunter? Temper of a Wolf? And what did he do and when did he do it?

Some Spartans at the table will tell us that he lived in the time of the very first Olympic games, but others will tell us that he lived later and reformed the games and instituted the Olympic truce. They will agree that there are "contradictions in every account of him—his family, his voyages, how he died, and, in particular, all his laws and the constitution we call Lycurgan."

They might not even agree on whether he was a man or a god or something in between. After all, when he visited Delphi, Apollo said to him,

> *Lycurgos, here you have come to my wealthy temple,*
> *You who are loved by Zeus and all the gods who live on Olympus.*
> *Are you human or are you divine?—I don't know what to say,*
> *But I think, yes, that you, Lycurgos, are divine.*

And when Lycurgos died, the father of the gods, Zeus, struck his tomb with a lightning bolt.

So much of his story appears to be legend, the telling of it might well begin, "Once upon a time" . . .

Different factions of Spartans—the people, the aristocracy, the kings—were arguing so violently that they had come to the brink of civil war and they sent missions to Delphi to seek some solution. One time the oracle told them that they would be friends again only if they brought the musician and singer Terpander from the city of Methymne in Ionia across the Aegean Sea. Terpander came and played the cither and sang so cleverly, and beautifully, that the harmony of his music brought them to tears and they embraced each other and wept.

Nonetheless, the violence continued. Lycurgos's father was killed by a Spartan sword (shaped like a meat cleaver). He, himself, was a member of the Agiad royal family, uncle and regent of the infant king, Labotas. Lycurgos was accused of plotting against his ward and so he left Sparta and traveled the Greek world to study the constitutions of cities in Crete and Ionia. He wanted to use this knowledge to create a polis that was as harmonious as Terpander's music. The ideal for which he strove is known as *eunomia*, which he defined as "everyone competing to be the best without resenting each other." He composed a constitution and presented it to the god at Delphi. When the god affirmed it, it became the Great Rhetra. (A rhetra is an utterance, in this case, the utterance of Apollo.)

"First [the Great Rhetra reads], dedicate a shrine to Zeus and Athena, then organize the tribes and obes, establish a gerousia of thirty including the kings, assemble at appointed times between the locations of Babyca and Cnacion, to approve or disapprove. The people in assembly are sovereign."

The Spartan poet, Tyrtaeus, in his poem, "Eunomia," presents a slightly different version.

The two kings "heard the voice of Apollo and brought home from Delphi oracles of the god and plans to be accomplished."

"The god-honored kings, in whose care is the delightful city of Sparta, shall lead the council and also the men who are senior and distinguished in birth; and then shall the men of the people (*damos*) reply to their proposals with honorable responses (*rhetras*)."

This simple document, with its clear statement of the people's rights and affirmation of their sovereignty, transformed Sparta into the most advanced democracy of its time. Under its terms the kings retained command of the army and kept their status as cult-leaders, but they ceded to the aristocracy all their civil power in Sparta except for their seats on the deliberative council, the *gerousia*, where the two kings sat with twenty-eight aristocrats, sixty years of age or older, who served for life.

One of the queens complained to her husband, "You are going to leave your son a lesser kingship."

"No, a greater," he replied, "because it will last longer."

The gerousia was the sole deliberative and policy-making body in Sparta and it also tried capital cases. In capital cases, the gerousia would deliberate over several days before rendering a verdict, and, even if they voted to acquit, the acquitted man was still liable to further deliberation and a possible change of verdict. A king explained, "They deliberate for many days because in capital cases if they make a mistake there is no changing it. And the acquitted man must still be liable to the law because it is always possible to reach a better verdict."

The kings and the aristocracy ceded to the popular assembly, as the sovereign body, the right to make the ultimate decisions, but they reserved to themselves an exception: "if the people make a bad choice, the elders and the leaders may set it aside."

The kings and the aristocracy under the Lycurgan reform divided the fertile valley of the Eurotas River, that is, Lacedaemon, and the heartland of Messenia into 9000 lots, each large enough to support an individual hoplite, and they distributed these lots to the men, whether aristocrat or not, who had fought to reconquer Messenia. Under the terms of the Great Rhetra they created and organized (in "tribes and obes") a new class, noble and non, called the Spartiates, that is, the citizens who served in the phalanx and met in the assembly.

The Spartiates—new citizens and old—were enrolled in the three Dorian tribes and then they were divided further into five obes (a uniquely Spartan division based on the five villages of Sparta). Thus they were woven together into the social and religious fabric of the state . . . and then frozen into a hereditary caste. The land they received freed them to live an aristocratic life of leisure devoted to the pursuit of excellence in athletics, music, dance, and war. Anyone who had not participated in the Messenian war, no matter what other qualifications he might have of descent, or wealth, or athletic ability, was excluded.

"If a man has not been brave in war," Tyrtaeus wrote, "if he has not endured the sight of wounds and corpses, if he has not stood close and struck at the enemy, I care nothing about him."

The new system was designed to produce and maintain a cohesive military force whose primary purpose was to dominate and control the helots whose labor supported the members of that force.

"Why do you Spartans put your fields in the hands of the helots?" a Greek asked King Anaxandridas, "Why do you not work the fields yourselves?"

The king replied, "We have them and we keep them because we do not work them."

Every year the Spartans declared war on the helots, so that a Spartiate, any Spartiate, could kill a helot without bloodguilt.

The new system was also designed to produce the perfect hoplite soldier, strong, disciplined, and fearless.

Imagine that you are a hoplite on a brown and dusty field in Greece in the hottest time of summer, a hot bright sun overhead, the temperature is 90 . . . 100 . . . 110 degrees, and four to five thousand men are putting on bronze armor, shifting their shields until they are comfortable, hefting their spears, adjusting their helmets—sixty-five to seventy pounds of equipment. You are in the front line of the phalanx. Your helmet muffles sound and limits your peripheral vision and you have to turn your head to see the other men in line. Are they holding up? Do they look confident . . . or afraid?

> The cowardly man's skin changes color,
> now to this and now to that,
> nor can he stand fast nor is his spirit calm,
> but he shifts from one foot to the other continually

and his heart beats violently in his chest,
as he thinks about his death, and his teeth chatter,
but the brave man does not change color
nor is he unduly perturbed,
and he takes his position quietly in the ranks,
and he wants to get right into the battle.

In the front line are the men in the prime of life who have experienced combat. They are calling out to the rest of the army, encouraging them, testing their war cries, while across the field, two hundred yards away, the enemy army, adjusting their equipment, calls out insults and shouts their war cries, and the watchword passes from right to left along the line and then back again to the right and the rightmost man moves forward. Drums beat on both sides, to keep the lines in time as they move.

Dust rises as the lines begin to jog and then to run. The drum continues to beat but the line becomes ragged. A soldier can not easily see left or right. He keeps looking to both sides to ensure that he is not ahead of the others, but behind him the rest of the phalanx is running and the line is developing gaps. The enemy are running at him and their line, too, has gaps. Their war cries can be heard. You feel a surge of adrenalin and the lines crash together and men jab with their spears and push. Some soldiers already have been wounded in the chest, a spear driven right through shield and breastplate, others have been wounded in the abdomen. They fall. The ground is slippery with blood. You push while the men just behind you jab past you at the enemy and push against your back to break the enemy line. And the enemy push and try to break your line. You have good reason to be afraid, because, if your line breaks, you are dead.

In the back of the formation the soldiers are already asking themselves, are we winning or losing? Are we being pushed back, is it time to think about myself, drop my shield and run? Are the lines getting tired, no longer pushing with their first vigor, and maybe even giving way slightly; if so, you have a decision to make. Stay and you could be involved in a chaotic situation, trapped by panic-stricken men, all trying to get away, and you could be killed, but if you drop your shield now and run, you can get away.

I ran and left my shield behind
left behind for an enemy to find
He will boast but I don't mind
I lived.

On the other hand, when you run, you help the enemy defeat your side and kill your fellow citizens.

In Sparta the expression for cowards, the tremblers (*tresantes*), described more than running away. It described the man who trembled so violently before battle that his armor rattled and also the man whose only sign of fear was the quivering of his lower lip behind his helmet. These were the tremblers, and no one would want to be one or be standing next to one in a battle line. A Spartan who ran away—and there were very few—lost his citizen rights: no one would shelter him, no one would give him food, no one would notice him—he was "dead."

The ideal of Sparta became the ideal of the hoplite, superb physique, training, self-sacrifice, courage, discipline, obedience to the law of the city, and reverence for their leaders.

—— 9 ——

The Spartan Way

All Spartan boys—except the kings' heirs—went through the course of training called the *agoge*.

Lycurgos considered the agoge fundamental to his reforms. He designed it to revolutionize Spartan society, to mix together the sons of aristocrats and the sons of commoners, and to train them all to be Spartiates. He convinced the aristocrats to accept the agoge by a simple demonstration. One day Lycurgos brought two dogs into the assembly. He explained that he had taken them, as puppies, from the same litter and he had raised one to be a pet and the other to hunt. He set out some treats and he released a rabbit: the house pet ran to the treats and the hunting dog chased the rabbit. "So," Lycurgos said, "can you not see that education is more important than birth?"

Under the Lycurgan system a newborn baby was subjected to an examination by the father and the tribal authorities and, if it was not healthy, it was exposed in a prescribed location and left there to die. If it was healthy, it was washed in wine and returned to its mother, who raised her children till their seventh year. At that time boys were enrolled with other boys (born in the same year) in a "herd" (*boua*)—an apt description of a group of boys without education and discipline—and they lived together in a barracks.

Until they were ten they underwent mild physical training, reading, writing, and music consisting mostly of the patriotic songs of Tyrtaeus. The boys were still visited by their mothers. The boys of ten to thirteen began competitive exercises in music, dancing, and athletics. In the next phase, if the boys were deemed fit to continue the agoge after the thirteenth year, they cut their hair, went barefoot, had one garment to last the rest of their training (six years), and they played and exercised naked. Each year from fourteen to twenty had its own designation: "babies," "almost itsy-bitsies," "itsy-bitsies," "boys (first year)," "boys (second year)," "almost an *eiren*"—an *eiren* was a youth in the last year before manhood—and "*eiren*."

The aim of the instruction was to control their energy and direct it into learning how to be a hoplite. They slept on mattresses of reeds which they collected themselves. They roamed Laconia and learned tactics and survival. They were not given enough to eat, so they would have to steal the food they needed—and thus learn to live off the land. They were wild and hungry.

They heard instructive stories: a Spartan boy stole a fox. (Apparently, he intended to eat it.) When an adult approached, the boy hid the fox under his cloak. The fox began to bite into his chest, but the boy never changed expression as he conversed with the adult. He kept talking until the fox gnawed its way into his heart and killed him.

The boys were punished for being caught, not for stealing, and they could be punished by any Spartiate. They were led by the recent graduates of the agoge and they were never instructed by a noncitizen. In adolescence they were not discouraged from forming liaisons with other boys or finding a mentor among the older men—but a sexual relationship with an older man was forbidden. They ate in a mess and were asked such questions as who was the best general. If they answered wrong, their thumb was bitten. They were the best mannered boys in Greece.

At eighteen the boy passed out of boyhood training and entered a provisional period in which he supervised other boys as "herd-leader" (*bouagos*)—perhaps one leader to ten boys—or he joined the *krypteia*. The krypteia was the secret police of Sparta, not used against the Spartiates, but against the helots. The Spartans declared war on the helots every year—so there would be no bloodguilt in killing them—and they employed the krypteia to watch them. The young men would sleep during the day and prowl at night. They killed any helots they found and disposed of the bodies, so no one would ever know what happened to them. They also watched the helots at work in the fields and, any helot who seemed especially big and healthy, or who exhibited leadership qualities, they killed and disposed of. Their objective was to convince the helots that they were under constant observation.

From the age of twenty-one to thirty, the Spartan men lived in barracks as Sparta's ready reaction force. They were forbidden to go to the agora. They were too young to hold office. They were not allowed to have a house, but they were expected to marry, although they had to conduct their courtship in secret. Slipping from the barracks, finding their way in the dark, meeting the woman they loved—thus they practiced those skills of maneuver and stealth which are so important to a soldier . . . and afterwards the "husband" would continue his normal, communal life with the men, returning to the barracks to sleep. The common joke was that a wife often did not know what her husband looked like until he was thirty. After the age thirty the Spartiate could have a household, in fact, he was expected to have children. If he did not, once a year, in the cold months, he had to run around the city, naked, chanting lampoons about himself.

All the Spartiates ate dinner together in common messes, by one account, fifteen to a table, but by another by military unit, the *enomotia*, and all Spartiates had to be a member of a public mess. Each member of the mess had to provide a stated amount of supplies or he was ineligible for the mess:

Seventy-two medimni (ninety bushels) of barley for himself
Twelve medimni for his wife
Fruit, olives, and raisins of an equivalent amount
Wine

To become a member of the mess you had to be approved unanimously by the members of the mess, a much more important decision, if the candidate would be fighting beside you. The members of the mess voted in secret by dropping chunks of bread into a container; if one chunk was squeezed solid, the candidate was rejected. Boys and young men could come as observers and guests at the mess, to see how they should conduct themselves as full citizens. Once in a while, as an object lesson, a helot would be gotten drunk, to demonstrate the evils of over-indulgence.

At the age of fifty a Spartiate no longer had to serve outside of Laconia and at the age of sixty he was released from military service altogether and became eligible for election to the gerousia, which was chosen from "the best of the Spartans."

Spartans wore their hair long, they had full beards, but no mustache—they plucked out the hairs from their upper lip to remind themselves that they had taken an oath to obey the law. They wore a severe cloak, they went barefoot at home, and they lived simple lives in a world without nuance. The Spartans were magnificent physical specimens, men and women both, the most handsome people in Greece, with the best-behaved children. They knew right from wrong and they practiced honor without compromise.

When King Charillos was asked why Lycurgos did not make many laws, he replied,

"Those who speak few words need few laws."

A sophisticated man in a conversation with an ordinary Spartan, at first, might believe that he was conversing with a simpleton who says little, but then the Spartan says something that perfectly hits the mark, as an arrow hits its target, and the sophisticated man seems like a child before him.

A Spartan observed a philosopher embracing a stone column in the winter (to prove that his mind could master his body's sensation of cold) and the Spartan asked him,

"Do you feel cold?"
The philosopher replied, "No."
The Spartan said, "Then what's the point?"

Spartans were as passionate about choral dance as they were about athletics and war and they celebrated their warrior spirit in the choral dance.

Choruses of old men sang, "We once were brave young men."
Serving soldiers sang, "We are brave, here is the proof."
And the youths sang, "We shall be better than you by far."

The Spartans had three major religious festivals devoted to Apollo (famed for his lyre): the Carneia, the Hyacinthia (conducted at Amyclae), and the festival of the Naked Boys (the Gymnopaedia)—a parade in the nude of all the boys and youths in the agoge; they participated in contests, wrestling, boxing, gymnastics, mock battles, processions with fantastic masks and dance. Young women danced and sang before an audience of Spartan men and women.

The Athenian Aristophanes wrote,

"Leave for a time the slopes of beautiful Taÿgetus, Muse of the Laconians, and come sing of the god of the Amyclaeans, worthy of our respect, and the goddess of the bronze temple and the Tyndaridae, who on the banks of the Eurotas take their measures . . . Let us celebrate that particular Sparta that loves the divine choruses, that beats its feet in time on the earth, where processions of young women dance along the banks of the Eurotas."

In Sparta—the Theban poet Pindar wrote—"are the counsels of the older men, the spears of the young, and the choruses, the Muse, and the festivals."

In the seventh century we know of fifteen poets and artists who lived in or around Sparta. In a collection of the eight best, or most representative, poets of this century, three lived in Sparta—Tyrtaeus, who was probably a native Spartan, Terpander, who migrated from Lesbos, and Alcman, possibly a native, who developed choral lyric, a combination of words, music, and dance.

One of Alcman's songs goes,

"Sweet, clear voiced Muse of many tunes and everlasting song, begin a new melody for the maidens to sing.

"Maidens with honey voice so loud and clear, my limbs can carry me no longer. Would, O would I were a kingfisher, such as flies fearless of heart with its mate over the bloom of the wave, the Spring's own bird, purple as the sea."

The Spartans created a new and distinctive form of choral dance—even the heirs to the throne vied for inclusion in the chorus . . . and might not be chosen—and then they repeated it over and over again: when a performer from Miletus added two strings to a lyre, an ephor cut them out.

Sparta was also noted for its ivory carvings and its ceramics. It took an active part in Greek life, exporting and importing, bringing sculptors to Sparta to create statues of their gods and to design and renovate their shrines. They took part in the Olympic games and dominated the games for some decades after the conquest of Messenia.

The Spartans, themselves, produced just about everything they needed, in their homes or on their estates, and for the rest they bartered with the outlying Laconian villages, or through them, from the outside world. They did have a market place—young men were forbidden to go there—but the Spartans outlawed the private possession of coined money. (They used lead spits for small change.)

Although every Greek polis was creating its own mint—the right to coin money came to symbolize independence—the Spartans decided not to establish a mint, not to collect taxes in coin, and not to deposit coins in a state treasury.

"Why not?" a visitor asked King Anaxander and the king replied,

"So that the guards would not be corrupted."

By the middle of the sixth century the outside world had lost interest in Spartan exports, but the Spartiates were famous throughout the Greek world as easy men to get along with and the most aristocratic. On the other hand, Spartan women were considered a disgrace. Instead of being locked away in a room of the house, they exercised in public in the nude, they learned to read and write, to keep the accounts, to run the house. They could own property, they chose their own husbands, and, once they were married, they could take a lover.

A Spartiate was asked what the penalty for adultery was in Sparta and he replied,

> "There is no adultery in Sparta."
> "But if there were adultery, what would the penalty be?"
> "To sacrifice a bull weighing twenty tons."
> "How could you ever find a bull that big?"
> "How could you ever find adultery in Sparta?"

The married woman truly—by Greek standards—was free. Women ran the house without men, who left at first light and only returned after dark. They had servants to clean and cook, to look after the small children, and to tend the looms and weave the cloth. Young women participated in the open in gymnastic and in dance. They wore loose and revealing costumes: one slit-dress was called the "thigh-flasher." They were expected to be chaste until they were married, as far as the peculiar marriage customs of the Spartans went, and they did not get married until they were eighteen or older, in contrast to the rest of Greece where girls typically were contracted to a husband at thirteen, fourteen, or fifteen.

As the man's duty was to fight, and, if necessary, die, in battle, so the woman's duty was to produce sons to fight in battle. As the noblest sacrifice of the man was death in battle, so the noblest sacrifice of the woman was death in childbirth. Spartan mothers were notoriously tough on their sons. One Spartan mother advised her son to return from battle "with his shield or on it." Another mother who was informed that her son had been killed in battle, said,

"That is why I had him . . . to give his life for Sparta."

—— PART III ——
THE ARCADIAN AND ARGIVE WARS

Table 3. The Kings of the Arcadian and Argive Wars

Eurypontid Royal House

Agiad Royal House

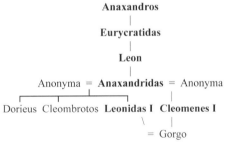

Eurypontid Royal House	Agiad Royal House
Anaxilas (645–625)	Anaxandros (640–615)
Leotychidas I (625–600)	Eurycratidas (615–590)
Hippocratidas (600–575)	Leon (590–560)
Agasicles (575–550)	Anaxandridas (560–520)
Ariston (550–515)	Cleomenes I (520–490)
Damaratos (515–491)	Leonidas I (490–480)
Leotychidas II (491–469)	

Kings highlighted in bold.

Illustration 4. Bringing Back the Dead (vase, photograph in author's collection) (Pamela M. Bradford)

— 10 —

The Spartan Alliance

Those Spartans who survived the Messenian revolt understood all too well the catastrophic possibilities of their situation—a subjugated but dangerous and inimical Messenian helotry, agricultural land abandoned, enemies scattered throughout the Peloponnesus, a powerful and hostile Argos—but, as the next generation grew up and went through the system of the agoge under the Lycurgan reforms, it developed into the finest army in Greece and the finest heavy infantry anywhere.

Imagine that you are back on that dusty battlefield, but, now, you are looking across two hundred yards at the Spartan phalanx. It is unlike any phalanx you have ever faced before. Every man is fully armed and completely equipped. The Spartans take their positions automatically, intent on the orders of their officers, without confusion or noise—no war cries, no threats or boasts—just silent efficiency. You know they expect to win. Your drummers begin the beat. Across the way, the Spartan flute-players play the "Song of Castor" and the Spartan phalanx advances, keeping time in perfect unison, almost like a choral performance. You see no gaps in their line. They just come on beautifully, perfectly.

You want to run, and, sometimes, the opposing army, witnessing this performance, does run. Sometimes it begins its charge, but before it closes with the Spartans, so many of the hoplites in the rear have halted—or never started—that the front breaks and runs before contact. Sometimes, already at a disadvantage because of the gaps that have opened in its line, it meets the Spartan line and then breaks and runs, leaving the dead and wounded behind. The Spartans do not pursue.

The superiority of the Spartan phalanx was not an illusion; the Spartans were in perfect physical condition and well-practiced with their weapons, individually and collectively, and they trained endlessly in the discipline and coordination required by phalanx warfare. Spartan courage was already becoming a subject of wonder.

"The Spartans are so ready to risk their lives in battle," King Anaxandridas said, "because we practice a reverence for life; we do not, like the rest of you Greeks, fear it."

Once, when one of Sparta's allies complained to the king that the Spartans had sent only a few soldiers while their allies had sent a lot, the Spartan king told the assembled army to stand up and then called out,

"Are any of you blacksmiths? Sit down. Farmers? Sit down. Merchants? Sit down."

And he continued until everyone was seated except the Spartans.

"You see," he said, "we are the *only* state to send soldiers."

This magnificent army, and the fading memory of the revolt, tempted the Spartan kings and the gerousia to advance Spartan power into Arcadia, reduce its population to helot or Laconian-neighbor status, to overwhelm Argos, and hunt down, kill, or expel from Greece all Messenian refugees.

King Eurykrates ("Power Far and Wide") sent envoys to Delphi to ask the god Apollo to grant them Arcadia. The king hoped that Apollo would sanction the war and guarantee Spartan victory. Instead, Apollo replied (through his priestess, the Pythia, of course),

"You want the whole of Arcadia? No, I will not give it to you. You are asking too much and the acorn-eating men of populous Arcadia can well protect their land. I will not promise all this to you, but in the land of Tegea, I say, the earth will resound with your dancing feet and you will measure their fertile fields with chains."

Tegea was the Arcadian city which blocked Spartan expansion north into central Greece.

The Spartans set out, complete with chains to bind their prisoners. And Apollo proved to be right, although not as the Spartans had expected, because they were completely defeated and some of them were taken prisoner and enslaved. Indeed, these slaves "danced" on the Tegean plain under the blows of the overseer's whip and they "measured" the fields with their feet as they were driven back and forth across them. (Two centuries later the Tegeans still displayed the chains they had taken from the Spartans.)

The Spartans were defeated for the simplest of reasons: the Tegeans preferred to die rather than become helots. Moreover, the Spartans were no longer fighting an army composed of aristocrats (3–5% of the population) but hoplites (15–20% of the population). The Tegean hoplites, unlike the aristocrats, had nowhere else to go.

The Spartans had been defeated, but they could only break the ring of their enemies, the Arcadians and the Argives, by first defeating the Tegeans. For a hundred years, down to the middle of the sixth century, four generations of kings led out the Spartans to fight Tegea, but the more they forced the Tegeans (and their Arcadian and Argive allies) to fight, the better their opponents became at fighting. The Spartans could not conquer Tegea, the Tegeans could not prevent the Spartans from attacking them. A century of warfare had resulted in a stalemate.

The royal families—the Agiads and the Eurypontids—had always been rivals and now they split on both foreign and domestic policy. The people wanted a real voice in the assembly, not just the right to vote *yes* or *no*, but actually to address the assembly, and to have the decision reached in assembly be the final decision. The aristocracy was caught in the middle.

The Agiad kings stood for royal power and foreign expansion. Their names reflect their policy: "Master of Men" (Anaxander, a name which was also the title of Agamemnon, the supreme king and commander-in-chief of the Greek army in the *Iliad*), "Powerful Far and Wide" (Eurykrates), "Lion" (Leon), and another "Master of Men" (Anaxandridas the "grandson of Anaxander").

The other royal family, the Eurypontids, accepted a more circumscribed role for the kingship within Sparta and sought another path in foreign policy. Their names reflected their policy—"Master of the People" (Anaxilas—*laos* is an elegant word for "people"), "Leader of the People" (Archidamos) and "Famous for his Leadership" (Agasicles). Agasicles summed up Eurypontid philosophy,

"If a man wants to rule securely without a bodyguard, let him rule the way fathers rule their sons." Agasicles and his fellow king Leon were successful in "all their wars" except the Tegean war and they dedicated a new temple of Artemis Orthia to commemorate Spartan success.

Agasicles invited and entertained philosophers at his table in the evening mess. He was interested in ideas, but he also had a straightforward requirement on their character: "I will not be the student of someone whose son I would not be."

Agasicles named his son "Best" (Ariston), a judgment with which the Spartans eventually agreed, and Ariston showed the results of a philosophic upbringing. When he was told that his fellow king, Cleomenes, had said that a good king should help his friends and injure his enemies, he commented, "Would it not be far better, my friend, to help one's friends and make one's enemies into friends?"

In the year 556 BCE, while Anaxandridas and Ariston were kings, and after a century of indecisive warfare, all the problems and conflicts came out in the open: should the kings have the sole power to direct foreign policy? Should the people (the *damos*) have a right to an independent voice? Should the gerousia retain the right to set the agenda? Should it have the power to ignore the assembly? What had the people gained from the incessant wars waged by the kings?

In this year—as in every year—the Spartans chose five new ephors. Ephors, originally, had been the representatives of the kings in Sparta when the kings were absent on campaign. Since then, the ephors had evolved more to be the representatives of the people. One of the new ephors was Chilon, a member of the royal families.

Chilon defined a statesman, or any wise man, as someone who was able to use his reason to see as far into the future as possible and he became known as one of the seven wise men of Greece. Chilon's aphorism—*Give a pledge ... and regret it*—was engraved in Delphi. This aphorism was a universal truth in Greece—and today, too, for that matter—but it had specific application to Sparta where trust between citizens was so low that the ephors stayed in session every day of the year to judge, and uphold, contracts, "so that"—King Eurykrates put a positive spin on it—"even in a hostile world we will be true to each other."

Chilon's world was a world of injustice. Philosophers, kings, and politicians debated the nature of the polis, citizenship, divine and human justice, law and order. Chilon's own brother complained to him that the Spartans did not treat them equally, but were unfair to him, the brother, because they had not chosen him ephor. Chilon told him, "You do not know how to put up with injustice and I do." King Leon described a kind of utopian society, "When the citizens have neither too much or too little and justice has power, then injustice will be weak."

Even at the Olympic games—supposedly the embodiment of manly perfection—Leon observed, as the runners were struggling over their starting position at the gate, "The runners are more concerned with speed than with justice."

King Anaxandridas (and rival of Chilon) told a man who complained that he had been exiled from his city, "Friend, consider that it is not as bad to be an exile from your city as it is to be an exile from justice."

And, in a conversation with someone who said that men would be happier if they did not care about their reputation, he said, "So then, according to your reasoning, temple-robbers should be happy, because they certainly do not care about their reputation."

Chilon's year as ephor coincided with the Olympic games. The Olympic truce was supposed to allow every city safe passage to Olympia even in time of war. Every Greek city sent a contingent and the Spartan contingent included the kings. The Spartans, and other Greeks, would come with wagons and servants, set up a tent village beside the river, and camp there during the games. The festival offered an opportunity for the leaders of different poleis to meet, get to know each other, and converse about the state of Greece. Each contingent demonstrated its character and its power to the other contingents.

When a lame old man was trying to find a place to sit down to watch the contests, a contingent of Greeks—some say the Athenians—called to the old man that there was a place to sit on the top row, even though there was no place, and, after he had struggled up to the top row, they laughed at him. When, however, the old man came to the Spartan contingent, every young man and many older men stood up to offer him a place. The other Greeks applauded and one Spartan said to another, "What curious people they are; they recognize justice, but they don't do it."

Chilon (who, as ephor, had to remain in Sparta) was an extraordinary and well-known individual. He composed songs which were admired for their Laconic style and wit. When a tyrant asked him for advice, he wrote him a letter, "Stay at home and consider yourself lucky if you die in bed."

Some of his precepts are quite familiar to us.

Gold is the test of men.
Watch your tongue . . . particularly at dinner.
Visit your friends more in adversity than prosperity.
Do not speak ill of the dead.
Honor the elderly.
Prefer a loss to a dishonest profit.
Don't speak without thinking.
Control your temper.
Obey the laws.
Accomplish something in your spare time.

Some are more rooted in Greek character and society—

Do not insult your neighbors or they will insult you.
Do not make threats.
Make a reasonable marriage.
Watch yourself.
Don't mock the misfortunate.
Learn how to administer your own house well.

And some are specifically Spartan—

Respect divination.
Don't rush in public.
Don't gesture when you speak—it makes you look crazy.

Chilon, then, was a thoughtful man who had the ability to examine what the future might be, and, within the context of the Great Rhetra (the constitution of Sparta), he intended to do no less than effect a revolution—to promote the ephors collectively to be an equal partner to the kings within Sparta, to limit the power of the aristocracy in the gerousia, and to transform Spartan foreign policy.

Chilon's chief rival was the king Anaxandridas. The whole of Sparta chose sides and almost came to blows. In the end, however, Chilon got his way and his reforms were ratified in the assembly. The reforms established the principle that all Spartiates were equal. Henceforth they called themselves *homoioi*, usually translated as "equals" but rather a word that meant "like one another." Neither in dress nor food nor house nor behavior would they appear different from one another.

After Chilon, for over three centuries, the five ephors were the chief civil magistrates of Sparta. Within Sparta they had almost absolute power. Aristotle called them "tyrants." They had the power to fine citizens and give orders to the kings inside Sparta. They saw to it that arguments did not develop into grudges—if two men seemed to have serious differences, they would insist that the two fight it out with fists right there and settle things. They had the right to speak for the damos in the assembly. At the evening mess, when all the other men rose at the arrival of the kings, the ephors, as the embodiment of the people, did not rise.

A visitor was amazed at this apparent discourtesy and asked King Anaxilas about it. The king said, "They do not rise for the same reason that they are ephors."

Once a month, now, the kings exchanged oaths with the ephors. The kings swore, "I will reign in obedience to the established custom of the state," and then the ephors swore on behalf of the people, "So long as you abide by your oath, we will preserve the kingship unshaken."

Chilon's civil reforms were fundamental to the future success of Sparta, but no less so than his reforms of Spartan foreign policy. If the Spartans, Chilon saw, could open a passage through Tegea into the Peloponnesus, now riven by rivalries between Argos and Corinth and Megara, between the cities of Arcadia, between Pisa and Elis over the control of Olympia and the Olympic games, and in so many cities ruled by tyrants, a strong polis like Sparta would be welcomed as an ally and could turn the situation to its own advantage—and neutralize Argos.

The kings, as always, turned to Apollo at Delphi for advice—how could they defeat Tegea and assume the leadership of Greece? Apollo replied (through the Pythia) that only when they had recovered the bones of Orestes and brought them to Sparta would they be successful. (Orestes was the son of Agamemnon the overlord of the Greeks in the *Iliad* and once, as Greeks believed, the ruler of all Greeks.) The Spartans kings, then, were advised by Apollo to prove that they were descended, not from Dorian invaders, but from the Achaean kings who had once ruled Mycenae and Sparta.

The Spartans asked Apollo where they might find the bones of Orestes and he replied,

> There in Arcadia lies Tegea of the broad fields,
> There two winds blow, driven by a mighty force,
> Blow and counter-blow resounds and evil comes from evil,
> There deep in the fruitful earth lies the son of Agamemnon.
> Bring home the body and you will defeat Tegea.

The Spartans could not figure out what this oracle meant, but the kings sent a man named Lichas, who was one of their five "Agents of Good" (the *Agathoergoi*), to Tegea. (They were not at war with Tegea just then.) These "Agents of Good" were chosen by the kings from the men who had become too old to serve in their elite guard. They were given the mission to travel around the Peloponnesus, or beyond, and seek information and situations which could be turned to the advantage of Sparta.

Lichas visited Tegea to investigate the oracle. He stopped at a smithy, drawn there by the sound of clashing iron, and he was struck by the sight of the smith beating the red-hot iron and the bellows forcing air unto the fire. The Spartan immediately recognized the elements of the oracle: the bellows were the "two winds driven by a mighty force" and the smith striking iron with iron (his hammer) was the "blow and counter-blow;" the "evil" was the evil of iron, the material of weapons. His amazement showed and the smith said to him, "Well, stranger, if you think this is something, you should see the body I discovered buried in my yard."

The smith told Lichas that he had unearthed a coffin while digging a well and he showed the Spartan the skeleton of an enormous man. Lichas returned to Sparta, explained the situation to the kings, and devised a plan to get the bones. He was publicly and ostentatiously exiled from Sparta, whereupon he "fled" to Tegea, settled there in a house beside the smithy, and, late one night, removed the bones to Sparta.

Now Chilon's plan came to fruition. The Spartan kings were sanctified as the legitimate leaders of Greece, even as they finally accepted that they could not conquer the Tegeans and they would have to find another way to accomplish their objective. "Don't desire the impossible," Chilon had said, and, "If you want your neighbors to respect you, not fear you, show mercy when you are strong," and so King Ariston offered the Tegeans a treaty on equal terms. The treaty, sworn to by the two kings, read something like this: the two parties are . . .

". . . to maintain friendship and peace always; to follow wherever the Spartans lead, both on land and on sea; to have the same friend and the same enemy as the Spartans. Never to make peace with anyone independently of the Spartans nor ever to fail to declare war upon whomsoever the Spartans declare war upon. Not to do wrong and receive fugitives from each other. If anyone should make war with an army on the land of the Tegeans, Sparta should come to help with its whole strength as far as it is able; if anyone should make war with an army on the land of the Spartans, the Tegeans should come to help with its whole strength as far as it is able . . ."

Sparta pursued a policy of expelling tyrants from Greek cities in the Peloponnesus and establishing hoplite oligarchies, which at the time, were the most democratic governments in existence. In return, the Spartans made alliances, one by one, with the new governments of all the cities of the Peloponnesus—except Argos—until the whole Peloponnesus was tied to Sparta by a system of alliances which the Spartans called "the Lacedaemonians and their allies," but we call "the Peloponnesian League." This system of alliances, to outward appearance equal partnerships between Sparta and the other states, gave the Spartans everything they wanted: they dominated the Peloponnesus, they marginalized Argos, and they got their new allies to expel all Messenian refugees and to refuse sanctuary to runaway helots. The members of the alliance received security and stability.

— 11 —

The "Strangers"

For five centuries—from the Dorian invasion down to the formation of the Peloponnesian League—the Spartans, and the other Greeks on the mainland, had been able to work out their own destiny without foreign interference, though not without foreign influence. They traded with Phoenicians and Egyptians, they served as mercenaries for the Chaldaeans in Babylon and throughout the eastern Mediterranean, and they founded colonies in the far west where they competed with the powerful city of Carthage. In the middle of the sixth century, however, for the first time, they attracted the attention of one of the empires of the Near East, the kingdom of Lydia in Asia Minor.

Lydia was ruled by a line of wealthy kings who commanded an elite cavalry. The Lydian kings campaigned against Miletus (the most powerful Greek city in Ionia) for years before they could force the Milesians to agree to an alliance on Lydian terms. Ultimately, the Lydians extended their empire to the shores of the Aegean Sea and compelled all the Ionian Greeks to pay tribute. The Lydians had established an eastern border with the Medes at the Halys River—this border seemed to have been sanctioned by the gods themselves when an eclipse of the sun in 585 BCE occurred just as the Lydians and the Medes were going to fight a battle. The eclipse convinced the two sides that the gods wanted them to make a treaty and this treaty held until 559 BCE, when the Median king was deposed by a Persian "king," Cyrus, the founder of the Persian empire.

The king of Lydia, Croesus, saw an opportunity to expand his borders at the expense of the new Persian empire and its new king, Cyrus, but he did have some doubts about the advisability of violating the treaty and initiating a war, so he looked for a trustworthy oracle to tell him what the future would hold. He tested all the oracles in the world and discovered just one oracle that could pass his test—Delphi. Consequently, he sent magnificent gifts to the temple along with some questions: How should he prepare for a war against Cyrus? Should he cross the Halys River (the border)? What would be the outcome of the war? And how long would his family rule in Lydia? He was elated with the response—if he crossed the river, a great empire would fall, and, furthermore, his dynasty would be secure until a mule assumed the Persian throne. He received additional advice to ask Sparta for an alliance and so he did.

The Spartan kings—Anaxandridas and Ariston—were amenable and, in mutual misunderstanding of what they were getting into, Croesus and the Spartans became allies. The Spartans did not—nor did Croesus—have any idea of the quality of their opponent, Cyrus, or the strength of the Persian empire, and Croesus did not understand that his new ally had other priorities, namely that they were going to have to fight the Argives, who were seeking to thwart the expansion of the Spartan alliance in the Peloponnesus.

In 547 BCE Croesus summoned his allies, including the Spartans, crossed the Halys River, and invaded the Persian empire. Cyrus reacted quickly and by the end of the summer he had driven Croesus back across the Halys River, at which point, satisfied—or so it seemed—with his summer campaign, Cyrus withdrew. Cyrus now, Croesus and his allies believed, would go into winter quarters and renew the campaign in the spring. Cyrus waited until the allies had departed—the Spartans returned home to prepare for their war with the Argives—and then he collected his army and attacked the Lydians in the dead of winter. He used a camel corps to frighten the Lydian horses and rout their cavalry, and then he laid siege to the Lydian capital, Sardis.

Croesus was in desperate trouble and he sent messengers to Sparta to summon help, but the Spartans did not come. Croesus' capital city, Sardis, soon fell to the Persians and Croesus, himself, was captured. Indeed, his crossing of the Halys River did cause a mighty empire to fall, his own, and his dynasty did end only when Cyrus, the son of a Mede and a Persian, metaphorically a "mule," ascended the throne.

While Croesus was still defending his capital, the Spartans and the Argives, by themselves with no allies, were preparing to fight a battle, ostensibly over the district of Thyreae, but, in fact, to determine who would be the master of the Peloponnesus. The two phalanxes were evenly matched, they comprised the flower of the citizen body, the outcome of the battle was not certain, and both sides risked losing so many men, even if they won the battle, that their polis would be weakened. Therefore the Spartans and the Argives agreed that they would each choose three hundred men and that these three hundred would fight, the victor to take the land, the loser to acknowledge defeat. The Spartans chose to send the elite unit of three hundred men, from whom came the bodyguard of the king (but without the king), and the Argives three hundred of the thousand men supported at public expense to train as hoplites. This battle, then, the Battle of Champions, in the year 546 BCE was both a battle and a duel.

The champions fought until dark. Of the six hundred men who fought that day only three survived, two Argives and one Spartan, Othryades. The Argives returned to their camp to claim the victory. The Spartan stayed, stripped the bodies of the Argive soldiers, carried the arms and armor to his side of the field, and piled them there as a trophy of victory. According to some accounts he was wounded and wrote a few words on the trophy in his own blood, and died. (His unintelligible scrawl became a riddle—what did Othryades write?) In another account he was not wounded but he killed himself in shame, because he had survived his comrades.

In any case, the Argive leaders claimed that they had won because two Argives had survived and only one Spartan, the Spartan kings claimed that they had won because the Argives had left the Spartan in control of the battlefield. They could not agree and so they fought a full-scale battle. They both suffered heavy losses, but the Spartans won and kept control of Thyreae, and, from that day on, the Argive men cut their hair in mourning and swore to keep it short until they had recovered Thyreae, while the Spartans stopped cutting their hair and wore it long. The Argives never accepted Spartan leadership and never joined the Spartan alliance.

When the Spartans learned, not long after the battle, that Croesus had been defeated and captured, they sent an embassy to warn Cyrus that Sparta would not tolerate Persian influence in Ionia.

"Who are these Spartans?" Cyrus asked.

He believed that the Greek poleis were merchant states like the Phoenician cities, and, as such, negligible, and he had contempt for a government without a single absolute ruler. And then, too, he knew that the Spartans had been allies of his enemies.

"I have never yet," he said, "been afraid of men who appoint a place in the middle of their town where they meet and deceive each other while swearing they tell the truth. And if I stay healthy, Spartans won't be discussing Ionia's problems—they'll be discussing their own."

The Spartans believed that they now had the right, and the duty, to protect, and to speak for, Greeks everywhere. Their system of alliances had brought them power and security, but the alliances had also involved them in the wider world. They had a tradition of opposition to tyrants—Chilon was supposed to have encouraged King Anaxandridas to free Sicyon from its tyrant—and, when their seagoing allies insisted upon their help against pirates, the Spartans joined in expeditions in the Aegean and in the north of Greece.

The most powerful pirate in the Aegean was Polycrates the tyrant (535–528/7) of Samos. After he seized power, he built a fleet of one hundred penteconters (fifty-oared galleys), recruited a force of a thousand archers, made an alliance with the pharoah of Egypt, and sent out expeditions to plunder the Aegean. He attacked friend and foe alike. (He said that a friend was happier to get back what had been taken than he would have been if he had never lost anything in the first place—such is the nature of gratitude.) He defeated the first expedition sent against him and set the prisoners to forced labor on the fortifications around the harbor and elsewhere on the island.

Samian exiles came to Sparta and begged the Spartan kings and magistrates for assistance. They spoke at length and when they were finished and asked for an answer, the Spartans said that the speech had been so long that by the time the speakers came to the end, the Spartans had forgotten the beginning. So the envoys came back with an empty bag and said,

"The bag needs flour."

The Spartans already had enough of a grievance because of previous acts of piracy, but, in addition, they were encouraged to act by their ally Corinth whose maritime trade was being injured by piracy. The Spartans led a fleet to Samos and attempted to land, but their first attempt was repulsed and they had to try a second landing before they could gain a foothold; they drove the Samians into their city and two Spartans pursued so vigorously that they got into the city itself, but the other Spartans did not keep up with them, they were cut off, and, after a desperate fight, were killed. The two Spartans' bravery impressed the Samians so much that the Samians gave them a public funeral and the son of one of the Spartans took the name "Samios" to honor the Samians and the courage his father had shown. Nonetheless, their courage came to nothing, because, after a siege of forty days, the Spartans grew discouraged and went home.

In the end Polycrates was done in by his own grandiose ambition—he was lured into a trap by the promises of the local Persian governor (the *satrap*), executed, and hung on a cross for the rain to drench and the sun to dry. With Polycrates out of the way, the Persians extended their empire to the coast of the Aegean Sea. While Cyrus conquered Babylon, campaigned on the borders of India, restored the Israelites to their homeland, and, in short, founded the largest empire the world had ever known, the Spartans cultivated their alliances and concentrated on their domestic affairs. The ephors became involved in the private lives of the kings, because neither King Anaxandridas nor King Ariston was having much luck producing a son.

Ariston had married and divorced two different wives and finally acquired a third by means not strictly honorable and with results that threw Sparta into crisis. The king suggested to his best friend that they prove what good friends they were by exchanging gifts. Ariston said that he would give his friend anything he asked for, no matter what, and, furthermore, he said he would swear an oath to it and his friend went along and also swore an oath. Ariston told him to choose first and the friend chose a horse he liked. Ariston then told him he wanted his wife. And he got her, but the friendship was over. Not long after the marriage, when he was seated in a chair in the presence of the ephors, a member of his household arrived and told him that a son was born to him, but Ariston counted up the months since he had married his wife and exclaimed,

"It is not mine!"

The ephors heard this, but took no action at the time.

In the other royal house, King Anaxandridas had married his own sister's daughter and he loved her, but they had no sons. The ephors summoned him—kings by custom refused the first summons—and at their meeting they insisted that he divorce his wife and remarry. Anaxandridas said that they were giving him bad advice—to divorce a wife who had done nothing wrong and replace her. And so the ephors consulted with the gerousians and then they summoned Anaxandridas again and told him,

"Since—we can see   that you are crazy about the woman you have now, then you must do what we say and not refuse—or the Spartiates may reach a certain decision about you. We do not insist that you divorce your wife, but you must marry a second wife and treat her as the equal of your first—so that your second wife will bear sons."

Anaxandridas gave way to the demands of the ephors and after this he had two wives and two separate households.

Before long the second wife bore him a son whom they named Cleomenes ("Famous for his Might"). And when this second wife had provided a royal heir-apparent, the first wife, who had been childless, became pregnant. She bore Dorieus ("Dorian"), and then a little later, Leonidas ("Son of a Lion"), and a little later Cleombrotos ("Famous Mortal"—although some say that Leonidas and Cleombrotos were twins). The mother of Cleomenes did not have any more children.

—— 12 ——

The Accidental King

By the time the father of Cleomenes, the Spartan king Anaxandridas, had died (c. 520), the Persian king Cyrus had already united the whole of the Asian Near East from the coast of Asia Minor down to the borders of Egypt and east to the Indus River (where in 530 BCE he died fighting). Cyrus's son Cambyses (530–522) had conquered Egypt and Cambyses's successor, Darius, who became king about two years before Cleomenes (and outlived him by a few years, 522–486 BCE), had established himself as king, put down rebellions, and transformed the valley of the Indus into the twentieth satrapy (province), one so wealthy that it paid a third of all tribute gathered from the eastern provinces,

In Sparta a dispute arose over the succession—the supporters of the first wife's eldest son, Dorieus—he was by all accounts a popular young man—claimed that Cleomenes was not mentally stable and should be rejected in favor of Dorieus, but custom was clear—the oldest son born while the father was king, and so engendered by a king, should be king and Cleomenes was chosen. Dorieus was outraged. He refused to live in a Sparta where Cleomenes was king, and he blamed the Spartiates. He and his adherents created so much ill-feeling that he was encouraged to take his followers out of Sparta and found a colony in Sicily. He tried and in the attempt he died. If he had remained in Sparta, he would probably have outlived Cleomenes and, since Cleomenes's only child was a daughter, become king.

Cleomenes's first recorded act (c. 519 BCE) was to lead an army up into Boeotia—we do not know why—and give advice to some envoys sent to him by the polis of Plataea. They asked Cleomenes to protect them from Thebes (the most powerful polis in Boeotia). Cleomenes told them,

"We live away in our own territory and would not be much comfort to you in yours. You could be enslaved several times before any of us knew about it. We recommend to you that you give yourselves over to the Athenians, for they are men who live in the land next to you and their help is not contemptible."

(Some said that Cleomenes wanted to make trouble between the Athenians and the Thebans. If so, he succeeded beyond anything he could have imagined—the Athenians came to the defense of Plataea and remained the enemies of Thebes for 160 years.)

In the next year (c. 518), when Cleomenes was back in Sparta, he received a visit from a Samian exile. The exile, Maeandrius, wanted to persuade Cleomenes to restore him to his city. He rented a house and invited Cleomenes to visit him, and, when Cleomenes visited him, Maeandrius made sure that the king saw his collection of gold and silver cups. He observed that Cleomenes was struck dumb by their beauty, and Maeandrius invited him to take as many as he wanted. When Maeandrius had urged him two or three times to help himself, Cleomenes recognized that he was being offered a bribe, but he thought, if he simply refused, Maeandrius would invite other Spartiates to his house and probably succeed in bribing some of them, so the king advised the ephors to expel "the Samian foreigner" from Sparta and also from the whole of the Peloponnesus. The ephors listened to him, issued an expulsion order (*xenelasia*), and Maeandrius departed.

While the Spartans were occupied in their own affairs, the Persian king Darius was planning to stop Scythia, once and for all, from raiding his empire. The Scythians were a nomadic horse-people who occupied territory along the northern borders of the Persian empire from the Black Sea to India. Darius planned to cross the Danube River and drive the Scythians all the way from the region of the Black Sea far to the east where he had set up blocking forces; there he would trap them between his two forces and annihilate them.

In response, the Scythians sent envoys to Sparta to try to persuade Cleomenes to make an alliance with them and to coordinate an invasion of the Persian empire. They proposed that they would invade the Persian empire across the Phasis River (between the Black Sea, into which it feeds, and the Caspian Sea) while the Spartans invaded the Persian empire from Ephesus (on the Aegean coast of Asia Minor) and the two armies would move towards each other until they met.

Cleomenes enjoyed the Scythians' company enormously—Greeks found them curiously engaging with their stereotypical snub noses, red hair, and amusing accents. The king associated with them rather more than he should have, and learned from them to drink his wine straight—instead of the typical Greek way of one part wine to three parts water. Ever after, the Spartans, when they wanted something stronger to drink than mixed wine, said they wanted to drink "like a Scythian," and they also said that the Scythians turned Cleomenes into an alcoholic.

Cleomenes, however, despite his personal affection for the Scythians, could hardly agree to the alliance. Sparta was not strong enough, even with all its allies. And, anyway, it had a critical situation of its own in Greece concerning the oracle at Delphi and the tyrant of Athens, Hippias. Hippias's Athenian opponents (whom he had driven into exile) persuaded the priestess (the *pythia*) of Apollo at the oracle of Delphi to respond to all Spartan visitors whether they were official sacred envoys or private individuals, "First free Athens."

The Spartans found themselves thwarted in their frequent consultations of the oracle and, finally, they concluded that Apollo, himself, commanded them to drive out Hippias and his family. They first voted to send a modest expedition by sea under the command of a prominent Spartiate. He landed at the smaller port of Athens, but Hippias had been warned that the Spartans were coming, he deduced where they would land, and he had the prospective battlefield cleared to facilitate the action of the elite cavalry of his allies, the Thessalians, who sent a thousand horsemen under the command of their king. In the ensuing battle the Thessalian cavalry overpowered the Spartans; killed many of them, including their leader; and drove the survivors back to their ships and back to Sparta.

In the next year (510 BCE) the Spartans voted to mount a major expedition against Athens under the command of King Cleomenes. He marched through the Peloponnesus, collected his allies along the way, and entered Attica. Cleomenes had learned the lessons of the defeat—if he let the Thessalian cavalry get around the flanks of his phalanx, he would lose control of the battle. As he entered Attica, he made sure that his flanks were protected. The Thessalian cavalry could not break the Spartan phalanx or outflank it, and, after a brief engagement in which forty Thessalians were killed, the Thessalians retreated, abandoned their allies, and returned to Thessaly. Cleomenes's victory established Sparta as the premiere military power in the Greek world.

He marched unopposed into Athens, joined on the march, and in Athens, by the Athenians who wanted to overthrow the tyrant. The tyrant and his family took refuge on the acropolis and Cleomenes lay siege to them there, but the Spartans never in their whole history figured out how to take a fortified site. After a few days Cleomenes became frustrated and debated whether to leave the Athenians to continue the siege themselves and solve their own problem, but, then, by chance, his forces captured Hippias's children. Cleomenes demanded that, if Hippias wanted his children back, he withdraw from Athens within five days. Hippias agreed and withdrew to the city of Sigeum on the Scamander River (near Troy and inside the Persian empire).

Cleomenes expected that the Athenians would now set up some sort of hoplite democracy friendly to Sparta and led by a friend of Cleomenes. (This Athenian had won the friendship of Cleomenes, rumor had it, by letting the king sleep with his wife.) But the Athenians had other ideas and chose someone else. Cleomenes's friend asked the king to drive out his rival, Cleomenes agreed (508 BCE), and sent a herald to Athens with his demands. Cleomenes came with a small force and expelled seven hundred Athenian families, whom his friend denounced. Then Cleomenes tried to dismiss the Athenian council and to transfer power to his friend. He had gone too far. The council refused, the Athenians gathered under arms, and Cleomenes with his friend (and his friend's three hundred supporters) seized the Acropolis.

On the way up to the Acropolis, Cleomenes passed a temple and decided to enter the sacred chamber of the goddess to pray. The priestess stood up from the chair of office before the door and barred his way. She said,

"Spartan foreigner, go back and do not enter the shrine, for it is a sacrilege for a Dorian to come here."

He replied,

"Woman, I am not a Dorian, I am an Achaean."

In that simple declaration was a world of meaning. Cleomenes meant that he was a descendant of Heracles, therefore an Achaean like Agamemnon and Menelaus, and, like Agamemnon, overlord of all Greeks. The Athenians, however, did not see things his way and they put him under siege. After three days he agreed to a truce which allowed him, and his Spartans, to withdraw, in exchange for the surrender of the Athenian rebels. Cleomenes disguised his friend as a woman and slipped him out with the Spartans. For the others, the Athenians let than die in prison. They invited the exiles to return and they sent ambassadors to Sardis, with the intention of making an alliance with the Persians, for they suspected—correctly—that the Spartans and Cleomenes were not done with them.

Sometime in this period King Ariston died and Damaratos succeeded him. Ariston was extremely popular and the Spartans considered it a tragedy that he had no children. They prayed that he would have a son, and a son was born to his wife. They named him "Prayers of the People," that is, Damaratos—and, although, at first, Ariston denied him, the son grew up and won his heart. Ariston considered Damaratos to be his son in all regards, and as the Spartans of his day considered Ariston to be the most distinguished of all the kings who had ever lived in Sparta, they followed his wishes and chose Damaratos to be their king, but they listened to Cleomenes.

Cleomenes had expected that the liberated Athenians would found a hoplite democracy, that Athens would become an ally of the Spartans, and that the Spartans, thereby, would extend their influence north of the Isthmus. His claim, made to the priestess, that he was not a Dorian but an Achaean, the heir to the kingdom of Agamemnon and Orestes, justified his—Spartan—rule over all Greeks. Now his expectations were shattered. He was furious at the way he had been treated, and he was determined to punish the Athenians. He planned to install his friend as tyrant in Athens. And once again (506 BCE) and without explanation he summoned an army from the whole of the Peloponnesus, formed an alliance with the Boeotians and the Chalcidians (in Euboea), and together with them, planned a coordinated invasion of Attica.

Cleomenes, with his fellow king Damaratos—it was the Spartan custom to send out both kings in command of the army during a major expedition—invaded Attica through the Isthmus, the Boeotians invaded from the north, and the Chalcidians invaded from the east. The Athenians decided to leave the Boeotians and Chalcidians for later and to confront the Peloponnesians. On the eve of the battle, the Corinthians, first, arguing among themselves that they were wrong to invade Attica, withdrew. When the Corinthians withdrew, King Damaratos also refused to participate, the other allies refused to advance, and the whole army was forced to withdraw. Cleomenes was furious and the Spartans were shaken. They decided that in the future only one king would be sent to command the army.

—— 13 ——

The King Who Saved Greece

Cleomenes was furious: personally, because of the way he had been treated, and politically, because the new Athenian state was now hostile to Sparta. The Athenians had already shown their power by defeating the invading Thebans and the Chalcidians in two battles. Cleomenes, while he was besieged on the Acropolis, had used the opportunity to explore the sacred precincts, the temples, and the temple records and among those records (he said) he had discovered a batch of oracles which predicted that the Athenians, if they were freed from the tyrant, would grow in power and become the equal of Sparta. He thought he was acting for the good of Sparta, when he freed Athens, but the Spartans had been better off before they expelled the tyrant.

Now, and only now, Cleomenes learned the whole story of the machinations of the Athenian exiles in Delphi and he addressed the Spartan assembly and told the Spartiates that they had been deceived by the false proclamation of the Pythia; on that basis, they had gotten involved in foreign politics, they had expelled Hippias and his family without cause, and, finally, they had done this without winning any favor from the Athenians.

In 505 BCE Cleomenes called a meeting of the Peloponnesian League and invited Hippias to come to Corinth from his refuge in the city of Sigeum (near Troy). Hippias accepted the invitation and the Spartan envoy addressed the assembled representatives:

"Allies, we confess that we have done something wrong. We were persuaded by corrupt oracles to drive from Athens men who were strangers to us and who were ready to obey us and we turned the city over to a people who were ungrateful, who, as soon as they were freed by us, abused us and drove us and our king out with violence. Now they are increasing in reputation so that those who live around them, the Boeotians and the Chalcidians, are suffering, and someone else will soon learn about them, if they annoy them. We made a mistake and we want, now, together with you, to correct that mistake. For that reason we have invited Hippias and you representatives from the Peloponnesus, to make a common plan and a common expedition to put him back in Athens and to restore to him what we took away."

The envoy finished his speech and then a Corinthian spoke.

"Now indeed earth and sky will change places: the earth will be above the sky, and men will live in the sea and fish will replace men, now that you, Spartans, who freed so many cities, want to restore a tyranny, for there is nothing more unjust among men, nor a greater pollution, than tyranny. But if you really think that cities should be ruled by tyrants, then first establish a tyranny in your own city, before you decide to establish it among others."

As the Peloponnesians were debating the fate of Athens, the Persian king, Darius, was going forward with his plans to annihilate the Scythians. He employed a Greek engineer to build a permanent bridge over the Bosporos and also to build a bridge of boats that could be transported up the Danube to a suitable crossing point. He assigned his Ionian subjects (under the command of their tyrants) to guard the Danube bridge while he invaded the Scythian homeland. Then he crossed into Scythian territory and advanced without resistance, but he soon found himself caught in the classic dilemma of a conventional army fighting a highly mobile force with no fixed place to defend.

Darius could not compel the Scythians to stand and fight. Furthermore, he could not prevent their burning and destroying the supplies he needed to support his army. He had miscalculated the distance to his blocking force, and, all too soon, he reached the point at which he could no longer advance without endangering his chances of a safe withdrawal. Rumors of disaster reached the Ionian Greeks defending the bridgehead. An Athenian named Miltiades—he was the master of the adjoining territory of the Chersonese—visited the Ionians and advised the tyrants to destroy the bridge and maroon Darius on the other side. At first the tyrants thought Miltiades had a good idea, but one of them pointed out, if Darius fell, all the tyrants would fall with him.

When Darius returned, and learned what Miltiades had done, he expelled him from the Chersonese. He was suspicious of the tyrants, even though they had done their duty, and he carelessly let his suspicions show. The tyrants decided to act against him before he could act against them; they laid down their tyrannies, installed free institutions in their cities, and formed a common council that created a League of Ionians and made plans to rebel from Persia. In the winter of 499/8 BCE they sent Aristagoras, the former tyrant of Miletus, as an envoy to Sparta to try to enlist the support of King Cleomenes. Aristagoras brought with him a bronze plate on which he had inscribed the whole circumference of the earth and the sea and all the rivers.

Aristagoras met with Cleomenes and said to him,

Cleomenes, don't be surprised that I am in a hurry. The circumstances are these: the sons of the Ionians are slaves to the Persians instead of free. Now, by the gods of the Hellenes, we call upon you to free the Ionians from slavery, men of the same blood as you. Indeed, it will be easy for you to do this, for the barbarians are not mighty men, and you practice always for war as the highest virtue. They fight like this: they go into battle wearing trousers and caps on their heads and armed with the bow and short spear. They are easy to beat.

He continued with a list of the people of Asia and their wealth and he pointed them out on the map and he added that if Cleomenes took just one city, he would be as wealthy as Zeus.

"You fight the Messenians, Arcadians, and Argives, although they have no gold and they have no silver, and yet you are willing to fight them to the death, when, if you made a different choice, you could easily rule the whole of Asia."

This is what Aristagoras said and Cleomenes replied to him,

"Stranger of Miletus, I will give you my answer the day after tomorrow."

When the appointed day arrived and they met, Cleomenes asked Aristagoras how many days journey it was from the Ionian coast to the seat of the Persian king. Aristagoras had been clever up to this point and had all but convinced him, but now he made a mistake and told him the truth—he said that the journey took three months—and he would have continued to say more about the road, but Cleomenes interrupted him,

"Stranger of Miletus, get out of Sparta before the sun sets. You have not said anything advantageous for the Spartans, when you want them to march three months from the sea."

Cleomenes went back to his house, but Aristagoras took up an olive branch, entered the house of Cleomenes as a suppliant, and pleaded with Cleomenes to hear him as a suppliant. Cleomenes's daughter, whose name was Gorgo, happened to be present. She was still a child, eight or nine years old, and Aristagoras suggested that Cleomenes send her into another room. Cleomenes told him not to worry about her. Aristagoras offered to give him ten talents, if he would do what he wanted. Cleomenes refused and Aristagoras added to the sum until he was offering fifty talents, and Gorgo exclaimed,

"Father, the stranger is corrupting you. Don't remain here. Please go away."

Cleomenes listened to the advice of his daughter and went into another room. Aristagoras fled immediately from Sparta—he should not have explained how long that road was—and he traveled to Athens, which had become the strongest Greek state outside of the Peloponnesian League. Aristagoras told the Athenians the same things he had told Cleomenes, about the wealth of Persia and the ease of fighting the Persians. He convinced the Athenian assembly (and also the Euboean city of Eretria) to send aid. The Athenians sent twenty ships, the Eretrians five. Together with the Ionians they attacked Sardis, the capital of Lydia, shut the Persian commander up in the citadel, and burned the town down. The Athenians and Eretrians then returned home, where they remained, while the Persians converged on the Ionians by land and sea.

The Ionian rebellion—mainland Greeks called it an "attack of sheep upon wolves"—seemed to be doomed to a quick end, but, unexpectedly, the Ionians defeated the Persians at sea (498 BCE) and Ionian allies, the Carians, annihilated a Persian army on land (497 BCE). The Ionians had a breathing space in which to organize and prepare to defend themselves from the inevitable Persian onslaught. Instead, they argued with each other, could not agree on a common strategy, and, individually, began to consider whether they might not be better off looking out for themselves.

As the Persians closed in on the Ionians, the Spartans faced a newly aggressive Argos, and one all the more dangerous because the Persians were looking towards Greece for allies. In 495 BCE Cleomenes had inquired at Delphi about a possible war and he had received the encouraging response that he would take "Argos." Elated by the oracle, Cleomenes led the Spartan army (without any allies) to the river Erasinos, which was the border of the Argolid. There, before crossing, Cleomenes performed a sacrifice, but the omens were unfavorable— the river god opposed their crossing into his territory. Cleomenes said,

"I admire Erasinos for not betraying his fellow citizens, but, nonetheless, the Argives will not be happy."

He marched his army to the edge of the sea, sacrificed a bull, collected boats, embarked his army, and landed on the coast of the Argolid. The Argives rushed to meet the Spartans and the two confronted each other near the little town of Sepeia. The Argives were not afraid of an open battle, but they feared that they might be beaten by some stratagem (for which Cleomenes was already famous), so they decided to be guided by the actions of the Spartan herald. When he gave orders to the Spartans to form up, to maneuver, or to withdraw, the Argives did the same.

Cleomenes soon figured out that the Argives were doing whatever his own herald signaled, and he put out the word to his troops that when the herald gave the sign to withdraw for the morning meal, they should withdraw, ground their arms, and then pick them up again and advance immediately upon the Argives. The Spartans did exactly as he ordered. They surprised the Argives as they were preparing their meal, and they slaughtered many of them, but many more escaped into the sacred grove of Argos. The Spartans surrounded the grove.

Cleomenes learned the names of some of the Argives who had taken refuge in the grove and he sent a herald to tell those men that he had received a ransom for them. (Among the Peloponnesians paying a ransom was a common custom, and the usual ransom for a soldier was set at two hundred drachmas—one drachma was a good day's wage.) Cleomenes succeeded in calling out about fifty of the Argives, one at a time. He had them seized and their throats cut. The men in the grove did not know what was happening because the woods were so thick that they could not see outside. Then someone climbed a tree and witnessed the murders. No one else accepted the invitation to come out.

Cleomenes then ordered the helots to surround the grove with cut wood and when they had obeyed, he set fire to the grove. As it burned, he asked one of the deserters to what god the grove was dedicated. When he heard that it was dedicated to "Argos," he groaned aloud and exclaimed,

"Apollo, giver of oracles, you've made a fool of me, when you said I would take Argos. Now I conclude that your oracle to me has been fulfilled."

Cleomenes, in the battle and the burning of the grove, killed 6,000 Argive soldiers. The king may have destroyed the Argive army as a step to taking the city or, in a wider purpose, to prevent the Argive army from helping the Persians. (The loss of adult citizens was so great that family slaves took over the running of the state as caretakers for the sons of the dead men.) The king, then, concluded a thirty-year peace treaty with Argos. He sent the greater part of his army back to Sparta, but he went with a thousand Spartiates to sacrifice at the Heraeon (one of the most sacred shrines of the Argives). He was opposed by a local priest, who forbade him to sacrifice at the altar, because it was impious for a foreigner to sacrifice there. Cleomenes ordered his helots to drive the priest away from the altar and whip him. After he had performed a sacrifice, he returned to Sparta.

No sooner had he returned to Sparta than his enemies (supporters of King Damaratos) charged him with accepting bribes not to take Argos, because, they said, he could easily have done so. He defended himself by saying that he had fulfilled the prophecy of Apollo, when he seized the sacred grove of "Argos," and he could not make an attempt on the city, before he had consulted Delphi and learned whether the god would give the city to the Spartans or stand in their way. He had gone to the Heraeon to seek a favorable sign, but, there, he saw a tongue of flame flash forth from the chest of the image, and he was forced to conclude that he could not take Argos. If the flame had issued from the head of the image, the sign would have shown that the city could be taken "from the top down," but, as it flashed from the chest, the sign showed that the expedition had done all that was allowed. The Spartiates concluded that his speech was persuasive and reasonable.

While the Spartans were fighting the Argives and judging Cleomenes, the Ionians were meeting the Persians in a great sea battle which would decide the whole rebellion. The four great Ionian naval powers, Chios, Lesbos, Samos, and Miletus, fought the Persians with a fleet of 300 ships at the Battle of Lade in 494 BCE; the Chians distinguished themselves by their bravery, but the Samians deserted the fleet, the Lesbians followed them, and the Ionian cause was lost. The Persians reduced Ionia, city by city, transported the population of Miletus to Mesopotamia, and hunted down traitors everywhere (except in Samos). Darius, however, was less interested in revenge than in stability and he appointed his son-in-law, Mardonius, to investigate the Ionians' grievances. Mardonius replaced the tyrannies with democracies, established courts to settle claims, and redistributed the tax burden. All in all, the Persians did not treat Ionia badly, but Ionia became a backwater of the empire.

Cleomenes, and some other Greeks as well—the Athenian Miltiades, for instance—realized that mainland Greece would be next on the Persians' list. The king did not believe, although many Greeks did, that Persia was invincible, but he had concluded that the disunity of the Ionians had cost them the war, and he was determined to assert the primacy of Sparta in Greece and the unity of Greeks under the leadership of Sparta. His first step had been the destruction of the Argive army. His second step was prompted by the Persian king.

Darius sent heralds throughout Greece to demand "earth and water," that is, submission to the Persians, and the moment of decision had come. The Athenians were barely convinced by Miltiades (one of the ten "generals" of Athens) to reject the Persian demands and to seek an alliance with the Spartans. The Spartans told the Persian ambassadors to find their own earth and water and they threw them down a well. Cleomenes swallowed his resentment at the way he had been treated by the Athenians and he convinced the Spartans to agree to an alliance with them. Cleomenes, also, transformed the Spartan alliance from a system of alliances between Sparta and the individual Peloponnesian cities into a new, more unified Peloponnesian League. This new league formed the basis for the alliance against Persia.

During the summer of 491 BCE the Athenians informed Cleomenes that the Aeginetans had given earth and water to Darius and had, thereby, betrayed Greece. Because of this accusation Cleomenes went to Aegina, where he intended to seize the Aeginetans responsible, but, as he tried to make the arrests, some of the Aeginetans resisted him. Their ringleader was a man named "Ram," who told Cleomenes that he would not be able to arrest a single Aeginetan, because he did this without the agreement of the Spartiates, that he had been bribed by the Athenians, and that the other king, Damaratos, opposed him. Cleomenes was forced to leave Aegina. As he was leaving, he found out what "Ram's" name was and he said to him, "Bronze your horns, Ram, as you're going to meet big trouble."

Damaratos opposed Cleomenes in everything. He was conscious that Cleomenes was the favored leader, and he was jealous. He demanded his own requisites, and he opposed the general policy of preferring the Athenians (Ionians) to the Aeginetans (Dorians and thus kin). Cleomenes, however, was a bad man to cross, because he had the unique ability to ask the right question and find the right answer. Now he asked how he could get rid of Damaratos and he discovered witnesses to the remark of Ariston, supposed father of Damaratos, denying that Damaratos could be his son.

Cleomenes convinced Leotychidas, who would be next in line for the kingship, should something happen to Damaratos, to bring an accusation that Damaratos was not the son of Ariston and therefore not a descendant of Heracles, not a Heraclid, not royal. Leotychidas already had a grievance against Damaratos because Damaratos had stolen away the woman Leotychidas wanted to marry. Leotychidas prepared the case.

The Spartiates decided to seek a response from the oracle in Delphi—was Damaratos the son of Ariston? Cleomenes had already persuaded an influential Delphian to influence the Pythia, the priestess who uttered the oracles, to say what Cleomenes wanted. Thus the Pythia replied to the inquiry of the ambassadors that Damaratos was not the son of Ariston. Damaratos was deposed and Leotychidas became king. Damaratos was still a Spartiate—he was not guilty of any wrong-doing, he was just not the king. But Leotychidas made his life miserable by mocking him, and so Damaratos decided, on his own, to leave Sparta and to travel to Delphi to investigate the oracle's response. He left the city secretly. When Cleomenes learned his intentions, he convinced the Spartiates that Damaratos was planning to join the Persians and the Spartans send out assassins to kill him. Damaratos, then, did escape to Persia (where he was welcomed and made one of the king's advisors).

As soon as Cleomenes got rid of Damaratos, he went with Leotychidas to Aegina. He demanded hostages and the Aeginetans judged that they could not resist both kings, so they turned over ten of their richest and most aristocratic men, among whom was "Ram." The kings took them to Athens and left them in the custody of the Athenians, who were the inveterate enemies of the Aeginetans.

Sometime after the summer of 491 the Spartans learned that Cleomenes had influenced Delphi. He did not await the repercussions. He escaped to Arcadia, but he had no intention of remaining there. He had so much prestige as the Spartan king that he convinced the Arcadians to accept him as their leader. He took the Arcadian leaders to the most sacred site in Arcadia, a site where the river Styx was supposed to bubble to the surface, and there, at this most sacred place, he had them swear an oath to follow him wherever he would lead. Cleomenes did not keep what he intended to do a secret—he announced that he was going to free the helots and the Laconian neighbors and revolutionize the Spartan state. The Spartiates were terrified and they invited him to return to Sparta and be their king just as he had been before.

Cleomenes was now about fifty years of age, or older, and, under the stresses of his situation, he descended (the Spartans said) into acute alcoholism. He would stroll through the city and tap the Spartiates he met on the head with his scepter. Perhaps he intended to display just how much power he had over them—a Spartiate had the right to strike dishonored men and push them out of the way—but the Spartans concluded that he was out of his mind and had his family confine him by fastening his feet in stocks.

Cleomenes found himself with only one escape possible and he demanded that the lone guard give him a short sword. At first the guard refused, but Cleomenes threatened him with what he would do when he was loose, and the guard, who was a helot, was afraid of the threats and gave him the sword. Cleomenes took the steel and, beginning at his shins, cut his flesh into strips up to his hips and to his belly. He died from loss of blood.

The Spartans concluded that he had killed himself in a fit of delirium tremens.

In his reign Cleomenes recognized the threat of Persia. He formulated Spartan policy, eliminated potential Persian allies, and created the alliance which would ultimately defeat the Persians. Cleomenes was the king who saved Greece.

── PART IV ──
THE PERSIAN WARS

Table 4. The Kings of the Persian Wars

Eurypontid Royal House

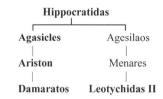

Agiad Royal House

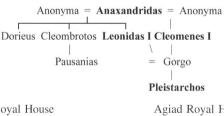

Eurypontid Royal House	Agiad Royal House
Hippocratidas (600–575)	
Agasicles (575–550)	Anaxandridas (560–520)
Ariston (550–515)	Cleomenes I (520–490)
Damaratos (515–491)	Leonidas I (490–480)
Leotychidas II (491–469)	Pleistarchos (480–459)

Kings highlighted in bold.

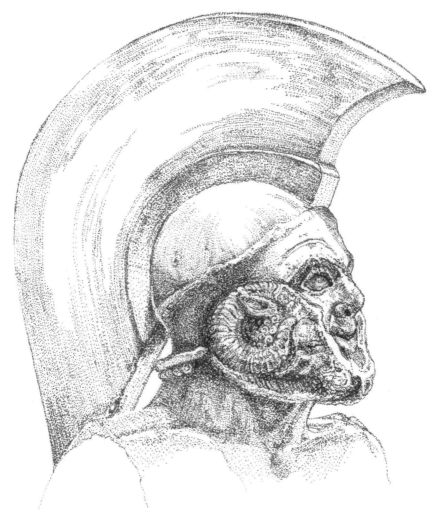

Illustration 5. Leonidas (from a bust in the Spartan Museum) (Pamela M. Bradford)

— 14 —

The "Greeks"

Cleomenes's death threw Sparta into turmoil at the very time that the Athenians needed the Spartans the most, because they anticipated that a Persian invasion might come any day. The Aeginetans demanded that the Spartans order the Athenians to return their hostages, the Spartans agreed, and they offered to let the Aeginetans have the king Leotychidas as a surety for the hostages' return. The Aeginetans wisely said *no*, even though the Athenians refused the Spartan request.

Meanwhile, as Cleomenes did not have a son, the Spartans chose Leonidas, who was the half-brother of Cleomenes, to be their king. Leonidas married Gorgo the daughter of Cleomenes (in order to preserve the bloodline and clarify the succession). Gorgo was about eighteen years of age, and Leonidas may have been about forty. He had a younger brother named Cleombrotos.

While the Spartans were sorting out the situation at home, Darius had authorized a plan to invade Greece by land and sea from the north under the command of Mardonius, but Mardonius was gravely wounded and a substantial part of his fleet was wrecked off Mt. Athos in the north. Darius then authorized an attack by sea with a fleet carrying infantry, cavalry, and the former Athenian tyrant, Hippias. The fleet was to attack both Athens and Eretria (the two poleis which had sent a fleet to help the Ionian rebels).

By the end of the summer of 490 the Persians had crossed the Aegean Sea and captured Carystus, the harbor on the southern tip of the island of Euboea; from this harbor they could attack either Eretria or Athens. They chose to attack Eretria first. The Eretrians hoped their walls and their 3000 hoplites and 600 cavalry could delay the Persians long enough for the Athenians to come to their aid, but the Athenians, faced with the Persian threat at Carystus, did not dare send any of their troops. The Persians captured Eretria and transported the population to the heart of the Persian empire.

An Athenian endurance runner ran the 150 miles to Sparta in forty-eight hours with the message: "Spartans, the Athenians need you!" and the Spartans replied that their law forbade them to venture out until the moon was full (probably the twelfth of September 490), but, as soon as the moon was full, they would come with their army. (The Athenians at that time—and historians ever since—have believed that the Spartans used the law to conceal their indecision in this moment of crisis. On the other hand, the Spartans were both conservative and cautious in religious matters. Should they violate religious custom and incur the displeasure of the gods? Their caution served a purpose—the Spartans needed to stay home to guard the helots and could afford to advance out of Laconia only under the most favorable conditions. They knew that Cleomenes had interfered with the Delphic oracle and he had come to a horrible end.)

The Athenians heard that the Persians had landed their army at Marathon under the guidance of the exiled Athenian tyrant, Hippias. (Marathon was a good place for cavalry and also a place with personal significance for the former tyrant.) The Athenians mobilized their army of 10,000 hoplites; they were joined by their neighbors, the Plataeans, with 1000 hoplites. The force was commanded by the Athenian *polemarch* (commander-in-chief) and the ten generals (one of whom was Miltiades). Miltiades had extensive experience of the Persians and believed that the Athenians could defeat them . . . under the right circumstances. The Athenians arrived in time to take up a position on a ridge, which effectively contained the Persian force between the ridge, two marshes, and the sea.

The Persians hoped that the Athenians would welcome Hippias, and the Athenians hoped that the Persians would be unable to supply themselves for long and would withdraw, or that the Spartans would arrive before the battle. After eight days (when the Spartan army was only two days march away) the Persians decided that they had to withdraw. They could not hope to carry the Athenian position on the ridge with their cavalry and light infantry, and they had to act before the Spartans arrived.

Five of the ten Athenian generals were content to let the Persians sail away, but Miltiades convinced the other four generals and the polemarch that they could fight and win, if they would wait until the Persians had loaded their horses on-board ship, before they gave the order to charge. At just the right moment, the phalanx charged down the slope of the ridge, slammed into the Persian light infantry, and scattered them. The Persian ships abandoned the infantry—6400 Persians were killed at Marathon, most of them hunted down after the battle. The Persian fleet withdrew back across the Aegean Sea. Two thousand Spartans arrived on the day after the battle, toured the battlefield, and congratulated the Athenians on a magnificent victory. The Athenians agreed—they thought Marathon was the greatest battle ever fought.

The battle of Marathon established that Persian light infantry was no match for the Greek hoplite, that the Athenians would fight, and that the Spartans would come to their aid (even if they had been dilatory). On the other hand, Marathon had also revealed how vulnerable the Greeks were to a naval attack. Many Athenians still believed that Athens, even with Sparta, was no match for the Persian empire.

The Persian king Darius died in 486 BCE, before he could avenge Marathon, and his son Xerxes (about thirty-two years old) had to put down an Egyptian revolt before he could consider avenging his father's defeat. Many Persians believed that their empire already contained too many Greeks—scribes, engineers, advisers, traders, soldiers, and sailors—but Xerxes's closest adviser was his uncle, Mardonius, and Mardonius, the strongest advocate for invasion, convinced Xerxes that he must avenge his father and demonstrate to his subjects and the world that no one could attack the Persian empire with impunity or refuse Persian demands without repercussions. Mardonius, also, as an expert on the Greeks, believed that in a crisis the mainland Greeks, just like the Ionians, would turn on each other and seek to make a deal with the Persians for their own safety.

Xerxes prepared for the expedition with all the care possible. He had a canal dug through the peninsula of Mt. Athos (where a Persian fleet had been destroyed), he built roads, bridged rivers and the Hellespont (following the design of a Greek engineer), ensured that his navy was outfitted with the latest ship, the trireme, and sent advance forces, army and navy, to occupy Thrace and Macedonia.

The Spartans may have had doubts about their policy towards Persia and debated whether to seek accommodation, but to the outside world they appeared steadfast in their determination to resist the Persian threat. The Athenians had lost Miltiades, but they had found another leader, Themistocles, who advocated an anti-Persian policy. Feelings ran hot in Athens and in the midst of the debate, the Athenians found themselves in a war (487–481) with Aegina over the hostages, and the Athenians were embarrassed to find that Aegina ("the eyesore of the Aegean") had a navy superior to their own.

When, therefore, in 483 BCE a large new vein of silver was discovered in the Athenian mines, Themistocles proposed that the silver be used to build and man a fleet of two hundred triremes. The objectives of the proposed fleet were, first, to defeat Aegina, second, to control the Aegean and defend Athens from the Persians, and third, understood if not stated, to provide employment for oarsmen and shipwrights. Themistocles's proposal was carried, the Athenians built a fleet, and the new fleet overwhelmed Aegina.

Meanwhile, the Spartans called a conference of their allies and the Athenians to meet in Corinth and establish a congress, where questions of strategy and command could be settled. We call the alliance "the League of Corinth" or the "Hellenic League," but the members called themselves "the Greeks," a title that implied that any Greek helping the Persians was a traitor. The "Greeks" settled questions of command—the allies would follow nobody but the Spartan kings—and they sent envoys all over the Greek world, but, in the end, the "Greeks" comprised the Spartans and their allies and the Athenians and their allies under the supreme command of the two Spartan kings, Leonidas, half-brother and son-in-law of Cleomenes, and Leotychides (who had superseded Damaratos). Themistocles the Athenian was second in command of the naval forces.

The "Greeks" decided to exploit the mountain ranges, rough sea, and the lack of provisions, to force the Persians to fight on Greek terms. They discussed where best to draw their first line of defense by land and sea. The Spartans wanted to fortify the Isthmus, the Athenians wanted Attica defended, and the Thessalians wanted Thessaly defended. Their envoys spoke to the representatives of the Greeks:

"Men of Greece, you must guard the Olympus pass, so that Thessaly and all of Greece is sheltered from war. We are ready to guard it with you, but you must send a large army, for, if you do not send it, you must understand that we will make an accommodation with the Persians."

The Thessalian statement put the situation in a nutshell—Greeks who found themselves on the northern side of the defensive line would join the Persians—so the Greeks sent an infantry force by sea to guard the pass. The Greeks, about ten thousand strong, camped between Mt. Ossa and Mt. Olympus where they were joined by the Thessalian cavalry. Their general was a Spartan polemarch, not a Heraclid. They remained there a few days, but then a message arrived from Alexander, the king of Macedon, that the position was untenable because there were too many alternate passes through the mountains, and they should withdraw, so the Greeks reembarked and sailed back to the Isthmus and the Thessalians asked the Persian king for an alliance.

The Greeks next decided to make their stand by land at Thermopylae and by sea at Artemisium. (Thermopylae and Artemisium are close enough together that the two forces could keep in touch with each other.)

Most Greeks believed that the Persians would win and most Greeks either joined the Persians (that is, *medized*) or remained neutral. Their divine guide Delphi was at best ambiguous—after the war some Greeks said that Apollo, himself, had *medized*—and responded to questions by saying that the Greeks should pray to the winds, for the winds would be their greatest allies. The Pythian priestess told the Athenian envoys,

"Why sit there? The roofs of the temples are running with blood and war is coming in a Persian chariot. Run, run as far as you can."

The Athenian envoys were appalled. They begged for some help, not just a prophecy, and they received an ambiguous and obscure pronouncement that "a wooden wall alone will remain unsacked. O divine Salamis, you shall destroy the children of women."

Themistocles convinced the Athenians that the second pronouncement was good news because the oracle would not have described Salamis as "divine," but as "baleful" or "fatal" or "cruel" if the Greeks were going to lose, and the "unsacked" wooden wall was the Athenian fleet. Thus encouraged, the Athenians voted to man their fleet and to move their whole population from Athens, partly to Salamis and partly to Troezen (in the Peloponnesus). They sent a large part of their fleet to Artemisium, to fight the Persian fleet there, while the Spartans and their allies guarded the pass at Thermopylae—this is an exceptionally narrow pass leading from Thessaly into Greece. The Spartan mission was to delay the Persians until the two fleets had fought. (The Persians employed a combined Ionian and Phoenician fleet.)

The Spartans had also received a disturbing oracle. The prophecy was written in hexameter verse like this:

> To you, o dwellers of the broad land of Sparta,
> Either your great and mighty city by Persian men
> Will be destroyed, or, if not, the land of Lacedaemon
> Will mourn the loss of a king of the race of Heracles.
> For not the might of bulls or of lions will hold
> With equal force, for he has the power of Zeus, and I say,
> He will not be stayed, before one or the other is fulfilled in its entirety.

Nonetheless, the Spartans decided to fight the Persians. They had intended to celebrate the Carneian festival (during which it was unlawful to send an army outside Spartan territory) and then to send out their whole army to help, leaving only a guard in Sparta. But events were coming to a head at Thermopylae. No one would defend it if the Spartans were not there, and so they decided to send an advance guard under the command of their king, Leonidas. Leonidas personally chose three hundred Spartiate hoplites who had "graduated" from the barracks and each of whom had a son to replace him, should he be killed.

He was joined by 2700 hoplites from the Peloponnesus, the whole army of the Opuntian Locrians (neighbors of Thermopylae), 1000 hoplites from Phocis, and 700 hoplites from Thespiae. The king demanded that the Thebans, whom he believed wanted to *medize*, to announce publicly whether they would go with him to war or draw back from joining the alliance of the Greeks. The Thebans did not want to join in a hopeless enterprise, as they saw it, but they were afraid to hold back so they sent a contingent of troops.

The Greek fleet at Artemisium numbered 271 ships: the Athenians had provided 127 ships (half their fleet, some manned by the Plataeans), the Corinthians provided forty ships, and the Spartans ten. The commander was Eurybiades, the Spartan naval commander of the year. He was not a Heraclid, but the allies had refused to serve under an Athenian, so Eurybiades was given the command. The Persians set sail against Artemisium in a storm and lost many ships, but the survivors caught the Greeks by surprise and captured three ships. They selected one prisoner, the handsomest of the Greeks, and cut his throat as a sacrifice.

The Greek defenders build a wall to defend the pass at Thermopylae. The Persians advanced faster than anyone had expected. When the Greeks heard that the Persians were near, they were terrified and the Peloponnesians wanted to go back to the Peloponnesus and guard the Isthmus, but the local troops, the Phocians and Locrians, were indignant at this decision and they appealed to Leonidas. Leonidas voted to remain.

—— 15 ——

Defeat and Victory

While the Greeks were preparing for the first encounter, Xerxes sent a scout to see how many Greeks there and what they were doing. He was curious, because he had heard in Thessaly that a small army was making a stand here, and that the leaders were Spartans and Leonidas, who was a descendant of Heracles. The scout could only see the guards outside the wall because the main army was behind the wall, but he observed that they were armed and he learned that they were Spartans. He rode back unmolested and he told Xerxes that he had seen armed men, that they were Spartans, and that some of them were exercising and some were arranging their hair.

Xerxes laughed at the scout's account, and he summoned Damaratos (who was with the army). When Damaratos arrived, Xerxes asked him what the Spartans were doing, exercising and fixing their hair. Damaratos said,

"You have listened to me before, when we set out against Greece, about these men. You laughed at me when I told you what has now come true. For now, O king, truly, the great struggle is upon you. Listen again now. These men intend to fight us for the passageway and they are preparing for that. For their law is this: when they are going to risk their lives, then they arrange their hair and beards. Understand this. If you defeat these men and those who remain in Sparta, there is no other group of people who would remain to fight you in close combat. Now you are advancing against the fairest kingdom and the mightiest men in Greece."

Xerxes did not believe a word he said, and he asked him again how such a small number could fight against his vast army. Damaratos said,

"O king, treat me as a liar deserves, if what I have said does not prove to be true."

Xerxes waited four days, hoping always that the Greeks would run away. On the fifth, when they had not departed and they appeared against all reason to have decided to stay, he ordered the Medes to attack them and take them alive while he watched. So the Medes rushed forward. Many fell, others took their place, and they did not retreat, although their losses were enormous. They made it clear to everyone and, most of all, to the king, that he might have massive numbers, but he had few real soldiers.

The struggle continued all day until, finally, the king ordered the Medes, who had been roughly handled, to withdraw, and he ordered the units of the Persians, whom he called the Immortals, to advance. The king thought the Immortals would handle the situation easily, but, although the Persians were brave men, they could accomplish no more than the Medes, even though the Greeks did not have many troops, because the Persians were fighting with short spears in a narrow space and they were no match for the Spartans. At one point, the Spartans suddenly turned their backs and, all in one bunch, ran away, and the Persians pursued them, each man as fast as he could run, and all shouting in triumph, until they lost their cohesion. Then the Spartans halted, spun around in formation, and killed a huge number of the Persians. A few of the Spartiates also were killed.

The Persians could not take the pass, no matter what they tried, and finally, defeated everywhere, they withdrew. The king (it is said) leaped up from his throne three times in fear for his army. Day after day, now, they fought for the pass, and each day they hoped that the Greeks, because they were so few, would be exhausted with wounds and unable to muster the men for battle, but the Greeks were arranged by national unit and each unit fought in turn, except the Phocians. The Phocians were guarding a footpath through the mountains.

While the two armies fought at Thermopylae, the two navies engaged in a full-scale battle at Artemisium. The sea battle lasted all day and ended in a standoff, except that the Greeks had the advantage of the prevailing current, which carried the wreckage of the battle to them, where they could salvage what could be salvaged and destroy the rest. Since half the Greek fleet was damaged and needed to refit, they decided to retreat to their second line of defense and they sent liaison officers to tell Leonidas that they were going to withdraw and that he need not defend the pass any more.

The Persian king, meanwhile, had learned of a pass around Thermopylae from a medizing Greek, and he sent a force to flank the Spartans. These troops set out from the camp at dusk, marched throughout the night, and, as dawn appeared, reached the highest peak of the mountains, where the Phocians had posted a thousand hoplites to guard the pass. The Persians approached without being seen, because of a dense oak forest, and the Phocians were unaware of them, until they heard the oak leaves being stirred, as though by many feet. The Phocians leaped up and grabbed their weapons and the Persians were upon them.

The Persians were so surprised to see men in armor, they halted, and the Persian commander, who was afraid that the Phocians were Spartans, asked his guide what army this was. When he learned who they were, he drew up the Persians for battle, and attacked the Phocians with a storm of arrows and javelins. The Phocians fled up the mountainside, because they thought that they were the object of the attack, and they prepared to defend themselves to the death, but the Persian troops ran past them and continued down the mountain as fast as they could.

At Thermopylae, before sunrise, the Greek seer Megistes performed a sacrifice, read the signs, and announced that death would be coming for them at dawn. Deserters arrived while it was still dark, and then, when day had already broken, three sentries ran down from their assigned position on the mountain, and they all reported the flanking movement of the Persians. Leonidas told the Greek commanders that he, and the Spartiates there with him, would not leave the post they had come to defend, but that they, his allies, should leave because he did not want them to be killed for no purpose.

The Greek historian, Herodotus, who knew men who had known Leonidas, believed that Leonidas had advised the allies to leave, because he recognized that they lacked heart for the fight, but he, himself, remained to fulfill the Delphic prophecy that either Sparta would be sacked by the enemy or a king would die, and he believed that, if he died there, he would fulfill the prophecy and guarantee the survival of Sparta.

Leonidas dismissed his seer, Megistes, but Megistes would not leave the king (although he did send his only son away). The Thespians and the Thebans, alone of the allies, remained with the Spartans. The Thespians refused to desert Leonidas and they died with him. The Thebans were compelled by Leonidas to remain, because he believed that they were going to medize the first chance they got and he wanted to use them while he could. (The Thebans remained, but at the first opportunity they surrendered to the Persians and Thebes became a Persian ally.)

As the sun rose, Xerxes poured a libation and then, when the sun was a quarter up the sky, and in accordance with the coordinated plan he had made with the encircling force, he marched forward and his mass of troops went forward with him. Leonidas and the Greeks recognized that now their path led to death and they preferred to advance into the wider part of the pass. They passed through the narrow way and fought against huge mobs of the enemy. In the back of the mobs the officers whipped on every man, always driving them to the front, where many fell into the sea and drowned and still more were trampled to death.

Thus Leonidas and the Greeks held their own and slaughtered the enemy, but, when they knew that the encircling force of Persians had arrived and death was certain, they displayed all their strength. In the constant fighting they broke their spears. Some fought the Persians with the broken spears and some fought with their swords. Leonidas fell in this struggle—the king. He was the best of all the men who came to Thermopylae, and others died with him, the best known of the Spartiates. (Herodotus was so moved by this feat of arms that he learned the names of each of the three hundred.) Two sons of Darius died here, too.

Persians and Spartans fought fiercely over the body of Leonidas, and in the greatest show of courage the Spartans drove the enemy back four times, picked the body up, and carried it back to the narrow part of the pass, where they took up a position on a hill. There they defended themselves with daggers, those who still had them, and with their hands and their teeth, as the enemy came on. Persian archers surrounded them, put up their barrier of shields, and shot arrows until they had killed all the Spartans.

(A hill has been excavated there with hundreds of arrowheads imbedded in it.)

Of the many brave Spartan and Thespian soldiers, the bravest and the best was a Spartiate named Dieneces. Herodotus heard from the Spartans that he had made a witty remark before the hand-to-hand combat with the Persians. He heard someone say that the enemy would shoot so many arrows, they would hide the sun. He said that he did not count as significant the numbers of the Persians, but the stranger had announced something good, if the Persians hid the sun, because then the battle against them would be fought in the shade. Dieneces was remembered for this saying and many others like it.

The dead were later buried on the battlefield and the following epitaph was composed and inscribed for the whole army:

Four thousand Peloponnesians fought
Three hundred times ten thousand here.

This epitaph was written for everyone, but there was one for just the Spartiates.

Go tell the Spartans, you who pass us by,
That here obedient to their laws we lie.

And the Spartans put up one for their seer.

This is the memorial of famed Megistias, whom once the Medes
At Sperchius' river crossed and killed, a seer,
Who saw clearly the fates of death coming,
But did not dare to desert the leaders of Sparta.

Xerxes examined the corpses and, when Leonidas was identified for him as the king of the Spartans, he ordered that his head be cut off and put on a stake. Ordinarily the Persians, and Xerxes, too, honored brave men, but Xerxes was more angry at Leonidas than he ever was at any other man.

Three of the three hundred survived the battle. Two of them, Eurytos and Aristodamos, had been dispatched with a message by Leonidas. As they were returning they were both stricken blind by an eye disease. When they learned that the three hundred had been outflanked and surrounded, Eurytos put on his armor and had a helot point him towards the fighting. He rushed forward and was killed. The other, Aristodamos, hid in a cave until his eyesight was restored and then he returned to Sparta. The Spartans called him "The Trembler" and deprived him of his citizenship rights. Not a single Spartiate would have anything to do with him or even speak to him. Aristodamos left Sparta and joined the phalanx of Tegea. (Perhaps if the two survivors had holed up together and then returned to Sparta together, they would have been accepted, but one had chosen to die and one had chosen to desert his king.) The third Spartan had been sent to Thessaly with a message. He hanged himself.

The Greek fleet reorganized at Salamis, the Athenians abandoned their city, and Damaratos gave advice to Xerxes,

"King, there is a large number of 'Lacedaemonians' and many cities in Laconia, but the city Sparta has at most eight thousand men. All of these are equals to those who fought here. The other Lacedaemonians are good men, but they are not the equals of the Spartans."

Damaratos advised him to occupy the island of Cythera off the coast of Laconia.

"From there you can terrorize the Spartans. With the war brought home to them, they will not be so eager to help the rest of Greece, as you conquer it, and, when you have enslaved the rest of Greece, only a weakened Laconia will be left.

"If you do not do this, here is what will happen. The Isthmus of the Peloponnesus is narrow. In this place the whole of the Peloponnesus will be gathered against you. Then expect harder battles than those you have fought already."

Xerxes rejected this advice. He marched his army down to Athens and sacked it, and then he opened secret negotiations with the Athenians to persuade them to betray their allies in exchange for favorable terms. The Athenians refused, even though their commander, Themistocles, had to threaten the Spartan commander that the Athenians would sail to the west out of the war and found a new city before the Spartan would agree to keep the fleet at Salamis and fight there.

Themistocles did not trust Greek resolve. He could see no sign that the Persians intended to initiate a battle, particularly in the narrows between Salamis and the mainland, where the Greek triremes, which were stouter if less maneuverable, would have the advantage, and so he sent Xerxes a secret message with just enough of the truth—the Greeks were divided and some of them wanted to withdraw from Salamis—that Xerxes believed the rest, that some would withdraw behind the island that very night while the others were in disarray and afraid to fight. Xerxes was ready to believe that Themistocles, or any Greek leader, would betray the other Greeks, and he ordered part of his fleet to sail around the island to block the escape route and ordered the rest to attack at dawn. An Athenian tragic writer gives us an eyewitness account of the battle as he imagined the Persians saw it:

"Our crews ate their dinner and got themselves in order; the rowers bound a thong around each oar, and, when the sunlight faded, every man was at his oar, every man at arms, and man encouraged man and they rowed the triremes to their appointed stations. All night the captains kept their crews awake, but the Greeks did not set sail secretly, and, when the dazzling chariot of the sun began to cross the sky, a songlike, happy tumult sounded from the Greeks, and echoed from the island rocks. We were afraid, for we had not expected this, and they, as though they never intended to flee, chanted a solemn paean, and rushed to battle. At once we heard the sound of oars striking the water and soon we saw them all. First the right wing and next the whole fleet advancing and we heard a great concerted cry,

" 'Greek sons, advance. Free your fathers' land, free your children, your wives, the sanctuaries of your paternal gods, the grave sites of your ancestors. Now the struggle is joined. All is at stake.'

"A Greek ship began the charge and sheared off the entire stern of a Phoenician vessel. Each captain drove his ship straight against some other ship. Triremes struck their bronze beaks together. At first the stream of Persian arms held its own, but when the mass of our ships had been crowded in the narrows and none could render another aid and each smashed its bronze beak against another of its own line and shattered their whole array of oars, then the Greek triremes recognized their chance, hemmed us in and battered us on every side.

"The hulls of our vessels rolled over and the sea was hidden from our sight, so thick were the wrecks and slaughtered men. The shores and reefs were covered with our dead and the foe kept striking and hacking our men in the water with broken oars and fragments of wrecked ships. Groans and shrieks together filled the open sea until night hid the scene."

Themistocles's general strategy and his particular stratagem at Salamis had won a stunning victory. The Persian fleet retreated to the Hellespont and the Greek fleet sailed out into the Aegean Sea. Leotychidas, the Spartan king, took command of it—the Spartans furnished twelve ships and a significant number of troops—and Xanthippos, the father of Pericles, was second-in-command. (The friendship between King Archidamos, the grandson of Leotychidas, and Pericles was probably based on the relationship developed between their families on this expedition.) Xerxes left Mardonius in command in Europe and returned to Asia. Mardonius withdrew into winter quarters and began a new effort to detach Athens from the league.

16

The Battle of Plataea

The Athenians wanted their city back. They wanted the Spartans to move out from the Isthmus and fight the Persians, and so they let the Spartans learn of the offer Mardonius had made to them, in effect to make them the satrap of a conquered Greece. The Spartans, in the end, decided that they could not afford to lose Athenian support. They mustered an army of 30,000 hoplites (10,000 from Laconia), and they also took 35,000 helots as light-armed troops. The army was commanded by Pausanias, the nephew of Leonidas and regent to the new king, Pleistarchos (the infant son of Leonidas).

As the Greek army advanced, Mardonius evacuated Attica and retired north to the vicinity of Plataea and pitched his camp on the north bank of the Asopus River. The Greeks, after some initial skirmishes, moved through the Plataean plain and occupied a ridge south of, and running parallel to, the Asopus River. Neither side could easily cross the river and attack the other, both sides debated what to do, turned to their soothsayers for guidance, and received the same report: the sacrificial signs were favorable for defense, but not for crossing the Asopus and initiating battle.

Mardonius, the Persian commander, was impatient. The two armies had already been sitting there eight days, which, for the Greeks, was an especially uncomfortable experience, as a veteran of such campaigns wrote, "In the open faced by our enemies we lay and from the sky, and from the ground, the meadow dews came out to soak our clothes and fill our hair with lice. And if I were to tell of . . . summer heat . . . under a windless sky—but why live such grief over again?"

Greek reinforcements kept arriving until a Theban convinced Mardonius to block the passes through the mountains of Cithaeron. Mardonius released his cavalry. The cavalry burst out into the plain and surprised a supply train of five hundred baggage animals with food for the army. The Persians slaughtered man and beast until they grew weary of the killing, and then they drove the survivors back to camp. From this time on, Mardonius's cavalry harried the Greeks constantly.

On the eleventh day of the stand-off, Mardonius, who was reported to have only a few days' food left, sent a herald to the Spartiates to say,

O Spartans, you say that you are the best men among the men here, who are amazed that you neither flee from war nor leave your formation but remain and either destroy your enemies or are yourselves destroyed. But none of this is true. You should have lived up to your reputation and sent us a herald to invite us to fight, us Persians alone, but we have found that you are not men enough to do this or to say this, but you tremble rather. Now then, since you will not initiate this proposal, we shall. Why do you not come out in front of the Greeks, since you are reputed to be the best, and we in front of our army, equal number to equal number, and we will fight? And, if the others decide they want to fight, they may fight later, but if they do not wish to, let us alone decide the issue in battle. Whoever wins, wins for his whole army.

The herald spoke and waited for a while, but, as nobody replied to him, he turned around, went back, and told Mardonius what had happened. Mardonius was elated. He was certain that he had won a moral victory and intimidated the Greeks, and he sent his whole cavalry force to harass and attack them. His horse-archers shot arrows at the Greeks and the Greeks did not know how to defend against them. The Persian cavalry fouled and ruined the spring from which the whole Greek army got its water. They could not get water from the Asopus River because of the cavalry and archers.

The Greek generals met with Pausanias and discussed the situation. They were cut off from water, their food supplies were low and resupply was difficult, and they were being harassed by the cavalry. They decided, if the Persians did not cross over on that day to force an engagement, that they would withdraw to a more defensible position with a ready source of water and protected supply routes in the foothills of the Cithaeron mountains. Further, they decided to move during that night at the second watch, so that the Persians would not perceive that they were setting out.

All through the day the Greeks suffered casualties from the horse-archers, but, as night came on, the horsemen withdrew, and, finally, the appointed hour arrived to move to the agreed upon place. Most of the Greeks fled in disorder, not to the appointed place, but, in a panic to escape the Persian cavalry; they fled for the polis of Plataea, and in their flight they arrived at the shrine of Hera, which is in front of the polis and about two and a half miles away from their original position. They grounded their arms in front of the shrine and camped there.

When Pausanias saw the allies setting out from their positions on the ridge along the Asopus River, he sent the word to the Spartans to take up their arms and to follow those ahead of them, for he thought that they were going to the agreed upon spot. All the unit commanders obeyed him except Amompharetos, the commander of the Pitanatan *lochos*. (A *lochos* is a Spartan unit equivalent to a battalion and comprising 512 men.) He said that he would not run from the "strangers," that he would not shame Sparta, and that he was amazed that they were not following their first plan, which they had all agreed on. Pausanias was furious with him for not obeying orders, but he decided that he could not just abandon the Pitanatan lochos, because, once it was alone, it would be annihilated, and so he kept the Spartans and their Tegean allies in place, while he tried to persuade Amompharetos not to do this. He told him that he, alone of the Spartans and Tegeans, would be left.

The Athenians were prepared to move, but they had noticed that the Spartans had not set out, and so they sent a scout on horseback to find out what the Spartans intended and to ask Pausanias what they should do. When the scout reached the Spartans, he saw that they were drawn up in their ranks and that the leaders were bickering. Pausanias was berating Amompharetos, but he was not able to sway him. Just as the scout arrived, Amompharetos took a rock in both his hands, dropped it at the feet of Pausanias, and said,

"With this ballot I vote not to flee from the strangers."

Pausanias said he was crazy and out of his head. The Athenian asked him what was going on, and Pausanias requested that the Athenians shift towards them and do what they did about the planned movement. The scout returned to the Athenians. Pausanias continued to argue with Amompharetos until just before dawn and then he decided to begin the movement without Amompharetos, because he did not think that Amompharetos would remain when all the other Spartans withdrew. He ordered the signal to be given, he began the withdrawal along the foothills of Cithaeron, because he feared the Persian cavalry, and the Tegeans followed. The Athenians in their ranks moved down into the plain.

Amompharetos, at the beginning, believed that Pausanias would not dare leave him and he continued with his refusal to move, but, when Pausanias had advanced a ways, Amompharetos realized that he was really being left, and he ordered the lochos to take up their arms and he led them at a walk towards the rest of the formation, which was about half a mile away. Pausanias stopped, by chance near a shrine dedicated to Demeter, and waited for the lochos of Amompharetos to catch up. No sooner had Amompharetos and his men rejoined them than they came under the attack of the Persian cavalry.

At dawn, as usual, the Persian cavalry had crossed the Asopus and ridden towards the ridge where the Greeks were stationed, only to discover that the Greeks were gone. A few rode back to inform Mardonius while the rest pressed forward on the tracks of the Greeks, until, at last, they caught up to them and attacked them. Mardonius, when he learned that the Greeks had withdrawn during the night and he saw the ridge deserted, said to an aide,

"What do you say now, when you see this spot deserted. Some said that the Spartans did not flee from battle, that they were first in war. Now we all have seen them run away in the night. It is clear, when they had to meet men who, in reality, are the best in battle, they proved that there is nothing to them and nothing to

Greeks. Now we must catch them, so that they pay to us the price for all that they have done to Persians."

He led the Persians on the run across the Asopus River along the track of the fleeing Greeks and he caught up to the Spartans and the Tegeans. He did not see the Athenians, who were marching in the plain, because of the hills. The rest of his army, seeing the Persians setting out in pursuit of the Greeks, raised their standards and pursued as fast as each one could, without any order or discipline, shouting with excitement.

When Pausanias saw the cavalry, he sent horsemen to the Athenians to say this,

"Athenian men, the great struggle is at hand, whether Greece shall be free or enslaved. We have been deserted by our allies who ran away in the night, we Spartans and you Athenians. Now we must defend and support each other, as best as we are able. Come help us. Or, if you are caught and are unable to come help us yourselves, send your archers."

When the Athenians heard this, they set out to bring help, but the Thebans and the other Greeks, who had sided with the Persians, were approaching them, so that they were no longer able to bring help. The Spartans and the Tegeans, and with them about fifty thousand light-armed troops, were alone. The Tegeans had about three thousand hoplites. The Spartan soothsayer performed the prebattle sacrifice, but the sacrifice was not favorable and Pausanias had to order his men to hold their position, defend themselves with their shields, and take no offensive action. The Persians advanced to close bow-range, fixed their wickerwork shields in the ground, and shot a mass of arrows at the Spartans and the Tegeans. A few Spartans were killed and many more were wounded. One of them, a Spartan named Callicrates, who was considered the handsomest man in the whole Greek army, fell in the ranks with an arrow-wound in his side. He was carried out of the battle line. He said that he did not regret dying for Greece, but that he had not struck a blow and that he had not done any deed worthy of himself, as he had longed to do.

With other Spartans falling around him, Pausanias looked off in the direction of the Heraeon of the Plataeans and called upon the goddess and prayed to her for her help.

At the moment that he called upon her, the Tegeans leaped forward, and the soothsayer proclaimed that the sacrificial signs for the Spartans were favorable. The Spartans charged the hedge of wickerwork shields, the Persians dropped their bows and used their spears, but still the Spartans advanced, broke down the barrier, and fought the enemy hand to hand. The Persians were not inferior in courage and strength, but they were unarmored and they were inexperienced and not equal to their opponents in skill. They rushed forward singly and in small groups, closed with the Spartiates, grabbed hold of the spears, and tried to break the oncoming phalanx. Mardonius himself was there, fighting on a white horse, and he had around him his elite guard of a thousand men. Here the fighting was the hardest and as long as Mardonius survived, the Persians fought and struck down many of the Spartans. When, however, a Spartan named Arimnestos closed with Mardonius and stabbed him and killed him, and his bodyguard died defending him, the rest turned and fled to their camp in complete disorder and hid behind the wooden wall which they had made in Theban territory.

Here, at last, was retribution for the death and desecration of Leonidas. Pausanias, the nephew of Leonidas and grandson of King Anaxandridas, won the greatest victory (Herodotus writes) of all we know about. Ninety-one Spartiates, sixteen Tegeans, and fifty-two Athenians died in the battle.

Now the other Greeks, those drawn up around the Heraeon, who had held back from the battle and were waiting anxiously for news, heard that there had been a battle and that the Spartans had won and that the Athenians had defeated the Thebans. When they heard that, without preserving their ranks, they rushed across the plain to the shrine of Demeter.

The Athenians, the Spartans, and the Tegeans advanced to the Persian camp and broke in. The camp dwellers panicked and crowded together without defending themselves, and all but three thousand of them were killed.

The Greeks voted on who had been the bravest. They agreed that, of the Persians, it was Mardonius, and that the Tegeans and Athenians had acquitted themselves well, but the Spartans had far surpassed them in courage. They also gave as their opinion that Aristodamos, the survivor of Thermopylae, had been the bravest and next to him the best had been the Spartiates Poseidonios, Philocyon, and Amompharetos. These last three men, all of whom had been killed, received public honors. Aristodamos did not, because the Spartans said he was a *dead* man, and the dead have no courage because they have no fear of death.

At the same time as the battle of Plataea—ancient tradition assigns it to the same exact day—King Leotychidas won the battle of Mycale. The Greek fleet was in the Aegean under the command of the Spartan king. While it was stationed at Delos, three representatives came in secret from Samos and informed the king that the people of Samos were ready to revolt from the Persians and that other Ionians would follow them, if he brought his fleet into action there. He listened to their proposal and he was uncertain whether they were telling him the truth and whether the proposed action was feasible, but when he asked the name of the chief informant and learned that his name was "Lead the Army" (Hegesistratos), the king said,

"I need no further information. I accept this portent."

The Greek seer, Deiphonus ("Voice of Zeus") and the Spartan king conducted the religious rites and the sacrifices. The seer announced that the sacrifices were propitious and the king ordered the fleet to sail for Samos.

The Persians withdrew from Samos without a fight and retreated to Mycale on the south coast of Asia Minor where there was a large force of Persian troops. The Persian leaders intended to beach their fleet and use their troops to build fortifications around it and protect it. They had begun the fortifications, quarrying local stone and cutting down fruit trees, when the Greek fleet arrived.

When Leotychidas arrived at Mycale and found that the Persians had beached their ships and that the fleet was protected with a palisade, he had to convince the

Greek commanders, who were disappointed that the Persians were not prepared to come out and fight in the open sea, to engage the Persians on land. Leotychidas ordered his ship to be brought as close to shore as it could be, and he shouted out a message for the Ionian Greeks serving in the Persian fleet.

"Men of Ionia, those of you who can hear me, listen to what I say. The Persians will not be able to understand what I say to you. When we fight, first, remember what you have to do to win your freedom and, second, remember our word of recognition, *Hera*. Those of you who have heard this, pass it on to those who haven't."

The message directed at the Ionians aroused the Persians' suspicions. They were afraid that the Ionians would turn against them, so they disarmed some of them and sent others on missions which carried them away from the battle.

The Greeks forced a landing and drew up their phalanx on the beach opposite the Persians, who had formed behind a line of overlapping shields. The Greeks advanced slowly and hesitantly, until they found the staff of a herald lying on the beach, and a rumor spread (as though brought by a herald) that the Greeks at Plataea had won a great victory. The morale of the Greeks shot up and they charged the Persian position.

The Greek plan was to divide their forces: the Athenians were to move directly at the fortifications and the Persians, while the Spartans were to cross a stream and a barrier of hills and then come down on the fortifications from the rear. The Athenians and their allies first fought the Persians in the open behind their line of shields. The Athenians forced them back into the fortifications and for a time were held there until their commanders called upon them for one more supreme effort. Then the Athenians broke through the wall. The Ionians still on the Persian side turned against them and the other allies fled. Now the Spartans came down from the rear and the last Persian resistance was broken. A few escaped by fleeing into the hills, but many were picked off there. The Persian fleet was destroyed.

The Greeks returned to Samos and there the commanders debated what they should do about the Ionians. By now they had confirmed that the Persians in Greece had been defeated and annihilated, but the Persians still had a presence at the Hellespont and still had enormous resources to bring to bear upon Ionia. The Spartan suggestion was to allow the Ionians who wished to be free of the Persians to move to mainland Greece and settle in the towns of the medizers—"If they love Persia so much, let them move there!" The Athenians objected and suggested rather that they bring the Ionians, beginning with the islanders, into their alliance. The Spartans acquiesced and the islands of Samos, Chios, and Lesbos, and, later, other islanders, joined the alliance. The islanders were required to swear an oath that they would adhere to the alliance and that they would fight for the freedom of all the members of the alliance.

The second Ionian revolt had begun. The League navy set out to the Hellespont to drive the Persians completely out of Europe. They laid siege to Sestos and took it.

"Various are the sounds of the voices of the conquerors and conquered, from the opposition of their fates. The conquered are stooping now to gather in their arms their dead husbands and brothers, children lean to clasp the aged who begot them, crying upon the death of those more dear, from lips that never will be free. The Greeks have their midnight work after the fighting that sets them down to feed on all the city has, ravenous, headlong, by no rank and file assigned, but as each man has drawn his shaken lot by chance. And in the enemy houses that their spears have taken, they settle now, free of the open sky, the frosts and dampness of the evening; without sentinels they sleep the sleep of happiness the whole night through."

Three Spartan kings forged the alliance, formulated the strategy, and led the forces which defeated the Persians. Cleomenes created the alliance and was one of the first to see the coming struggle and what Sparta must do. Leonidas was the first Spartan king to engage the enemy, and his aggressiveness and his sacrifice were crucial to the ultimate victory. Leotychidas commanded at the culminating victory of Mycale.

— 17 —

The Treason of Pausanias

The Spartans and Athenians together had defeated the greatest military power in the world, and yet half a century later the Spartans and the Athenians fought such a war against each other that, in the words of one Greek writer, they "murdered Greece." The Athenians blamed the Spartans. They claimed, first, that Pausanias let the victory go to his head, that he began to treat his allies as though they were helots, and that he conspired with the Persians to enslave the Greeks. Second, they claimed that the Spartans tried (in vain) to prevent the Athenians from rebuilding their city walls.

After the Persians had been defeated both on land and sea by the Greeks, and their army had been destroyed or been forced to withdraw from Europe, and those who fled in their ships had been destroyed at Mycale, Leotychidas, the king of the Spartans, and the leader of the Greeks at Mycale, withdrew home, taking with him his allies from the Peloponnesus. After Sestos fell, the Greek contingents sailed away from the Hellespont to their separate cities.

The Athenians returned to their city and began to rebuild the wall. The Spartans, when they learned what the Athenians were going to do, sent an embassy to inform them that they much preferred that neither the Athenians, nor anyone else outside of the Peloponnesus, have walls, in case the Persians returned and used a walled city, as they had Thebes, as a strong point. The Athenians sent an embassy, headed by Themistocles, himself, to Sparta to delay and obfuscate. The kings received him and wined and dined him. When they asked him about rumors that the wall was being built anyway, Themistocles advised them to send an embassy to see for themselves. He sent a messenger secretly to Athens to detain the Spartan embassy until the walls were high enough to protect the city. When word reached him that the walls had been completed, he told the Spartans, "We decided that it was better for our city to have a wall and it will be of more use for our citizens in private and for our allies. For it was not possible, except from equal resources, to give equivalent or equal advice."

The Spartans did not reveal anger to the Athenians, but they said that they had not given this advice out of ill will, but for the common good, and they had the warmest feelings for those who, next to themselves, had shown the greatest zeal against the Persians, and they were hurt that their good advice had been so misunderstood.

Pausanias was sent out from the Peloponnesus with twenty ships to command a fleet which included thirty Athenian ships and a large number of allies. They conquered most of Cyprus and then they sailed to Byzantium, which the Persians held, and they besieged and took it, but the other Greeks, in particular the Ionians, were upset because of Pausanias's violent temper.

Pausanias dressed in Persian garments which he had taken in Byzantium, and, when he traveled, he had Persian and Egyptian spear-bearers accompany him. He dined at a Persian table. He showed a terrible temper towards all equally, so that no one was able to get in to see him, and he was not able to conceal his cast of mind, but he revealed in the littlest actions that he intended in the future to do even greater things.

Pausanias on his own authority had had two lines inscribed on the tripod, which the Greeks set up in Delphi as part of a thank offering from the Persian spoils,

The Leader of the Greeks, as he destroyed the army of the Persians
Pausanias, sets up this memorial to Phoebus Apollo.

The Spartans chiseled out the couplet from the tripod and inscribed the names of the cities, which together defeated the barbarians, and then they set it up. The arrogant inscription, the Spartans and other Greeks believed, revealed the autocratic nature of Pausanias.

The Ionians went to the Athenians and asked them to assume the leadership of the naval alliance as they were of common blood. The Athenians listened and replied that they would not ignore their request and that they would do what seemed best to them.

Meanwhile the Spartans recalled Pausanias, to question him about what they had heard. Greeks accused him of many crimes and, in particular, that he had rather emulated a tyrant than a general. Pausanias was censured for some of his private acts of injustice, but he escaped the greater charge of criminal behavior. Other Greeks, but not the Spartans, were absolutely convinced that he had medized. During his absence, the Athenians assumed the command of the naval alliance. They had a free hand in the Aegean, because Sparta did not recognize any immediate threat from Athenian naval operations, and Corinth, the only Spartan ally that could have contended with the Athenians for control of the Aegean, turned west and continued to develop and enlarge its trade routes and influence in Greater Greece.

Pausanias, in private, took a trireme from Hermione and traveled to the Hellespont to oppose the Persians, he said, but, in fact, the Greeks believed, to help the Persian king enslave Greece so he could become satrap. He had done a favor for the king at Byzantium. During that operation he had captured some Persians, who were close to the king, and he had released them with a letter for the king.

"Pausanias the leader of Sparta, wishing to do you a favor, sends back these men, captured by the spear. I have made up my mind, if it suits you, to marry your daughter and to put Sparta and the rest of Greece under your hand. I think that I can do this with your help. If any of this pleases you, send a trustworthy man to the coast and we will carry on the rest of our discussion through him."

Xerxes was delighted with the letter. He sent a confidant to take over the neighboring satrapy, and he wrote to Pausanias,

"Thus says King Xerxes to Pausanias: for those men whom you rescued and returned to me from across the sea in Byzantium, there will be recorded in my house gratitude that will last forever. I am pleased with your words. Let neither night nor day hold you back from doing what you have revealed to me, nor let expenditure of gold and silver, or throngs of troops, cause you to hesitate, if it is of any help to you. Cooperate with my satrap, a noble man, whom I sent you. Be bold and your affairs and mine will turn out for the best and most prosperous."

Word reached Sparta that Pausanias had settled in Colonas near Troy and that he was up to no good and corresponding with the Persians. The ephors sent a herald to him with a coded message that he was to accompany the herald back to Sparta, or the Spartiates would declare him an enemy. Pausanias wanted to avoid suspicion and he was confident that he could free himself of the charges through influence and bribes, so he returned for a second time to Sparta. When he arrived, the ephors threw him into prison—they have the power to confine even the kings—but he arranged his release and prepared to answer the charges of those who wanted answers.

The Spartiates had no clear proof, and he was a man in whom they had always had confidence, whom they had honored as a Heraclid, and who was regent to King Pleistarchos, the son of Leonidas. But, nonetheless, he had provided many reasons for suspicion by his unlawful actions, by his enthusiasm for barbarian ways, and by his autocratic nature. They learned that he was meddling somehow with the helots, that he had promised them freedom and citizenship if they stood by him and did everything he wanted, but, still, the Spartiates did not entirely trust the information they received, and they did not want to rush to judgment against him because they never took an irrevocable action against a Spartiate unless they had absolute and incontrovertible proof.

Now, however, a confidant of Pausanias, a boyhood companion (called a *mothax*) who had accompanied Pausanias through the agoge, brought to the ephors a letter which Pausanias wanted him to take to the Persian satrap. (The man had opened the letter and found in it an instruction to kill the messenger.) Even then the ephors wanted evidence from Pausanias's own lips, and they devised a scheme to trap him. The man went as a suppliant to Taenarum and the ephors hid behind a double wall they had had constructed. Pausanias came and asked the man why he had sought sanctuary. The man blamed him for what was written in the letter about himself and he enumerated everything he had done for Pausanias, the whole plot came out, and Pausanias reassured him that all would be well. The ephors heard everything clearly and they returned to Sparta.

The ephors intended to arrest him as he entered the city, but when he saw them and he observed the expression on the face of one of the ephors, he knew why they had come, and he ran to the nearby shrine of Athena of the Brazen House and took refuge there. He went into a small room within the shrine, in order that he might not suffer from the elements, and there he lay low. The ephors did not enter the shrine, but they took the roof off the room so they could observe him; they bricked him up inside the shrine, sat down around the outside, and waited for him to starve. When they perceived that he was on the point of death, they knocked down the bricks, dragged him outside, still breathing, and watched him die right there on the spot. They were going to throw his body into the chasm, where they threw common criminals, but in the end they decided to bury him nearby.

The conversations at the evening mess during this affair must have been interesting, particularly afterwards, when some of the members reported that the ghost of Pausanias was haunting the temple. Finally, the Spartans asked Delphi what they should do and the oracle advised them that they should establish a tomb where he had died and that they should give back two bodies in place of the one in the Brazen House to rid themselves of the pollution. They set up two bronze statues at the place where he had died.

The ephors also took action against King Leotychidas. He was tried and convicted of corruption—accepting a bribe to cut short an expedition in Thessaly—and he went into exile.

Between 478–465 the Spartans not only had two royal crises, but they also had to fight two major wars, one against an alliance of Tegeans and Argives, whom they defeated at Tegea, and a second against an alliance of Arcadians (except for the Mantineans) whom they defeated at Dipaea. In this same period the district of Elis, against the wishes of Sparta, reorganized, designated the polis of Elis as its capital, and expanded the rights of its citizens into a limited democracy.

— PART V —
THE ATHENIAN WARS

Table 5. The Kings of the Athenian Wars

Eurypontid Royal House

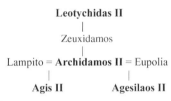

Agiad Royal House

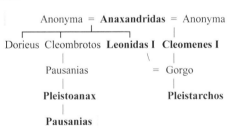

Eurypontid Royal House	Agiad Royal House
Leotychidas II (491–469)	Pleistarchos (480–459)
Archidamos II (469–427)	Pleistoanax (459–445, 426–409)
Agis II (427–399)	Pausanias (445–426, 409–395)
Agesilaos II (399–360)	

Kings highlighted in bold.

Illustration 6. The Spartan Phalanx (Chigi vase) (Pamela M. Bradford)

—— 18 ——

The Precarious Entente

With the rise of the Athenian navy and the growing enmity of the Athenians, the Spartans' influence was limited to points they could reach by land. When they contemplated a war, they had to consider marching distances, the availability of allies, and food supplies, how long would their allies stay in the field, could they accomplish their objective in that amount of time, how long a campaign could they sustain, and would they have to fight their way through hostile territory? With the Athenians, now, they were facing a whole new way of war. In a world in which the phalanx was not supreme—or the supreme expression of the polis—what was the role for Sparta?

The Athenians were quite conscious that they had a new source of power, the democratic navy, and a new form of government—Democracy. Democracy, one Athenian wrote, is despised by all the right people, because it gives power to the wrong people, but, nonetheless, it is justified, because the people man the fleet and the fleet has brought Athens its power.

The Athenians not only had the largest fleet in the Aegean, they had also developed battle tactics so sophisticated and so demanding that no one else could perform them. The Athenian navy was as far superior to other navies as the Spartan army was to other armies. The Athenians' hoplite force was not as good as the Spartan hoplite force, but it was good enough and far better than any force its subjects could muster and so was sufficient to control them even if the subjects could somehow combine against them, which they could not do because the Athenians controlled the Aegean Sea.

The Athenians recognized the military advantages of naval power: even confronting a stronger land power, such as the Spartans, they could keep the enemy off balance, land somewhere they were not, plunder and burn, and, by the time the enemy could react, reembark and sail away. They could undertake distant expeditions, because a fleet could carry its own provisions and travel without hindrance wherever the sea reached.

The Spartans did not yet grasp how profoundly the fleet of the Athenians had changed the balance of power. They relied on their friends in Athens, men who admired aristocratic virtues, despised the democracy, and opposed Athenian imperialism. Principal among them was the son of the hero of Marathon— Cimon. He believed that the future of Greece depended upon the cooperation, if not the partnership, of Athens and Sparta, and only through such cooperation could the Greeks be secure and stable and effectively oppose their greatest enemy, the Persians.

While the Athenians did have legitimate grievances against the Spartans, the Athenians, for their part, were far from blameless in the increasing hostility. Without any consultations with the Spartans, they had assumed command of the allied fleet and the naval alliance (the Delian league). They ran it as they pleased: they forced every island to join, punished those who wanted to withdraw, and determined the amount of money, ships, and crews each member owed. The first payment they exacted from the members was 460 talents, which could commission and crew forty-six triremes and keep them at sea for the eight-month sailing season. The Athenians, in time, took over the fleets of all the cities except Chios and Lesbos and they demanded a fixed tribute to be paid in coin. In contrast, the Spartans did not impose tribute on their allies, but they did impose oligarchies, the only government acceptable to them.

Under the leadership of Pericles, the Athenians became the masters of the Aegean Sea. Pericles recognized, and, perhaps, exaggerated the power that command of the sea gave Athens, but he also recognized that Athens itself was vulnerable to siege, and, therefore, he converted Athens into an "island" on the mainland by having walls (the "long walls") constructed from the city of Athens to the Piraeus (its port). As the only potential enemy strong enough to put Athens under siege was Sparta, the Long Walls seemed to be a clear statement of Athenian expectations and policy.

In the meantime, while the Spartans concentrated on their problems in the Peloponnesus and at home, the Athenians were continuing the war against the Persians throughout the whole of the Aegean and beyond. In the process they transformed the Delian League into an Athenian empire. When the Aegean island of Thasos tried to withdraw, because the Thasians considered the war with the Persians all but over, the Athenians treated them like rebels. The Athenians defeated the Thasian fleet and put the city under siege and the Thasians sent envoys to the Spartans and asked them to help by invading Attica. According to the Athenians, the Spartans agreed, but their plans were disrupted by an unforeseen event. (Without Spartan help and, after a three-year siege, the Thasians were forced to surrender to the Athenians. They had to tear down their walls, hand over their fleet, pay for the war, pay tribute, surrender their mainland possessions, and give up the right to mint coins—the symbol of freedom and independence.)

Illustration 7.   Mountains in the earthquake zone (Pamela M. Bradford)

In Sparta, after the exile of Leotychidas, Archidamos, his grandson, was chosen king. He was born about 490 BCE, became king at the age of about eleven, and was under the guidance of a regent until 469 when he turned twenty-one. He had already made a good impression on the Spartans. (His name was a "democratic" declaration, "First among the People.") In the year 465/464, in the middle of the day and without any warning, Sparta was struck by a devastating earthquake. The earth cracked open in many places, several of the peaks of Mt. Taÿgetus were torn away, and the whole city of Sparta was destroyed with the exception of five houses.

The young men and boys were exercising inside a colonnade a few moments before the earthquake struck; a rabbit suddenly ran through the colonnade, and the boys, still naked and covered with oil, chased after it, while the young men remained behind and were all killed when the colonnade collapsed on them. (They were buried in a common tomb and the tomb, called *Seismatias*—*seismos* is Greek for "earthquake"—was still to be seen in the second century CE.)

INTERLUDE IN THE MOUNTAINS

The earthquake was caused by a vertical movement along the fault line at the base of Mt. Taÿgetus. It is estimated to have been of a magnitude of 7.2. (The 1986 earthquake at Kalamata—in which a large part of the city was destroyed and part of the river bed of the Pamisos River dropped a foot-and-a-half—was estimated to be a magnitude of 5.8.) The Kalamata earthquake left a fault-scarp about thirty-six feet high and about twelve miles long.

I wanted to explore the fault scarp in the Taÿgetus Mountains. I was in Sparta in the third week of June and we could see snow on the tops of the mountains. While I was having dinner at *En Hatipi* I explained to the owner, Michael, my interest in seeing the fault scarp and the modern evidence of the ancient earthquake. He explained that the roads were rugged and would wreck Aristoteles' car, but Aristoteles could rent a motorcycle and I could ride behind him. I was lukewarm about that idea, so Michael studied the map I had and said he would take us in his car.

"I have ridden over that area a thousand times and I have always wondered how the little rocks from up above got down below."

He picked us up the next morning and for two and a half hours we drove through the earthquake zone of Taÿgetus. He knew the area intimately, but he had not known that its abrupt drops and sheer cliffs were due to the Great Earthquake of 464.

We began on a winding, blacktop road that gave us a spectacular view of the Frankish fortress of Mystra. The road wound across the property of a monastery and through a small village, Taÿgete. Michael explained that the "pops," the church fathers, have money and use it to improve their property, including the roads. Beyond the monastery the road, which proceeds on to other villages, is just rock and ruts, soft shoulders, and steep drop-offs.

Spartans today—and ancient Spartans, too—love the Taÿgetus mountains.

We stopped to look at a tortoise and Michael pointed out a plane tree and said, "Where there is water, there are plane trees; where there are plane trees, there is water. Water is life."

He picks oregano and nuts in the mountains for his restaurant. Goatherds today, just like ancient herdsmen, drive their goats up in May and back down in October.

The goatherds receive money from the government to buy feed so they will not pasture their goats on the mountain, but they take the money and pasture the goats anyway. If the trees grow too thick for the goats, the goatherds set them on fire. Michael said that he had chided a goatherd for the destruction that goatherds, and goats, caused in the mountains and the goatherd said,

"But the mountain belongs to me."

(Michael's cell phone rang during the drive in Taÿgetus. It was his brother-in-law in Boston.)

Everywhere in this region we saw broken and shattered mountains—some cut in half, as it were, by a cleaver—and evidence of the subsistence of the earth. The sound alone, above and below the earth, must have been deafening and terrifying, and, to a people who believed in the gods, a manifestation of the power—and displeasure—of Poseidon.

Had it not been for Archidamos, this earthquake—*The Great Earthquake*—would have been the last chapter in a history of the Sparta.

Standing in the ruins of Sparta, King Archidamos at once understood that the immediate shock could be followed by others, that everyone was dazed and acting as individuals, trying to rescue survivors and salvage their most valuable belongings, and that the security of Sparta, the king's primary responsibility, was at stake. He ordered the trumpet to be blown, which gave the signal that an enemy was about to attack. Every Spartan trained constantly to react to that signal, to grab his equipment and form up outside the city with the kings. Now every able-bodied Spartan rushed to his assigned position. Not long after they had formed up, helots arrived from the surrounding country to see what had happened. (The Spartans later concluded that the helots had not come to help, but to attack them. This conclusion poisoned an already delicate relationship.) The helots found the Spartan phalanx ready to fight and they spread the report that the Spartans could still defend themselves. Archidamos's quick thinking in this crisis saved Sparta. Nonetheless, the disaster convinced some of the Laconian neighbors to rebel and the Messenian helots joined them.

In their desperation the Spartans sent an envoy to Athens. An Athenian eyewitness wrote (as though speaking to Spartans),

"He sat down as a suppliant at the altars, his face bloodless against the purple of his cloak, and he begged us to send an army, for the Messenians had attacked you and the god had shaken you. And Cimon led out 4000 hoplites and saved Sparta."

Cimon told the Athenians that they should "not allow Greece to go lame, or their own city to be deprived of its partner." His political opponent, the foremost democratic leader of Athens (and predecessor of Pericles) opposed the request and exhorted the Athenians not to attempt to rescue or restore a city which was their rival, but, rather, to let Sparta's pride be trampled underfoot. Cimon won the debate and the Athenians helped the Spartans regain control of most of Messenia. The fighting was desperate and brutal—Arimnestos (the Spartan who killed Mardonius) was ambushed in Stenyclaros and he and the three hundred men with him were killed. The Spartans, the Athenians, and other allies forced the rebel Messenians to concentrate on Mt. Ithome. The Athenians returned home and the Spartans put the Messenians under siege, but the Spartans were notoriously inept at conducting effective sieges and they asked the Athenians for more help. The Athenians returned, but, by the time they arrived, the Spartans believed that they had the situation under control and they were afraid that the Athenians might support the rebels, so they dismissed them.

The Athenians were furious at this treatment. They ostracized Cimon, accepted the Messenian refugees, and resettled them at Naupactus on the Corinthian Gulf, where they would provide a base from which the Athenians could interdict Corinthian trade. The Athenians under the leadership of Pericles pursued an aggressive policy: they reduced the island of Aegina, forced the people to leave, and resettled the island with Athenians. They detached Megara from the Peloponnesian League—to secure the isthmus. They sent a colonizing expedition to Italy—Athenians joined by other Greeks—to secure a foothold in the west. They formed an alliance with Argos, the inveterate enemy of Sparta, and they sought to detach other poleis in the Peloponnesus and to set up a coalition of land powers to oppose Sparta. Finally, they completed the Long Walls that turned Athens into an "island" on the mainland.

The Athenian leaders presented to the Athenian people a picture of the Spartans as a duplicitous and crafty people who depended more on intrigue and deception than on military power—from the advice given to the Plataeans in 520 to seek aid from the Athenians (and so create enmity between Athens and Thebes) to the treason of Pausanias, the opposition to the walls, the dismissal at Ithome, the planned raid into Attica—in short, a people who said one thing and thought another. They convinced the citizens that the Spartans were their implacable enemies, that regardless of what the Spartans said, what they promised, what they did, regardless of any professions or gesture of peace, the ultimate and unwavering objective of the Spartans was the destruction of the Athenian democracy.

In response the Spartans sent an army into central Greece. In the name of the liberty and independence of Delphi the Spartans invaded Phocis and made an alliance with the Thebans—formerly anathema to them because the Thebans had medized. The Spartan commander was the regent for the young king Pleistoanax the son of Pausanias. (Pleistarchos had died while still young and without leaving a son.) The regent was successful in Phocis, but, in the face of active Athenian opposition, he found himself stranded. He did not want to risk a seacrossing in the face of the superior Athenian navy, and he did not want to have to force a difficult passage through the Isthmus past the Athenian army and their allies the Megarians. He had also heard that the opposition to the democracy in Athens might overthrow the democracy and he wanted to remain in the area, in case he could support the oligarchs. Consequently, he remained with his army in Boeotia.

The Athenians, however, suppressed the oligarchs and marched into Boeotia to confront the Spartans. They were joined by their allies, the Argives and the Thessalian cavalry, and they fought the Spartans in a battle at Tanagra. However, the Thessalians deserted and the Spartans won, despite heavy casualties on both sides. The victory opened up the Isthmus again—Megara returned to the Peloponnesian League—and checked the Athenian plans to build a land alliance against the Spartans, but, in retaliation for the defeat, an Athenian fleet sailed around the Peloponnesus and burned the dockyards of the Laconia port, Gytheion. The Spartans and the Athenians agreed to a five-year truce.

The Athenians were stretched thin and the great Athenian democratic leader Pericles had to recognize the limits of Athenian power—his land alliance had been defeated by the Spartans, foreign expeditions against the Persians had been a disaster, and the Athenians were unable to gain supremacy at sea. In 448 BCE the Persian king issued a decree which ended the Persian wars, and many "allies" of the Athenians concluded that the reason for the alliance was over and they should be allowed to withdraw.

After the five-year truce expired, the Spartans believed that they could humble the Athenians. They had sympathizers within Athens, the Thebans were attempting to reduce Plataea and to create a League of Boeotians that would secure their borders against the Athenians, and the cities of Euboea were in revolt. The Spartans sent their young king, Pleistoanax, to invade Attica. He reached Eleusis with an army and from there, it seemed, was poised to deliver the coup-de-grâce to the Athenians, but he and his adviser, Cleandridas, were convinced by the Athenians to negotiate and he withdrew. The withdrawal of the Spartans insured that the Athenians could defend their border from the Boeotians and reconquer Euboea. In Sparta the king and his adviser were accused of accepting a bribe. Cleandridas was executed. Pleistoanax went into exile in Arcadia and his son, Pausanias, became king. Pleistoanax was so afraid that the Spartans would send men to assassinate him that he built his house half within the sacred precinct of Zeus where he could take instant refuge. He spent nineteen years in exile in Arcadia, before he was reinstated because of an oracle.

Nonetheless, and perhaps in consequence of Pleistoanax's withdrawal, the Spartans and the Athenians did initiate negotiations for a truce: the Athenians gave up all their mainland possessions except Naupactus, they agreed (as did the Spartans) to respect the independence of Delphi, and they agreed not to commit aggression against Sparta or Sparta's allies, as the Spartans agreed to respect theirs. All parties not included in the truce, except for Argos, were free to join either side and to be covered by all the conditions of the treaty. Both sides guaranteed freedom of the seas for trade, and they agreed to submit their differences to arbitration. Both sides listed their allies, recognized the other's allies, and in 445 BCE concluded a truce which was supposed to run for thirty years. (One of the effects of the peace was that King Pausanias was free to visit the battlefield of Thermopylae, recover the bones of King Leonidas, and return them to Sparta.)

The 30-year truce was supposed to stabilize the Greek world by recognizing that each of the two powers had legitimate spheres independent of the other, but the concept was flawed. Sparta's ally Corinth was threatened by the Athenians' encroachment on their maritime interests and the Athenians were not satisfied with the status quo. They constantly sought new members for the Delian League, that is, their empire, and, over time, the Spartans became apprehensive—and justly so— for themselves, while their allies looked to them as their only hope against Athenian aggression.

The war with Persia was over. The war with Athens was about to begin.

— 19 —

King Archidamos Gives Sound Advice

Three events broke the thirty-year truce and precipitated the great war between Athens and Sparta. Pericles, determined to demonstrate Athens' power, proposed to the Athenians a decree barring the Megarians from trade within the Athenian empire. This decree was, in fact, a blockade, since ships could hardly move without touching at a port within the empire. Secondly, the Athenians demanded that Potidaea (a city within their empire but a colony of Corinth) demolish the city wall next to the sea—to give Athenians access to the city whenever they pleased. When the Potidaeans refused, the Athenians put them under siege. Third, the island of Corcyra, which was not included in the thirty-year truce, asked the Athenians for help against Corinth, and the Athenians agreed, because they hoped to enhance their own position by facilitating the destruction of both the Corinthian and the Corcyraean fleets.

The Corinthians could not help but consider themselves an Athenian target. The Athenians had sponsored the foundation of a colony in Italy, they had supported the Corcyraeans (a way station to the west), they had occupied Naupactus from which they could close the Gulf of Corinth and interdict Corinthian trade with Italy and Sicily, and in the northern Aegean they had put the Corinthian colony of Potidaea under siege.

Late in 432 the Spartans called a meeting of their allies. At the meeting the Corinthians pressed them on two issues, Corcyra and Potidaea, the Megarians on the decree impoverishing their city, and other Greeks, in general, on the tyranny of the Athenian empire. The Corinthians, in particular, castigated the Spartans for being slow to act, for always doing less than they could, for waiting until their enemies had become strong rather than attacking them while they were still weak, and for wanting to preserve the status quo, which was impossible, because the Athenians were ambitious and aggressive, always seeking ways to increase their power, and quick to act. The allies asked the Spartans to declare war on Athens.

Some Athenians, by chance, were present, not as ambassadors, but on other business, and they asked for permission to speak to the Spartan assembly. They did not offer any defense of their actions except that they had fought the Persians and they had been forced to make some tough, and unpopular, decisions. In particular, they had been forced, when the Spartans became hostile, to hang on to their empire in self-defense, and, moreover, they were managing their own affairs as the Spartans managed theirs. They were a sovereign state, the equal in reputation, dignity, and power to the Spartans. Finally, they suggested that the Spartans think about the power of Athens before going to war.

Archidamos, the Spartan king, whom Greeks knew to be moderate, moral, sensible—and a friend of Pericles—advised caution.

"I, myself, have fought in many wars, Spartans, and I see some of you who are about the same age as I am. [He was fifty-eight.] No experienced man wants war, in which many suffer, nor does he consider war either good or predictable. You will realize that this issue you are debating is not a small thing, if you think about it rationally. Our strength depends upon our ability to march suddenly upon our neighbors, who are much like ourselves, but the Athenians live far away, and, moreover, have extensive experience of the sea.

"They have as much wealth, in private and public, and as many ships and cavalry and hoplites and people as any single place in Greece, and they also have numerous allies from whom they receive tribute. How can we have confidence in a war with them? Our ships? We are inferior to them. Build them? We need time, if we are only going to plan for the future and begin to prepare now. Money? We have no money in a treasury nor are we ready to pay personal taxes.

"Some one may dare to suggest that our hoplites and our light-armed troops can quickly occupy their land and ravage it. Well, they control other land from which they can be supplied by sea. And if we try to detach their allies, then we must have a fleet to help those allies, most of whom are islanders.

"What sort of a war will this be, if we can not defeat their fleet or deny them the revenues by which they support their fleet? We will suffer more than they. Nor will it be easy to end this war, if we are the ones thought to have started it. And we should not depend upon that hope of bringing the war to a quick conclusion by invading and ravaging their land. Athenians are not slaves to their land nor are they so inexperienced that they will whine about the reverses of war. I fear rather we will bequeath this war to our children.

"I am not suggesting that you ignore our allies and dismiss their complaints, but that you not rush to arms. Perhaps the Athenians will listen to our ambassadors, but if not, after a few years, when we are in a better situation, then we can go against them. We should not openly threaten war, but we should not reject it either. We should put our grievances before them and we should seek new allies, both Greek and barbarian, whoever can help us, because we are all potential targets of the Athenians. We should get our own house in order.

"Perhaps they will listen to our grievances—that would be best. And perhaps when they see that we are prepared and that our deeds equal our words, with their land not yet ravaged, and their present prosperity, they will decide they have too much to lose. You should think of their land as your prisoner, and you should protect it unharmed. If, urged on by our allies, to act before we are prepared, we ravage it, we could do nothing worse for the Peloponnesus or more futile. Complaints from cities and private individuals can be resolved, but a war which involves everyone, when undertaken for a few, and unclear in its outcome, can not so easily be set right.

"Don't let anybody think that we lack courage because we do not immediately march out and attack one single city. They have allies who are as prosperous as they are. War is not as much about weapons as it is about money through which weapons are bought, especially when the people of the mainland fight against a sea power.

"Do not be ashamed of that slowness to action for which we are criticized. When you rush into something for which you are not prepared you end up farther back than you thought. We live in a free city, the best known in the world. And it is mostly because of our common sense. We are not immoderately buoyed up when things go our way and we do not despair when things go against us. We are not inordinately pleased at the praise of someone urging us on, and if someone denigrates us, well, we aren't so concerned about that either.

"We are tough in war and wise in council because we are well organized at home. We are brave because we are sensible and honorable and have an inner moral sense. We advise ourselves well. We have trained ourselves to obey the laws and to be content with them and, by our wise and rigorous training, not to be deaf to their voice. And we are not very clever at futile things, like picking apart the schemes of our enemies in words, and then falling short in action. We are not so different from our neighbors and we know that it is futile to analyze something which will be determined by chance. Always, when we plan well, then we are prepared indeed for our enemies. And we need not cling to the hope that they will make a mistake, but we have self-confidence, because of our foresight. We shouldn't think that there is much difference between one man and another, but that whichever man is trained in the hardest school will be the strongest.

"These practices our fathers handed down to us and, because we owe everything we have to them, we should not abandon them. Let us not in the brief space of a day make a decision which concerns so many persons and money and cities and our reputation, but let us deliberate at leisure. This is possible for us, because it is our particular strength, not that of others. Send envoys to the Athenians about Potidaea, send them on those matters in which our allies say they have been wronged, and otherwise be ready to arbitrate as they have expressed their willingness to arbitrate, for it is neither the custom nor is it right to injure those who have offered to submit to arbitration. Meanwhile, however, prepare for war. In this way you will make the best decisions and be most frightening to your enemies."

After Archidamos had spoken, an ephor addressed the Spartan assembly and said that as far as he was concerned the Athenians had not answered any charges and had only spoken about themselves, but the question for the Spartans was. *Have the Athenians broken the treaty?*

The assembly voted *yes* and the Peloponnesian War had begun.

The Peloponnesian War was a war between two systems, superficially a democratic navy against an oligarchic army, but also a coercive empire against a loose confederation of independent states. The Spartans had the advantage on land—they and their allies could march to the walls of Athens—but, to an extent, they had to consult their allies. The Athenians had the advantage that they did not have to consult anyone but themselves and they could go anywhere their fleet could sail.

The Athenians had a large fleet, a reserve of 6000 talents, an empire of perhaps 300 states that paid a tribute of 400 talents/year and an income of 400 talents/year from Athens itself. (It cost ten talents to commission a trireme and keep it at sea for the eight-month sailing season.) They set aside 100 hulls and 1000 talents to be used only if Athens was attacked by sea. The Spartans as leaders of the Peloponnesian League and allies of Thebes, could muster an army of 50,000 hoplites.

In a sense the war was a stalemate from its inception—neither side had any experience in this kind of war, an army against a navy; neither had the means to defeat the other; and neither had formulated a strategy which could win the war. Neither the Athenians nor the Spartans expected to be able to destroy the other polis and their ultimate objective was not total victory and annihilation of the other. The Spartan objectives—to force the Athenians to rescind the Megarian decree, lift the siege of Potidaea, and tear down the Long Walls—would reduce the power of Athens and lead to the disintegration of its empire, an issue as distasteful to the Athenians as the disintegration of the Peloponnesian League and the loss of Messenia would be to the Spartans, but the Spartans' objectives, at least, were clear, if unobtainable with their resources at that time, while the Athenian objectives were ill-defined: the Spartans should accept the Athenians' right to run their empire as they saw fit, even if a Spartan ally suffered thereby?

Many Spartans expected that they would invade Attica, bring the Athenian army to battle, defeat it, negotiate the terms of peace, and go home victorious. This common belief put Archidamos in an uncomfortable position—he understood the nature of the power of the Athenians, and he was a friend of Pericles. While friendship would not keep him from leading the Spartan army in an invasion of Attica, he understood Pericles' character better than any other Spartan, he expected that Pericles would restrain the Athenians from giving battle, and, therefore, he would be unable to meet Spartan, and allied, expectations.

── 20 ──

The Archidamian War

The Peloponnesian forces mustered in May 431 BCE at the Isthmus, and, from there, Archidamos sent an envoy to the Athenians, but the envoy was turned back without a hearing. He remarked,

"This day is the beginning of bad things for Greece."

Archidamos summoned the generals from each polis to a meeting and addressed them,

"Peloponnesians, our fathers conducted many campaigns inside the Peloponnesus and outside of it, too, and the older men among us are not inexperienced in war. We are as prepared as ever our fathers were, but now we are marching against one of the most powerful of cities and they have many good soldiers, so it is right that we appear no worse than our fathers nor that our reputation should suffer in comparison with theirs.

"The whole of Greece is involved in this undertaking and, out of hatred for the Athenians, wishes us well in what we intend to do. Now, if we think we are advancing with a mass of men and with so much security that the enemy will not dare to meet us in battle, we are liable to advance in a careless way with our preparations neglected, so each general and each soldier from each city should be ready to encounter danger at any moment.

"War is filled with uncertainties. Those who attack often attack from anger and many times those lesser in number, motivated by fear for their own survival, have defeated greater numbers.

"We should advance on the enemy with the expectation of victory, but we should also look to our security, for we are marching against a city well able to defend itself, prepared superlatively in every way, so that we may expect them to advance on us to give battle, now, or whenever we actually enter their land and lay waste to it.

"Think about the great city you are attacking and about our ancestors from whom we are descended: follow where you are led, keep good order, keep on your guard at all times, and be quick to obey orders. We will be most secure when we all act together under one discipline."

Archidamos began his campaign with an attack upon an Athenian fortress on the border of Attica. The attack failed and so he abandoned the operation and advanced slowly into Attica. Some Spartans believed that his heart was just not in the war and that, even at this point, he still hoped the Athenians would agree to negotiate, but he, finally, had to accept that they would not and, in the middle of the summer, when the crops were ripe—and the Athenians had the most to lose—he fought his way through a detachment of Athenian cavalry and advanced into the heart of Attica.

There he established a camp and began a systematic devastation of Athens' most populous district, the home territory of some 3000 hoplites. Archidamos hoped these hoplites would convince the Athenians to come out and fight, or, if not, that the disagreement would cause a division within Athens. The Athenian young men, in particular, did want to fight the Spartans, but Pericles would not allow the assembly to meet and possibly vote to send the army outside the walls. The Athenians were furious with Pericles, but he stuck to his resolve to conduct a naval war exclusively. Archidamos shifted his troops from place to place and continued to devastate Attica.

While Archidamos was in Attica, the Athenian fleet sailed around the Peloponnesus, established some forts, and made a surprise attack on a poorly fortified Laconian city, Methone. The Athenians' attack almost succeeded, but a Spartan general named Brasidas—he happened to be nearby with a special unit—broke through the Athenian forces into Methone and then beat off the Athenian attack. He was the first Spartan leader in this war to be specially mentioned in Sparta.

The Spartans continued to devastate Attica, the Athenians continued to raid the Peloponnesian coasts and press the siege of Potidaea, and neither side could formulate a winning strategy—the Spartans were at a loss how to respond to the Athenian strategy, but, for their part, the Athenians did not appreciate how expensive the war would be and how difficult it would be to break the will of their enemy.

The next year, in 430 BCE, in the early summer after Archidamos had conducted operations in Attica for forty days, a plague broke out in Athens. The plague was carried to Athens by sea, borne by the merchant ships which brought supplies to Athens, and was particularly devastating because Pericles's strategy required all Athenians in Attica to crowd into the city. The plague (430–429, 427–426) killed thousands, caused public order to break down, and, in 429 BCE, killed Pericles. Without Pericles the Athenians lost strategic direction, but they continued the siege of Potidaea—even though a quarter of the Athenian troops there died of the plague—until the Potidaeans, driven to cannibalism, agreed to Athenian terms to leave their city with their lives and the clothes on their backs. The siege of Potidaea cost the Athenians 2000 talents (that is, two-and-a-half-years income).

In the summer of 429 BCE Archidamos led the Spartan army to ravage the land of Plataea and put the city under siege. The Plataeans send envoys to Archidamos to remind him that the Spartan commander of the army that fought the Persians at Plataea had sworn oaths in the marketplace of Plataea that Plataea would be free and independent forever. Now Archidamos was about to violate that oath by attacking Plataea.

Archidamos replied,

"You are right, Plataean men, to mention that oath and now you should join with those others, ourselves, who swore that oath and are running risks to free those who have been enslaved by the Athenians. This is how you would really live up to those oaths you swore. But if you prefer to live in peace at home, then open your city, allow a free intercourse, and do not give access to the enemy."

The Plataeans returned to their city to discuss what he had said and then they returned to tell him that they were afraid that they would be attacked by either the Thebans or the Athenians or both. He offered to occupy their city and their land and keep it safe for the duration of the war. They said that they needed to get the Athenians to agree, because the Athenians had received the Plataeans' woman and children and could use them as hostages. When the envoys returned from Athens, they called to him from the walls that they could not agree to his terms.

Archidamos then addressed the land of Plataea.

"You gods and heroes, who hold the land of the Plataeans, be our witnesses now that we have not begun this war unjustly nor were we the first to abandon our oaths, when we entered this land, where our fathers prayed to you when they defeated the Persians. You were with us, then, the Greeks, and now witness that we are not acting unjustly in what we do. We are right to call upon you to be our allies in curbing the injustice of those who committed the first injustice. Now help those who act according to law and custom."

Archidamos initiated a siege. Spartan officers kept the work crews working night and day for seventy days and nights to build a mound up against the city wall. The Plataeans built a second wall within the first and dug out the earth which the Spartans were piling up. The Spartans brought battering rams against the walls, but the Plataeans constructed a kind of swing with chains and logs which they dropped on the battering rams and broke them. Frustrated, the Spartans gave up on the idea of siege works and kindled a huge fire, but the wind did not cooperate, and the city was not burned down. Finally, the Spartans decided that they would have to starve the Plataeans out and the largest part of the army returned home. The Spartans spent two years in an effort that was all out of proportion to the strategic value of Plataea.

In 427 BCE half the Plataean garrison, and their Athenian allies, broke out under the cover of a stormy night and escaped to Athens. The remaining Plataean defenders were exhausted, they could no longer hold the walls, and they agreed to surrender on the condition that they would be given a trial and no one would be put to death unjustly. Five judges, who came from Sparta to try the survivors, asked the defendants a single question, Have you aided Sparta or its allies in this war? None of the survivors could answer yes and all of them were executed.

At sea, meanwhile, the Athenians defeated the Peloponnesian fleets and proved themselves as superior to the Peloponnesians on the sea as the Spartans were to the Athenians on land. When (in June 428) a member of the Athenian empire, the city of Mytilene, on the island of Lesbos, rebelled, the islanders, as Archidamos had predicted, begged the Spartans for assistance and the Spartans were unable to comply, because they had no creditable navy. The Athenians besieged Mytilene and compelled the Mytilenians to surrender.

The Athenian assembly followed the advice of Cleon (a demagogue and Pericles's successor) and voted to execute every adult male in Mytilene and enslave the rest of the population as an example for the rest of their subjects. They dispatched a trireme with the orders, but, after a night of reflection, they changed their minds and dispatched another trireme to rescind the first order. The oarsmen kept to their task all day and by their exertions managed to arrive just as the orders brought by the first trireme were about to be carried out. Still, the amended terms were severe enough. The Athenians executed 1000 men, dismantled the walls of the city, confiscated all their ships and all their possessions on the Asian coast, and divided all the land on the island—except for the land of Athens' one ally— into 3000 lots, dedicated 300 lots to the gods and distributed the rest to Athenian settlers. The settlers required the Lesbians to work the land and pay 100 talents a year rent for it.

Every Greek city was divided into factions, one pro-Spartan, the other pro-Athenian, and in many cities the factions were fighting; the most brutal of all the civil wars was the one being fought in Corcyra, the city that had provoked the war. The democrats murdered sixty oligarchs and levied a heavy fine on the rest; the oligarchs armed their slaves, set parts of the city on fire, and fought the democrats in a battle that ended only when twenty Athenian ships arrived with 500 Messenian hoplites on board. The Athenians restored the peace in Corcyra, but, later, when the Corcyraean fleet (their strongest arm) sailed out to meet a Peloponnesian fleet, the crews fought among themselves, two ships deserted, and thirteen were captured. Finally, the democrats began to hunt down and murder every oligarch. Corcyra was in shambles and it was not the only victim of civil war. Civil war spread throughout Greece and left it weaker: money became scarce and the crops withered in the fields.

Sometime in the winter of 427/6 King Archidamos died and his son Agis—the name means "Leader"—became king. Agis proved not to be an especially aggressive leader, he appeared to have major reservations about the war itself (as his father had), and he was liable to accept every omen as a reason to cut a campaign short. Also, at this time, the Delphic oracle issued a pronouncement to the Spartans that if they did not restore the descendant of the divine offspring of Zeus, they would plow the soil with a silver plowshare. The oracle was obscure—it may have meant that the Spartans were going to have to spend a lot of money if they disobeyed the god—but its purport was clear and the Spartans, in response to the oracle, invited Pleistoanax to return and be their king again. Pleistoanax returned, although many Spartans believed that he and his brother had "persuaded" the priests to produce that oracle, and they were ready to attribute every reverse in the war to the sacrilege committed by the "persuasion." The two Spartan kings, then, had their own personal reasons for wanting the war to end.

In Agis's first campaign he led the army to the border of Attica, but, before he could cross, he experienced severe earthquakes; he accepted the earthquakes as a sign that he should not advance any farther and so he returned to Sparta. In the next summer, however, he invaded Attica and ravaged the land. He was conducting operations there when events unfolded off the coast of Messenia which were to dramatically change the course of the war.

In 425 BCE the Athenians raised the league tribute to 1000 talents and they voted to send a fleet to Sicily. With the fleet they sent their best general, Demosthenes, and a force of soldiers for him to use against the Peloponnesians, if, on the way, he saw any opportunity to harm them. The fleet put in at Pylos on the coast of Messenia and Demosthenes decided that he could best harm the Spartans by building a fort there, but the fleet commanders wanted to press on to Sicily. By chance, however, a storm forced them to remain at Pylos. The Athenian troops grew bored, they liked Demosthenes's scheme, and they worked hard, on their own, to build a fort for him and his troops. When the weather cleared, the fleet continued on its way and Demosthenes remained behind with his detachment of troops and five ships.

In Attica Agis received word that the Athenians had seized Pylos and he and his advisers decided to cut short their invasion—the weather had been cold, rainy, and unpleasant—and return to Sparta. Meanwhile, as the Spartans were celebrating a festival and did not consider the Athenian presence at Pylos as particularly dangerous, they waited for the end of the festival and the return of their king. When Agis did arrive, the Spartans dispatched a division reinforced by Laconian neighbors. Agis and the rest of his army remained behind in Sparta to recuperate from their campaign.

The Spartans believed that the Athenian fort was in a precarious position, insufficiently garrisoned, poorly fortified, and meagerly supplied, and, if they could prevent the Athenian fleet from seizing the harbor of Pylos, they could starve the Athenians into submission. To prevent the Athenians from landing on the island of Sphacteria (an island that partially closes off the harbor of Pylos) and using it as a base, they sent a detachment of 420 hoplites with attendant helots to the island. They chose the hoplites by lot from all of the units (lochoi) of the Spartan army.

Then, having gathered their fleet and their forces, they prepared to assault the Athenian fort by land and sea. The Athenian commander, Demosthenes, sent his ships to recall the Athenian fleet and advised his men not to think about the danger they were in, but to fight as hard as they could. He anticipated where the Spartans would land and led sixty hoplites to the point of greatest danger. There the

Spartans pressed the attack, but the landing spot was narrow and rocky. The captains of the ships were afraid they would wreck their vessels. One Spartan commander distinguished himself. Brasidas—the man who had saved Methone—urged on the ships, but had to withdraw when he was badly wounded. After a day and a half of effort the Spartans gave up the assault and began to organize supplies for a siege, but, at that moment, the Athenian fleet returned and caught the Spartans by surprise, put their fleet out of action, and marooned the Spartan soldiers on the island of Sphacteria.

The Spartan command panicked and Pleistoanax advised them to ask for an armistice, while they send envoys to Athens. The Athenians granted the armistice on two conditions: first, that the Spartans hand their ships over to the Athenians for the duration of the armistice and, second, they neither remove their troops from Sphacteria nor supply them with more than one-day's rations at a time. The Spartans agreed and sent envoys to Athens. They offered the Athenians peace and an alliance, if the Athenians would only allow the Spartans on the island to leave. The new democratic leader in Athens, Cleon, convinced the assembly that the Athenians could not trust the Spartans to keep their word and, anyway, if the Spartans were so desperate for peace now, what would they be like when the Athenians actually captured the soldiers on Sphacteria?

The Athenians had 14,000 troops and total control of the sea around Sphacteria (because they refused to return the Spartans' ships), but the Spartans promised helots their freedom and some money, if they could get supplies to the island. Some helots swam underwater with leather bags filled with a mixture of poppy seed, linseed, and honey; others crashed their boats—filled with provisions—on the shore. Soon, the Athenians found themselves conducting an uncertain blockade which had lasted over two months and was approaching the stormy season when it would be difficult to patrol the waters around Sphacteria.

Cleon urged the assembly to send out someone who would do something and the assembly chose his arch rival Nicias to go. Cleon boasted that, if he, himself, had been chosen, he would have captured the Spartans in thirty days. Nicias offered to withdraw in his favor, Cleon tried to back out, but the assembly chanted, "Sail! Sail!" and he had to accept the command. By chance, when he got to Sphacteria, a fire broke out on the island and burned off all the cover. For the first time Demosthenes was able to estimate the number of Spartans on the island (more than he had thought), study their dispositions, and plan a campaign.

Eight hundred Athenians landed at dawn, overran the first Spartan guard post, killed the thirty or so hoplites there, and secured the landing site. Demosthenes then disembarked all the rest of the Athenian soldiers except for the garrison of the fort at Pylos, and also his Messenian troops, 800 archers, and 800 peltasts. (The *peltast* had a small round shield—a *pelta*, from which he got his name—no body armor, a leather cap instead of a helmet, and, for weapons, several javelins.) His army seized the high ground around the Spartans.

The Athenian hoplites were reluctant to come to grips with the Spartans—these were Spartans after all—but their light-armed troops kept up such a barrage of arrows, stones, and javelins that they forced the Spartans to pull back and encouraged the hoplites to be more aggressive. The Spartans could not see through the dust and ash swirling over the battlefield, they could not hear commands because the Athenians were shouting, and they were being hit from every side. After some had been killed and many wounded, they retreated to a fort on the upper end of the island and there, all day, they held out against the Athenians' attack, until a band of archers led by a Messenian circled around the cliffs and got behind and above the Spartans. The Spartans had to abandon their position or be annihilated.

At this point Demosthenes and Cleon halted the Athenian attack and offered the Spartans a truce to discuss surrender. The Spartans conferred with heralds from the mainland, the heralds passed on to them the decision of the commanders,

"Do whatever you think best so long as it is not dishonorable."

The Spartans surrendered. Of the original 440 hoplites, 292 surrendered, of whom 120 were Spartiates. Their surrender sent shock waves through Greece.

One of the Athenians said to a Spartan prisoner, "I guess the arrows killed all the brave ones."

The Spartan replied, "That would be a valuable arrow, indeed, which could pick out just the brave."

The Athenians transported their prisoners to Athens, and they sent word to Sparta that, if there were another invasion of Attica, the prisoners would be executed. The Athenians placed a Messenian garrison at Pylos, helots deserted in droves, and Pylos became a running sore in the side of Sparta. The Athenians captured the island of Cythera, they almost took Megara, they raided the Peloponnesian coasts with impunity, and the coasts of Laconia, but they suffered losses, too—1000 hoplites killed and 200 captured at the battle of Delium, their land ravaged, and thousands dead of the plague. Many Athenians wanted peace, although the majority led by Cleon rejected all Sparta's offers.

This Athenian intransigence forced the Spartans to adopt a desperate scheme proposed by one of their leading citizens and finest soldiers, Brasidas. Brasidas proposed that he lead an expedition north to free the Athenian subject cities in Chalcidice. He was allowed to enlist 700 helots (whom he was to train as hoplites) and enough money to hire 1000 mercenaries in the Peloponnesus. Brasidas marched rapidly through the territory of friend, foe, and neutral, arrived safely in Chalcidice, and proceeded to win over many cities by the force of his personality—the Chalcidians believed him when he assured them that he would never deceive them, that the Spartans had no hidden agenda and no interest in ruling the Chalcidians, but only in defeating Athens and freeing the Greeks.

Brasidas persuaded the citizens of the most important Athenian possession in the region, the city of Amphipolis, to come over to him. He garrisoned Amphipolis before the local Athenian commander could react. (That commander was condemned to death, lived in exile, and wrote the definitive history of the Peloponnesian War—the historian Thucydides.) Other Chalcidians contrasted the moderation of Brasidas with the harsh and autocratic Athenian commanders and rushed to join the rebellion.

Brasidas transformed the war. The Athenians accepted a one-year truce on the basis of the status quo and with the understanding that the two sides would meet to discuss a full treaty. They were desperate to prevent the loss of Chalcidice, which was the major source of their ship-building timber and a significant part of their (now) 2000-talent/year tribute from the empire. Moreover, they feared that Brasidas might reach as far as the Hellespont and choke off the grain that fed them. The one-year truce was signed in March of 423 BCE. Two days after the signing, Brasidas accepted the surrender of Scione. (He was unaware of the truce.) The Athenians demanded that Scione be returned. Brasidas offered to submit the matter to arbitration. The Athenians sent an expedition with instructions to capture Scione and execute the entire citizen body. Then Brasidas accepted the surrender of Mende, on the grounds that the Athenians had broken the truce. The Athenians extended the decree of execution to Mende and, when the truce expired in 422, the Athenians refused to renew it and prepared an expedition under the command of Cleon to retake Amphipolis and the other Chalcidian cities.

Cleon had a force of 300 cavalry, 1200 hoplites, and a sizeable fleet. Brasidas had a force of 1500 Thracian mercenaries, about 2000 hoplites, 300 cavalry, and several thousand light-armed troops. Cleon arrived in Chalcidice, recovered several rebel cities, and then camped on the coast in the vicinity of his principal objective, Amphipolis. There he proposed to wait until his ally, the king of Macedonia, showed up, but his troops ridiculed him for the delay, they compared his inaction with the daring of Brasidas, and they accused him of cowardice. Cleon decided he had to do something to satisfy them—they were, after all, citizens who would deliver the verdict on his performance when they were back in Athens—so he led a reconnaissance in force.

Cleon intended to march up to Amphipolis and then march back to camp, but when the army reached Amphipolis, the men could see into the city, and they could see that Brasidas had his army in formation and that a troop of cavalry was at the gate opposite them. Cleon thought he had enough time to withdraw. He ordered his left wing (facing the city) to retreat, and he began to turn the right wing (under his personal command). This movement exposed the unprotected right sides of his troops to Brasidas and also threw the Athenians into confusion. The city gates burst open and Brasidas led a charge right at the center of the Athenian line. The Athenian troops closest to the sea immediately broke and fled to their camp. Brasidas hit the center, and the Athenians in the center, already panicked because they had been deserted by the left wing, broke and ran. (Cleon ran, too, and was killed by a peltast.) Brasidas turned on the right wing already under attack by his second-in-command. The Athenian right wing fell back, reformed up a hill, held out for a while, and then—under a storm of missiles—broke and fled. Six hundred Athenians were killed, including Cleon, and seven of Brasidas's troops . . . and Brasidas himself.

The Amphipolitans gave Brasidas a state funeral and voted to honor him with religious rites and a shrine as hero and founder. They sent a delegation to Sparta to commend Brasidas. (His mother thanked them, but told them Sparta had many men just as good as her son.) Brasidas, of all the figures of the Peloponnesian War, made the greatest impression on his contemporaries. He was quick-witted, had both strategic and tactical sense, and he was a leader who inspired his own men, the people he wanted to win over, and even his enemies. His influence lived on: Athenian subjects believed that all Spartans were like Brasidas and that the Spartans were fighting selflessly for the freedom of Greeks.

Brasidas was dead and Cleon was dead. For the moment only the peacemakers survived, and their leaders, Pleistoanax of Sparta and Nicias of Athens, worked out the terms of a peace. The treaty—the "Peace of Nicias"—was signed in 421. The Spartan kings Pleistoanax and Agis, and an entourage of prominent Spartans, took the oaths and poured the libations.

For the Spartans the peace was an acknowledgment that Archidamos had been right: the war proved to be far more difficult than they had ever expected and the Athenians far more formidable. Oddly enough, the kings, who were the war leaders and who were at their most powerful when they were in command of an army in the field, showed the least enthusiasm for the war. Perhaps they were better acquainted with the Greek world than the ordinary Spartan was. Perhaps they recognized that in war other leaders, like Brasidas, could emerge to challenge the whole assumption of kingship. Perhaps they had enough prestige within Sparta that they did not need war to distinguish themselves. Perhaps, as they entered the public mess in the evening, they observed the diminishing number of tables of Spartiates and they sought to protect those who were left. In any case, Pleistoanax, Archidamos, and Agis all preferred arbitration and negotiation to battle.

For the Athenians the peace was an acknowledgment that the war had cost them far more than they expected and that their empire was more vulnerable to attack than they had expected. Nonetheless, as they repaired the damage done, they grew dissatisfied with the peace.

— 21 —

War within Peace

The Peace of Nicias was supposed to last fifty years: it enjoined the two powers to commit no acts of war against each other or each other's allies, to submit disagreements to arbitration, to allow access to shrines, to guarantee the independence of Delphi, to liberate all prisoners of war, to return all the places that either side had taken, or, at least, to remove all garrisons, and to make no changes in the terms of the treaty without the agreement of both sides. A majority of the council of the Peloponnesian League accepted the terms and the treaty was ratified, but peace never had a chance. Corinth, Megara, and Elis rejected the treaty and seceded from the Peloponnesian League. Thebes and the Boeotian League also rejected the treaty. Mantinea joined an association of democracies to resist Spartan domination and the Argives saw a chance to take advantage of the turmoil in the Peloponnesus and take Sparta's place. The Argives chose 1000 young men of the hoplite class to form an elite unit which would be supported by the state and have no duties except to train for battle.

In reaction, the Spartans negotiated a new treaty with the Athenians by which the two powers became allies, and so, in theory, deprived Argos of Athenian assistance, but there was a clause that the Athenians and Spartans could change any part of the treaty they mutually agreed upon. The Spartan allies in the Peloponnesus considered this clause to be aimed at them, to deprive them of their freedom, and they had come to the conclusion that the Spartans were not as formidable as they once had been, that they had been weakened considerably by their losses in the war, and that they had profoundly fallen away from the courage and virtue of the Spartans of old. Would Leonidas's Spartans have surrendered at Pylos? Would the Spartans of his time have readmitted the prisoners of Pylos—released by the Athenians in accordance with the treaty—to full rights in Sparta, as the Spartans of this time did? The Spartans seemed to have become ineffectual.

The Arcadian city of Mantinea challenged the Spartans by constructing and garrisoning a fort on the border of Laconia and capturing a border town allied with the Spartans. In 421 the Spartan king Pleistoanax led out an army to destroy the fort and to liberate their Arcadian ally. The Mantineans brought out their whole army to fight the Spartans. (Their allies, the Argives, guarded Mantinea in their absence.) The two armies met and fought a battle. King Pleistoanax and the Spartans defeated the Mantineans, freed the border town, and destroyed the fort, but their victory was not enough to overawe Mantinea, let alone their other enemies in the Peloponnesus.

The Spartans had aroused the suspicions of their own allies without being able to quell the suspicions of the Athenians. And now the Athenian aristocrat and nephew of Pericles, Alcibiades, personable, wealthy, ambitious, and a general of real ability, assumed Cleon's role as the leader of the war party and rival of Nicias (the architect of the peace treaty). He played upon the suspicions of the Athenians, elevated himself into the role of the foremost opponent of Sparta, and (in 420 BCE) persuaded the Athenians to join a defensive alliance with Argos, Mantinea, and Elis.

Between the years 420 and 418 the Spartans brought Megara and Corinth back into their alliance and checked the expansion of Elis by seizing the city of Lepreum on the border of Elis, freeing the helots who had served with Brasidas, and settling them there as a garrison. (The Eleans then declared that this attack was a violation of the Olympic truce—which had been declared in Elis, but not yet in Sparta—levied a fine on the Spartans, and refused to allow them to compete in the Olympic games of that year, 420 BCE.)

No sooner had the Spartans concluded their action against Elis, than they learned that Alcibiades and the Athenians were attacking Epidaurus in the Argolid, clearly with the intention of using it as a forward base for operations in the Peloponnesus, but King Agis had his doubts about the wisdom of intervening. Earlier, when the ephors had introduced Agis to a man from another city and said,

"Take our young men and follow this man. He will admit you into his city,"

Agis replied, "Is it right, ephors, to entrust our young men to someone who would betray his own fatherland?"

When Agis arrived at the Laconian border and conducted the sacrifices, the results were unfavorable and he returned to Sparta.

Meanwhile, the Argives' operations were running up against the beginning of the month Carneus, a sacred month, when Dorians were prohibited from campaigning. Nonetheless, they were able to continue their campaign against Epidaurus by declaring that every new day was the fourth day from the end of the month. A month passed and again Agis led the Spartans out to the border and again he determined that the sacrifices were unfavorable, returned to Sparta, and concluded campaigning for the summer, but the Argives pressed the war during the winter, and, once again, the Spartans seemed ineffectual and their situation in the Peloponnesus deteriorated.

In the next summer, 418 BCE, Agis summoned the allies to meet for a campaign, but, as he was marching to join the main army with his Spartans, the Argives intercepted him, too late in the day to fight, but they intended to fight him the next morning. During the night Agis gave the Argives the slip, joined his allies—thus forming one of the largest armies the Spartans had ever commanded—and formulated a plan of campaign. He divided his army into three divisions. He led his own division by a difficult and circuitous route around the Argive army and into the plain of Argos; the second division, he ordered to march by the route the Argives had expected Agis to take; and the third, he ordered to occupy the hills. When the Argives entered the plain to fight the Spartans, they were caught between these three divisions, their retreat was cut off, and the Spartans were between them and the city of Argos.

The Argives could not retreat, but, if they joined battle with the Spartans, the Spartans' allies would attack them from the rear and the flanks. Two of the Argive generals recognized that the battle was going to be a disaster and they asked Agis to negotiate. Agis did, entirely on his own without consulting his allies, and he agreed to a four-month truce during which the Argives would carry out all Spartan demands. The Argive army then returned in safety to Argos, but the Argives in the ranks had thought that they were in a favorable situation, that they had trapped the Spartan army between themselves and their city, and that without any reason they could understand they had been denied a great victory. Once the army was safely back in Argos, the Argives repudiated the agreement.

The Spartans were furious with Agis. The ephors publicly rebuked him, fined him, and threatened to tear down his house. He begged for another chance and swore that he would do something worthy of Sparta and his own reputation. The ephors ordered him out anew, this time accompanied by a board of ten Spartiate advisers. Agis had no trouble finding the Argives. They were drawn up on a hill awaiting his attack. He advanced into javelin range, and he appeared to be about to order a charge up the hill, until a veteran shouted out to him that he was trying to right a wrong with another wrong, and he withdrew. Agis had now broken off battle twice, and the Argives believed that he was afraid to fight them. They pursued him and came upon him unexpectedly near Mantinea.

Some of his advisers were concerned that they were heavily outnumbered. Agis told them,

"We have to be willing to fight against many if we want to rule many."

Some Spartans said later that they had never been so surprised in their lives. Nonetheless, the Spartans had time to form up and perform their customary rituals. They were drawn up on the right of their battle line, with the troops of Brasidas and the *neodamodeis* (a class of Spartans without political rights) next to them and their allies to the left. Agis had about 3600 Spartans, formed eight deep, with a front rank 448 men long.

"The king explains what must be done to the polemarchs, the polemarchs to the commanders of the lochoi, the commanders of the lochoi to the commanders

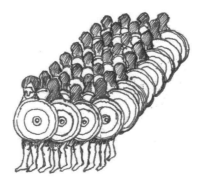

Illustration 8.   An Enomotia (Alfred S. Bradford)

of pentekostyes, and these to the commanders of the enomotiai and these to their enomotiai."

An Enomotia is thirty-two men.

A Pentekostys ("fifty") is four enomotiae, 128 men.

Each Lochos is four pentekostyes (512 men).

Seven lochoi contain 3584 men.

"Commands travel very quickly for nearly every one of the Spartans is a leader.

"The army of the Spartans appeared larger, but it is not possible to give an exact number for the Spartans, for the number of Spartans is kept secret, but an approximation can be made thus: they were fighting with seven lochoi, not counting the Sciritai (who were 600 in number) and in each lochos were four pentekostyes and in each pentekostys were four enomotiae, each enomotia had a front of four and they were drawn up, on average, eight deep, so the front rank, excluding the Sciritai was 448 men long."

(The *Sciritai* came from a small district in Arcadia on the border of Laconia. They had the status of Laconian neighbors and, by agreement, drew up on the left of the Spartan phalanx.)

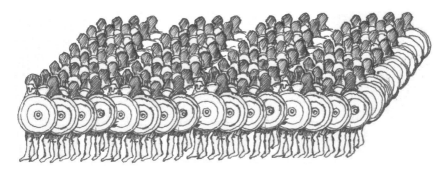

Illustration 9.   A Pentekostys (Alfred S. Bradford)

"At this point when the armies were poised to come together the leaders of their own contingents addressed their troops. The Mantineans said that the battle was for their fatherland and the difference between freedom and slavery, the Argives that the battle was for the leadership of the Peloponnesus, the Athenians that it was a noble thing to be fighting beside such allies and that if they beat the Spartans here there would be no one in the future who would dare oppose Athens. The Spartans according to their old customs did not say much but that each man should obey orders, for they knew they would find safety in their long training and experience rather than in words."

On the opposing side the Mantineans were on the right; next to them were their Arcadian allies, then a unit of 1000 elite Argives (who were supported in their profession of arms by the city), then the rest of the Argives, their allies, and on the far left flank (directly opposite the Spartans), the Athenians, so the armies were drawn up thus:

Phase One
Mantineans|Arcadians|Elite Argives|Argives|Argive allies|Athenians|Athenian cavalry

Cav|Sciritae|Brasideans|helots|Spartans - - - - - - - - - - - - - *Spartans|H|T |Spartans|Cav*

Cav = Cavalry   *H = Heraeans| T = Tegeans*

Illustration 10.   Battle of Mantinea phase one (Alfred S. Bradford)

The armies approached each other, the Argives and their allies shouting their war cries to rouse their spirit, the Spartans quietly and steadily, keeping in step as their flutes played the "Song of Castor."

In general, as two phalanxes approach each other, their right wings extend to the right, and both armies tend to extend beyond the left wing of the enemy, because each man is motivated by his fear to place his unprotected side behind the shield of the man drawn up next to him on his right and he thinks that the compactness of the formation is his best protection. For this reason the rightmost man in the front line becomes the guide, as he strains always to get his unprotected side past the enemy and he draws everyone else in the formation after him.

The flank of the Mantineans extended far beyond the left of the Spartan line, and the Spartans were even farther extended past the Athenians: Agis thought that the enemy might turn his left, so he ordered his leftmost units to move to the left, opening a gap in the middle of his line, and he ordered his two rightmost units to march down and fill the gap. The commanders on the right refused, because the lines were already advancing—later they were found guilty of cowardice and exiled—and Agis did not have time to close the gap before the two armies met.

Phase Two

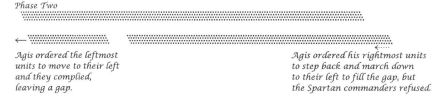

Agis ordered the leftmost
units to move to their left
and they complied,
leaving a gap.

Agis ordered his rightmost units
to step back and march down
to their left to fill the gap, but
the Spartan commanders refused.

Illustration 11.   Battle of Mantinea phase two (Alfred S. Bradford)

Agis's left wing was overwhelmed by the Mantineans, Arcadians, and the elite unit of 1000 Argives. It was routed and driven from the field with the enemy in pursuit. On the right, however, King Agis and his elite guard and the rest of the Spartans and Tegeans routed the enemy before the lines even met and sent them into such panicked flight that some of them were trampled to death.

The Athenians were boxed in and cut off and would have suffered heavily, but Agis saw the predicament of his left wing, which by then was in flight, and he wheeled his phalanx around to save it. His advance across the battlefield caused the Argives, who had defeated Agis's left, to break and run, and he cornered and killed some Mantinean soldiers, but he did not initiate a vigorous pursuit of the defeated enemy—Spartans generally fought steadily and tenaciously until the enemy broke but then let them escape. Agis lost about 300 men, mostly on his left wing, his opponents about 1100.

After the battle heralds from the Argives arrived to ask for a truce to recover their dead, and they acted so arrogantly that Agis had to reassure some of his allies. He said,

"Don't worry. If you, the victors, are feeling some fear of them, how do you think they, the losers, feel about us?"

This battle convinced the Mantineans to rejoin the Spartan alliance and the Argives to conclude a fifty-year treaty with the Spartans. (The Spartans helped the elite Argive guard seize power in Argos.) The Spartan alliance was again intact and Sparta's prestige was restored. Alcibiades' reputation was damaged in Athens and Nicias's peace policy was reaffirmed.

In the next year the democrats in Argos waited until the Spartans were celebrating the festival of the Naked Boys (the *Gymnopaedia*), then attacked the oligarchs, killed some, exiled others, and regained control of the city. The Spartans put off an expedition against them until the winter, when they learned that the Argives with Athenian help had built long walls to the coast. Agis led out an army, invaded the Argolid, captured and sacked one Argive town, and seized and destroyed the long walls, but he failed to overthrow the democracy.

In 416 BCE Alcibiades convinced the Athenians to send an expedition to the tiny island of Melos. The Melians were no threat to the Athenians, except that they did not want to give up their freedom and become part of the Athenian empire; Athenian policy, however, allowed no room for neutrals—all Greeks were either with them or against them—and the Athenians presented the Melians with an ultimatum: enter the Athenian alliance or die. The Melians resisted, and the Athenians put them under siege for close to a year before they compelled them to capitulate; the Athenians executed all adult males and sold the women and children into slavery.

In the spring of 415 the Athenians received sixty talents of silver and a request for an alliance against Syracuse from Segesta, a town in Sicily. The Athenians had always suspected that the Syracusans might help their mother city, Corinth, the ally of Sparta, and they believed (erroneously) that the Sicilians were enormously wealthy and would support the whole Athenian fleet for as long as it took them to force Syracuse, and the rest of Sicily, into the Athenian empire. Alcibiades saw this expedition as his big chance. He supported it in the assembly, overrode Nicias's objections, and convinced the Athenians to approve a budget of 3000 talents and a force of 60 triremes, 40 troop ships, 1500 hoplites, 700 marines, 30 cavalry, and (if the ships had full crews) 10,000 oarsmen. The Athenian people appointed Nicias, Lamachos (a steady and experienced general), and Alcibiades to lead the expedition.

On the day the fleet was to sail the Athenians awoke to find that someone had mutilated the sacred herms (little busts of Hermes scattered throughout Athens). The people of Athens attributed the sacrilege to the opponents of democracy, that is, to the oligarchs, and, in particular, they suspected Alcibiades because, rumor had it, he had once held a mock religious ceremony. The Athenians allowed him to sail but then decided to send a ship after him, to summon him back for trial.

When the Athenian fleet reached Sicily, they found no money and no allies—the western Greeks were terrified of them—and the generals could not decide what to do. Nicias proposed that they attack Selinus (the stated objective of the fleet), make a show of force along the coast, and return home. Alcibiades proposed that they send representatives to the native population and to all Greek cities except Syracuse and Selinus to determine who would help them. Lamachos proposed that they attack Syracuse, while the Athenians were at full strength and the Syracusans were most unprepared and most frightened. In the end the generals compromised: they made a reconnaissance in force and then went into winter quarters.

At this point the ship arrived to take Alcibiades back for trial. On the way back to Athens he escaped to Sparta and earned his keep there by making himself as useful to the Spartans as he could—he advised them that the Athenians intended to conquer Syracuse as a first step in a renewed war against Sparta and that the Spartans should respond immediately by sending help to Syracuse and by invading Attica. And this time when they invaded Attica, they should build a fort and keep their army in Attica all year round. The Spartans were not ready to confront the Athenians directly, nor send a Spartan army as far away as Sicily, but they did send the Syracusans one expert, a Spartan named Gylippos.

Gylippos had been a *mothax*—that is, a boy enrolled into the agoge without the familial right to the training, but through the influence of a full citizen and as a companion of a (future) full citizen. Gylippos would have been born about 455, that is, the son of someone who had survived the Great Earthquake—in the case

of Gylippos, the son of a man who had lost his citizenship for corruption. He—
and Lysander, another prominent Spartiate reputed to be a mothax—may have
been enrolled in the agoge to replace the Spartans killed in the Great Earthquake
and the subsequent Messenian war.

Meanwhile, the Athenians had begun their campaign. They seized the plains to
the west and above Syracuse, built a fort ("the circle fort") in the center of the
plains and extended walls north and south to blockade Syracuse by land while their
fleet attempted to blockade Syracuse by sea. When the Syracusans began a counter
wall to the south of the Athenian wall, an Athenian elite force of 300 men stormed
it and took it. The Syracusans counterattacked, killed Lamachos, and almost
captured the circle fort, but the Athenian fleet rowed into the Great Harbor
and forced the Syracusans to withdraw into their city. The Athenians went on to
complete their southern walls (two of them to enclose the beach the fleet used
and to protect the supply lines from the sea to the circle fort).

The Syracusans were so discouraged that they debated whether to accept
Athenian terms, but, in the midst of their debate, Gylippos arrived and put new
heart into them. He cut off the Athenian wall to the north with a new counter
wall, and he forced Nicias to move his camp to the Plemmyrium (the southern
jaw of the Great Harbor). Nicias fell ill, he became depressed—he had never
had faith in the expedition and now he alone was responsible for it—and he sent
a letter to Athens asking to be relieved.

"Our fleet and men were in prime condition when we arrived, the timbers were
dry and we had full crews. Now because of the time they have been at sea the
ships' timbers are waterlogged and our crews are no longer at full strength. We
cannot beach our ships and repair them because we need every ship in case of
an enemy attack on us and we must keep watch night and day to prevent a surprise attack. And even if we outnumbered them and were not forced to keep
watch everywhere, still we would be in trouble because we can barely get our
supplies past them and we are continually losing foraging oarsmen to enemy cavalry. Our slaves are deserting and the Sicilians are returning to their cities. In
short, I am writing to inform you that the moment when we had full crews was
brief, that those with the expertise and spirit to get the ships going are few, and
that we have no place to recruit new crew members, and, Athenians, you are
not easy to command because of your difficult nature."

The Athenian people (in the winter of 414) voted to send the generals Eurymedon
and Demosthenes to reinforce Nicias, and, in addition to the Syracusan campaign,
they launched attacks on Amphipolis and, in retaliation for the actions of Gylippos,
on the coasts of Laconia. The Spartans demanded redress (through arbitration)
and the Athenians refused. The Spartans now believed that war had been forced
on them unjustly and they were confident that heaven would aid them and they
would win in the end.

The Spartan king, Agis, invaded Attica in early spring 413 and (in accordance
with the advice of Alcibiades) constructed a fort at Decelea in Attica. Decelea is
about fourteen miles from Athens with easy access to Boeotia and has a mythical

connection with the Spartans. It is visible from the walls of Athens. The king's primary objective was to lure the Athenian army to come out and fight, but, failing that, his secondary objectives were to confine the Athenians to their city, force them to stand guard on the walls night and day, wear down their cavalry through constant daily patrols and skirmishes, and, generally, lower Athenian morale. In addition, the fort cut off supplies coming from Euboea through Attica and limited the Athenians totally to supplies brought by sea through their port, the Piraeus. Decelea also became a refuge for Athenian slaves; as time passed, nearly 20,000 slaves deserted. All farm animals were confiscated or killed. The Spartan king's constant presence at the base also emphasized the importance the Spartans assigned to this new strategic initiative and influenced the allies to fulfill their duty to supply troops for their assigned rotation. As Agis was accessible and had an army, he became the de facto commander of the war. He also received much advice, which, though good in intention, was difficult to execute and he said to one such adviser,

"Your scheme is good, but where are your men and where is the money?"

Another speaker told him, when the king didn't seem very impressed with his speech, that words were more important than anything else. Agis said,

"Do you mean, when you aren't talking, you are worthless?"

In the spring of 413 the Syracusan fleet attacked the Athenian fleet in the Great Harbor. The Athenian fleet barely held its own, and, while the Athenians in the Plemmyrium were watching the battle, Gylippos made a surprise attack on them and seized the Athenian camp there. Then, in July 413, the Syracusans reinforced the bows of their ships and, once more, attacked the Athenians in the Great Harbor, while Gylippos assaulted the southern walls. The Athenians were on the brink of defeat when Demosthenes and Eurymedon rowed into the Great Harbor with seventy-three triremes, and 5000 hoplites. The Syracusans withdrew.

Demosthenes assessed the condition of the ships and men at Syracuse, and he advised Nicias to withdraw immediately. Nicias refused. He knew what happened to generals who did not fulfill the expectations of the Athenian people and he preferred to die fighting. Demosthenes then proposed that they try a night attack on the counter wall to the north, with the understanding that if the attack failed, the Athenians would withdraw. The night attack did fail and Demosthenes finally persuaded Nicias to agree to withdraw, but their decision was undone by an eclipse of the moon (August 27, 413). The soothsayers advised the Athenians not to move for thrice nine days, and Nicias took their advice, which agreed with his own inclinations.

Gylippos and the Syracusans were confident now that they could not only defeat the Athenians but annihilate them, and they began to construct a wall of ships across the mouth of the Great Harbor. The Athenians attacked with every one of their 110 ships; their first attack penetrated to the barrier of ships, but when they tried to break the line of tethered ships, the Syracusans attacked them from all sides. The Athenians had no room to maneuver. Ship crashed into ship, marine fought marine; the oarsmen and the steersmen held nothing back. No one could make sense of what was happening, or give direction, with the noise of ships crashing, and the shouts of so many men, and the confusion of two hundred ships fighting in a crowded harbor. No one could hear orders. The army on shore shouted encouragement when they thought their fleet was winning and cried out in despair when they saw part defeated. In the end the Syracusans broke the Athenians' will to fight and the Athenians rowed to the land, beached their ships, jumped out, and ran to safety. Panic infected the Athenian camp. The oarsmen refused to man the ships for another attempt, even to try a dawn attack to break out of the harbor and escape. The generals had never considered what to do if they were defeated and they vacillated for two days before they decided to retreat overland.

The Syracusans pursued and quickly surrounded Demosthenes's division; they accepted Demosthenes's surrender, granting only one condition—they promised not to kill the prisoners on the spot. They pursued Nicias's troops and caught them at the banks of a river; the Athenians and their allies had broken ranks to quench their desperate thirst and the Syracusans slaughtered them. The Syracusans executed the generals, sold the allies of the Athenians as slaves, and threw the Athenians into a quarry. Of the 40,000 men in the expedition, the Syracusans took 7000 prisoners and left them to rot. A handful escaped during the night and the Syracusans later released a very few.

The Athenians' fundamental error was not so much their overconfidence in the power of their fleet, but in their failure to understand the need to operate from a secure base. While the Syracusans could attack at a moment of their own choosing or retreat to safety within their walled city and live a fairly comfortable and regular life, the Athenians in their camp before Syracuse deteriorated in health just as their ships deteriorated, but, despite all this, the Athenians would probably have won, if the Spartans had not sent Gylippos.

22

The Decelean War

At the end of 413 the news of the Athenian disaster raced through the Aegean. The island members of the Athenian empire revolted and the Spartans negotiated a secret agreement with the Persians. At first, the Persian king demanded that the Spartans cede to him all Greek cities which he had once possessed. That demand would have reestablished the Persian Empire all the way to the Isthmus of Corinth. The Spartans rejected this demand, but they finally agreed to abandon the Ionians of Asia Minor in exchange for Persian money to build a fleet and hire oarsmen.

When Agis learned of the defeat of the Athenians, he led a force out of Decelea and campaigned to the north along the borders of Thessaly to punish Athenian allies and to raise money to build a fleet of 100 ships. Agis received delegations from many Greek states, which believed that the Athenians were finished, the war would be over by the end of the summer campaigning season, and, if they wanted to get credit with the Spartans for opposing Athens, they needed to stand up now.

From 413 to 411 the Athenians held their own at sea. Meanwhile, Alcibiades left Sparta. He had seduced Timaea ("Chastity"), the wife of King Agis, although Agis did not tumble to the fact until a son, Leotychidas, was born and he counted up the months since he had last had intercourse with his wife. The one time he could have fathered this son he had felt an earth tremor, right in midact, and he had run from the house. Since then he had been on campaign and he had not had relations with her, so a son born ten months after the last time was obviously not his, and he said so. Alcibiades was not very gracious—he explained that he really had little interest in the woman, he just wanted his sons to be kings in Sparta.

In 411 Alcibiades arrived in Persia, where, like a good sophist, he urged the Persians to let Sparta and Athens fight each other to exhaustion, while, in secret, he advised the Athenians that, if they would abolish the democracy, he could persuade the Persians to help them. The Athenians believed him and they voted to institute a new government, the "government of 400" leading citizens, who would choose 5000 citizens to be the sovereign body of Athens, to oversee the war and bring peace. They sent envoys to Agis to inquire if he would be willing to open peace negotiations. They told him that he would never get more favorable terms than now, but he was wary and he told them that they would have to take their proposals to Sparta. (The Athenians in the fleet at Samos did not recognize the new government and they set up a government in exile.)

Agis received envoys from Euboea and from Lesbos, each wanting help in rebelling from Athens. Agis directed troops—some three hundred freed helots—and ships to Lesbos. He also received envoys from Abdera. They spoke at length about the need for the Spartans to help them and, when they had finished speaking, they asked the king what they should report to their fellow citizens. He replied,

"Tell them that you spoke at length and I listened politely."

In this year, in the middle of war, the pan-Hellenic Isthmian Games were celebrated and the Athenians, as part of the Greek community, were invited to attend. They accepted the invitation, used the opportunity to gather gossip and ferret out possible rebellions and weaknesses in their empire, and learned about a plot by the Chian oligarchs, abetted by the Spartans and Alcibiades, to over-throw the Chian democracy and revolt.

Although Agis supported the attempt, his rival Endios, an ephor, who was a friend of Alcibiades, tried to gain credit for the revolt and to appoint Alcibiades as quasi-commander/adviser of the small Spartan fleet which sailed to Chios. The Spartans succeeded in getting the Chians to revolt and then proceeded to Miletus and raised Miletus in revolt. From there the Spartans went on to Lesbos. The Athenians, meanwhile, used the 1000 talents that had been placed in reserve and, reenergized, took to the sea to stem the growing revolts. They attacked the enemy forces at Lesbos and retook the island and then they defeated the Chians and ravaged their land. The Spartans abandoned their plan to campaign against the Athenians in the Hellespont.

In 411/410 Alcibiades was restored to citizenship and appointed general. He commanded the fleet with some success, but in 410, after the new government had not received Persian money nor ended the war, the Athenians restored the democracy. Agis, headquartered at Decelea, was beginning to get frustrated. He could see transports coming into the Piraeus with loads of grain and he couldn't stop them. He paraded his troops to try again to induce the Athenians to fight a battle. He moved up close to the walls near the Lyceum, but the Athenians would not fight, so he withdrew. During the withdrawal the Athenian light armed troops attacked the rear guard of the Spartan army and inflicted a few casualties.

In 408 he sent one of his officers with a small fleet to the Hellespont to attempt to extend the blockade there, but, otherwise, he sat tight and awaited develop-ments. The Athenians continued to employ Alcibiades and by the beginning of 407 they had forced a standoff at sea, they had regained their confidence, they were becoming more aggressive—the Spartans had to pay their oarsmen three times what the Athenians paid theirs—and they welcomed Alcibiades back to

Athens. In this year King Pleistoanax died and his son Pausanias became king (again).

Alcibiades's first official act was to raise Athenian morale by leading the state procession along the Sacred Way to Eleusis (the first time the festival had been celebrated since Decelea was occupied), and then he returned to the fleet. There he found that the situation had changed. Early in 406 the Spartans had appointed a new admiral-in-chief named Lysander; Lysander, the story went, had been a mothax. Born in the later 450s, he was the son of someone who had survived the Great Earthquake, perhaps the product of a helot mother and a father who was a Spartiate and possibly even a Heraclid.

Lysander had won the friendship—and rumor suggested much more—and the support of the son of the Persian king, Cyrus the Younger. Alcibiades returned to Athens to report the new situation and, in his absence, his fleet was defeated by the Spartans. The defeat turned the scales once more against Alcibiades—he had already disappointed the Athenian people by his failure to produce Persian money—and he was forced into exile.

Nonetheless, the Athenian position was not hopeless. When they heard that the Spartan commander Callicratidas (Lysander's replacement) had blockaded their own commander, Conon, at Mytilene on Lesbos, the Athenians mustered every man old enough to row, slave and free, rich and poor, crewed 110 ships in thirty days, collected ten ships from Samos and thirty more from their other allies, and met Callicratidas with his fleet of 120 ships at the Arginusae Islands. The Athenians incorporated the islands into their line to stretch it out still further and force Callicratidas to break his fleet into two divisions to engage the left and right wing of the Athenians. Callicratidas's navigator thought that there were too many Athenian ships, and he suggested that Callicratidas order a retreat. Callicratidas replied that Sparta would be no worse off with him dead.

The weather was stormy and soon after the two formations met, they scattered and fought ship to ship. Callicratidas's ship rammed an Athenian ship, Callicratidas fell into the sea, and he was never seen again; the Athenian right wing routed the Peloponnesians. The battle of Arginusae was an Athenian victory—the Peloponnesians lost more than seventy ships, and the Athenians lost only twenty-five ships. But because of the stormy weather, the Athenian generals could not rescue the 5000 oarsmen thrown into the water, and the people were so furious at the loss of these irreplaceable men that they condemned the generals to death.

Even so, the victory at Arginusae gave the Athenians one last chance for peace. They received an offer from the Spartans to evacuate Decelea and end the war, if the Athenians would accept peace on the basis of the status quo. The Athenians refused and soon found themselves facing a new fleet, commanded by Lysander (who had persuaded Cyrus to furnish the necessary money), and stationed at Lampsacus on the Asian side of the Hellespont, where it threatened Athens's grain supply. The Athenians sent their whole fleet (180 ships) to Aegospotami ("the River of Goats") on the Chersonese side of the Hellespont where the Hellespont is about one-and-three-quarters miles wide. Once again, as at

Syracuse (and at Arginusae, where storms had prevented the Spartans from launching a surprise attack), the Athenians rejected a safe harbor (Sestos) in favor of an exposed position close to the enemy.

The Athenians were still confident that they could defeat the Spartan fleet, and for five days the Athenians rowed across the Hellespont and offered battle to Lysander. For five days he refused to leave his safe harbor, and the Athenians came to believe that he was afraid of them and would never come out. On the fifth day, when once more he refused to come out, the Athenians returned to Aegospotami, beached their ships, and scattered across the countryside in search of firewood and food. Lysander chose that moment to attack. He caught the Athenians totally by surprise and captured the majority of their ships still beached. He executed all Athenians taken prisoner.

When the news reached the Piraeus, the first people to hear it began to wail, and the wailing traveled along with the news all the way up the Long Walls to Athens , itself. The Athenians feared that what they had done to so many others would now be done to them, and not without reason. When the news reached Sparta, King Pausanias was sent with the remainder of the Spartan and Peloponnesian troops to join Agis and advance on the city. He camped in the Academy. Lysander arrived with the fleet and the combined Spartan forces put Athens under close siege.

The Athenians tried to make peace with Agis on the basis that they would join the Spartan alliance, keep their walls, and the Piraeus. Agis told them that he had no authority to negotiate and sent them to Sparta, but the ephors refused to even allow them to enter Sparta with those terms and ordered them to go back to Athens until they were willing to make a serious proposal. The Athenians held out for as long as they could, but in the end they surrendered. Some of Sparta's allies wanted to murder the whole population of Athens, but the Spartans refused "to destroy the city which had served Greece so well in the Persian wars" and accepted its surrender—the Long Walls and the walls of the Piraeus were demolished, the fleet except for twelve ships was surrendered, all Athenian garrisons everywhere were removed, all exiles were recalled, and a new antidemocratic government was installed.

The Spartans won the war more because of Athenians failings, perhaps, then their own brilliance, but they had the consistent leadership of their kings and one brilliant leader, Brasidas, and one more superb leader, Lysander. The Athenians rejected Pericles's conservative policy—to defend Athens and the bulk of the fleet while raiding the enemy. They had no clear objectives in the war. They overrated the power of their fleet and they never understood the necessity of securing the fleet, not at Syracuse, not at Arginusae, and not at Aegospotami. While the democratic assembly voted to adopt the (ultimately) disastrous policies proposed by its leaders, the Athenian people can hardly be blamed for the strategic and tactical failings of those leaders, although they exacerbated those failings by their narrow intolerance of the setbacks inevitable in war.

The Long Walls were torn down to the sound of flute players and Greeks everywhere rejoiced because now, at long last, they were free.

—— 23 ——

The Man Who Would Be King

Even as the Greeks were celebrating their freedom, Lysander was planning to take it away from them. He had, like the regent Pausanias (the victor of Plataea), let the victory go to his head. Everywhere he went in the one-time Athenian empire, he was treated like a god—he was the subject of hymns, gifts, and memorials—and he commissioned a grandiose monument in Delphi, with himself at the center of an admiring crowd of staff officers and gods. And, personally (and illegally), he had amassed a fortune. Now he advocated a policy in Sparta to replace the Athenian empire with a Spartan empire.

Lysander replaced the democratic governments supported by the Athenians with "boards-of-ten" which were charged with reestablishing the "ancestral constitutions," but the new governments were, in fact, narrow, pro-Spartan oligarchies supervised and supported by a Spartan commander with a garrison of mercenary soldiers (whose salaries were paid, ultimately, by the people they had "liberated"). The members of the boards-of-ten owed their positions, and gave their loyalty, to Lysander. Lysander treated Athens much as he had the other cities: he installed a board of thirty men (later called the "Thirty Tyrants" because of their brutal, autocratic rule).

Lysander, like the regent Pausanias before him, was repulsed by the possibility that he might return to Sparta and be treated like just another citizen. Rather he thought that the Spartans should choose their "best man"—him—to be king and so, to that end, he visited Delphi and other oracles and made surreptitious requests for their divine sanction. (They delivered a blunt *no!*) Nonetheless, for the moment, Lysander was a hero to most Spartans and he convinced King Agis and a majority of the ephors to continue him in his command and to support his imperial ambitions and policy, from which, he promised, the Spartans would profit doubly—they would become wealthy and they would be secure.

King Pausanias, however, the grandson of the regent Pausanias, opposed not only Lysander's policy, but Lysander, himself, and the king was supported by a couple of the ephors and a substantial minority of the citizen body. As for wealth, he could point out the example of Gylippos who had embezzled money taken from Athens and had left Sparta in disgrace. And there were others. If such men could be corrupted by money, who was safe from corruption? As for security, he advocated a withdrawal inside the Peloponnesus and a return to the traditional policy of Sparta, to protect their interests within the Peloponnesus and to observe affairs beyond . . . and thus to maintain their reputation as liberators. (Pausanias, as it turned out, was absolutely correct—Sparta had neither the money nor the manpower to maintain an empire.)

Pausanias, first, in pursuit of his policy—and over the vehement protests of Lysander—withdrew the Spartan garrison from Athens and he also removed some of Lysander's men from other cities, as he, and now Agis, too, recognized the extent of Lysander's power in the Aegean. He also offered to mediate a reconciliation between the oligarchs and the democrats of Athens, but, ultimately, he failed, and the Thirty Tyrants, without the support of the Spartans, tightened their control over Athens with a program of intimidation and murder; their democratic opponents seized and held the port, the Piraeus. Pausanias refused to intervene in the dispute, and, without Spartan intervention, the democratic army was able to defeat the army of the Thirty.

Lysander proposed that the Spartans send an expedition to recover the Piraeus and Athens—he would lead an army to blockade Athens by land and his brother would command the Spartan fleet and would blockade the Piraeus. Pausanias suspected that Lysander's plan was really an attempt by Lysander to install himself as tyrant of Athens. After all, once he had Athens, who could make him give it up? By this time Pausanias had already defeated the democrats in a battle and had convinced their leaders—and the oligarchs within the city—to come to his camp and confer with him. From there he sent them on to Sparta, with his support, and the delegates convinced a majority of the ephors to accept Pausanias's plan to let the Athenians settle their own affairs and keep Lysander out. In the end, the democrats overthrew the Thirty (Lysander's allies) and restored the democracy. (Ironically, the Athenians were the only participants in the Peloponnesian War who did not believe they had been treated unfairly by the Spartans.)

Elsewhere, the boards-of-ten completed their tasks and restored the "ancestral constitutions," but still the garrisons and the Spartan commanders remained, and, wherever they remained, their narrow, brutal, and hypocritical policy antagonized Greeks and cost the Spartans all the good will they had acquired during the war. Admittedly, two ideals treasured by Greeks were in conflict—first, Greeks believed each and every polis should be free and autonomous, to determine its own form of government and its own foreign policy, and, second, Greeks believed that all Greeks should act together in the interests of collective security and stability.

Up to this time the Spartans had provided unity and security through the Peloponnesian League—in the Peloponnesian League, although the member states were required, in fact, to obey Sparta, still they had enjoyed limited free expression, control over their internal affairs, and even, to some extent, control over foreign policy, but, when all was said and done, the League depended upon the power of Sparta. Now, as Greeks sought security in local leagues and alliances, the Spartans determined, not unjustly, that such associations were aimed at them and a possible threat to them, so they tried to break them up, wherever they were: Arcadia, Elis, Chalcidice, Boeotia. Their pretext was that, as "liberators," they supported the "ancestral constitutions" of Greece and the independence of individual poleis.

For the first time since the wars with Tegea, Spartan policy was far more ambitious than Spartan resources could support. The Spartans had to hire mercenaries to crew their ships—and they could not maintain the overseas empire without a fleet—and they had to hire mercenaries for the garrisons in the dozens of subject states and more mercenaries for the armies to fight their former allies in Greece and to carry out foreign policy abroad, and they paid the mercenaries' salaries with the tribute they collected from the empire. In addition, Sparta concealed a dirty little secret: Lysander and Cyrus, the younger son of the Persian king, had formed a personal relationship and Lysander had made a disgraceful pact with Cyrus. Cyrus would subsidize a Spartan victory over the Athenians and, in return, the Spartans would help him overthrow his older brother, Artaxerxes (the heir to the Persian throne), and become king. Cyrus, as king, would let the Spartans administer Ionia.

In 401 BCE, when Cyrus mustered his army of revolt (with 13,000 Greek mercenaries under the command of the Spartan exile Clearchos), the Spartans supported him with their fleet. Cyrus marched his army into the heart of the Persian Empire and fought a battle against his brother, Artaxerxes, at Cunaxa. The Greek phalanx dominated the battle, but Cyrus was killed and the Greeks were isolated, their generals were lured away and murdered, and the survivors were called upon to surrender. The Greeks elected new leaders and marched out of the Persian empire.

Artaxerxes ordered his satraps to occupy Ionia and Sparta's duplicity was revealed. When Artaxerxes's satrap in Asia Minor, Tissaphernes, began to reduce the Greek cities, the Spartans sent a force of 1000 *neodamodeis* (the non-Spartiate soldiers resident in Sparta) and 4000 Peloponnesians to stop him. By the year 399 the several Spartan commanders had forced the satraps to offer terms—if the Spartans would withdraw all their forces from Asia Minor, the Persians would guarantee that the Greeks of Asia Minor would be free and autonomous. The satraps waited while the Spartan commanders sent a representative to Sparta for advice, but the Persian king, in the meantime and just in case, ordered the Persian fleet to be rebuilt. Before the year was out, he had a fleet the equal of Sparta's and a commander better than theirs—he hired Conon, an Athenian veteran of the Peloponnesian War.

In the same year (399 BCE) the Eleans, the hosts of the Olympic Games, took the first steps to form a league. They intended to combine the separate poleis in Elis and cooperate with each other for greater security and power within the Peloponnesus. The Spartans opposed the formation of this league, as they opposed any potential change in the balance of power, and, because of their opposition, the Eleans forbade Sparta to participate in the Olympic Games. They caught an elderly Spartan man, who had come to watch the games anyway, whipped him, and expelled him. They also committed another affront: they refused to allow Agis to consult the oracle of Zeus at Olympia, as he had been instructed to do by another oracle. The Eleans said that the oracle should not be consulted in a war of Greek against Greek.

Agis heard someone praise the Eleans for the justice they showed in administering the Olympic Games and he said,

"I don't see that it's such a big thing or so wonderful that they practice justice on one day in four years."

The ephors ordered Agis to lead an army against the Eleans, but soon after he entered Elis, there was an earthquake and he withdrew. The Eleans now sought allies, while the Spartan ephors authorized another campaign and Agis summoned his allies—all joined him including even a unit of Athenians and several Elean cities that deserted the nascent league. Agis marched to Olympia where he sacrificed to Zeus and consulted the oracle. (No one tried to stop him.) He then advanced on the city of Elis and gathered so much booty that the news spread through the Peloponnesus and more contingents of troops arrived from Arcadia and Achaea just to loot. The Spartan invasion caused a civil war in Elis between the anti-Spartan democrats and the pro-Spartan oligarchs. The oligarchs conspired to murder the leader of the democrats, when he kept a certain appointment, but he missed his appointment because he had a hangover and stayed home to sleep it off. He and his followers then defeated the oligarchs and seized control of the city, but they were unable to defend their territory from the depredations of Agis's force, and after a year they agreed to dissolve their league.

Agis traveled to Delphi and dedicated a tenth of the spoils of the Elean war to Apollo. Agis was now an old man and not in the best of health, but he still had his wit. Another elderly man complained to him that Sparta was in a mess, the old customs were dead and bad new ones had been introduced and everything was turned upside down.

Agis replied, "Yes, I remember when I was a boy, my father complained to me that everything was turned upside down and he said to me, when he was a boy, his father complained that everything had been turned upside down, so we should not wonder that things get worse. We should only be surprised if they get better."

Soon after this, he fell ill and he died (in 399 BCE). The Spartans gave him a magnificent funeral—if, sometimes, he had seemed overly cautious on campaign, nonetheless, he was the son of a popular king, he had commanded the army in the victory at the battle of Mantinea, and, from his headquarters at Decelea in Attica, he successfully prosecuted the war against Athens.

Agis had all the Spartan attitudes and prejudices. When he examined the massive walls of Corinth, he said, "A suitable place for women." He observed, "If you want to remain free, you must not be afraid to die." But he also understood that the Spartiates were a precious resource and needed to be preserved and that battle was risky and should be avoided, if at all possible. This single fact—the vulnerability of the Spartiate core—would determine the course of Spartan history in the fourth century.

After the funeral of Agis, the Spartans chose a new king.

── PART VI ──
THE THEBAN WARS

Table 6. The Kings of the Theban Wars

Eurypontid Royal House

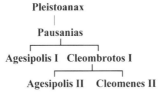

Lampito = **Archidamos II** = Eupolia

Agis II   **Agesilaos II**

Leotychidas   **Archidamos III**

Agiad Royal House

Pleistoanax

Pausanias

Agesipolis I   Cleombrotos I

Agesipolis II   Cleomenes II

Eurypontid Royal House	Agiad Royal House
Agesilaos II (399–360)	Pausanias (445–426, 409–395)
Archidamos III (360–338)	Agesipolis I (395–380)
	Cleombrotos I (380–371)
	Agesipolis II (371–370)
	Cleomenes II (370–309)

Kings highlighted in bold.

Illustration 12. Archidamos III (from a Spartan coin) (Pamela M. Bradford)

— 24 —

The Common King

Agis was survived by a boy, Leotychidas, who was fifteen years old, and by a half-brother, Agesilaos (the son of Archidamos), who was about forty. Unlike Leotychidas (the putative heir to the throne), Agesilaos had gone through the agoge. Agesilaos had not distinguished himself, but he had learned obedience and amiability. He was short of stature—true to the ephors' warning that Archidamos, if he married the short woman he loved, would create a race of "midget kings"—and he had a limp. He fought in the phalanx near his father, Archidamos, and, although he was aggressive, he did not stand out in battle. His father advised him, "Son, either get stronger or become more modest about your abilities." To his friends he seemed the very type of the noble Spartan, a plain-speaking, simple man with common sense, not pretentious but magnanimous, courageous, and energetic.

Leotychidas should have been chosen king without any controversy, but Spartans remembered that Agis had said in the hearing of others, when he learned of the birth of Leotychidas, that the child was not his. Many Spartans suspected that Leotychidas was the son of the Athenian Alcibiades, and was, therefore, not a Heraclid, and was not eligible to be king, even though Agis, on his death bed, had claimed Leotychidas and had entreated the ephors to support him and protect him.

Some Spartans were swayed in this controversy by Lysander's strong support for Agesilaos. The two were close friends and Lysander, whatever other reasons he might have had, thought that he could manipulate Agesilaos. But other Spartans supported the claim of Leotychidas, they accepted that he was the son of Agis, and they cited a prophecy, furnished by a prominent soothsayer, that the Spartans would suffer a disaster if they ever had a "lame" king. Lysander responded that the word "lame" was metaphorical and referred to Leotychidas's "lame" ancestry. In the end, the Spartans were convinced by the advocacy of Lysander, they disinherited Leotychidas, and they bestowed the kingship—and the king's property—on Agesilaos.

Agesilaos found himself in an uncomfortable position. He had made many enemies during the dispute, and, particularly, he had alienated the mother of Leotychidas, who had been denied Agis's royal property, and he had also alienated her powerful family. He conciliated them by giving them half his inheritance and he set out to conciliate the rest of the Spartans through his personal charm and amiability. The ephors thought he went too far and they fined him for trying to supplant themselves in the affections of the people. Thereafter, Agesilaos demonstrated his subservience to the representatives of the people by not standing upon the royal prerogative of ignoring the ephors' first summons.

However, he also faced opposition because he was perceived to be Lysander's man and a proponent of his policy—to take Athens' place at the head of an empire and to preserve Sparta's exclusive social structure and distribution of property. Thus he found himself opposed by the other king and by a large number of Spartans who believed that the ranks of the Spartiates, depleted by the wars and by the earthquake, should be filled with new citizens drawn from the very many "good" men who fought in the phalanx but did not have citizenship—these non-Spartiate hoplites were called *neodamodeis*, a cryptic term which indicated only that they had some place within the damos (the "people").

The Spartans could have introduced new blood into their system through the custom of the *mothax*—a noncitizen boy (Laconian neighbor or helot), who accompanied a young Spartiate through the agoge. The mothax, who graduated from the agoge, could be awarded a parcel of land, admitted to the barracks with the others, enrolled in a mess, and granted all the rights and privileges of a citizen. Two prominent Spartiates, Gylippos (whose father had lost his citizenship) and Lysander, were said to have been *mothakes*. The rub was that, in the Spartan system, membership in a mess, and hence full citizenship, depended upon meeting a monthly quota of rations produced from one's own land, and the land, by the time of Agesilaos, had already passed into the possession of a narrow group of citizens who just were not willing to let any of it go.

In this tense situation, Agesilaos conducted the new-year sacrifices. The seer told him that the signs were as bad as though they were surrounded by enemies, and, not long after, the ephors were informed that Cinadon (a young man who served in the army but was not a Spartiate) was plotting a revolution.

"He took me to the edge of the public area," the informer told them, "and he said to me, 'Count the number of Spartiates in this place.' I counted: the kings, the ephors, the gerousians, and about forty others. That was all I could find. Then he said, 'These are the enemy. All the rest are our allies and there are more than four thousand in this area.' "

Cinadon was arrested and tortured. He named names and everyone he named was arrested, questioned under torture, and executed. One of the conspirators he denounced was a Spartiate, a seer named Tisamenos; he was executed. Cinadon was executed. The executions thwarted any possible revolution and, also, any possibility of reform.

Not much later, Agesilaos was sacrificing a bull at the shrine of Athena of the Brazen House and a louse bit him. He caught it and crushed it in front of everyone and he said,

"How sweet it is, to kill someone who plots against you, even at the altar."

In 396 BCE the Spartans were persuaded by Lysander to reject the Persian offer of peace and to send him in command of a new expedition to Asia Minor. Agesilaos was to join him with thirty Spartiates, 2000 Neodamodeis, and 6000 allies. Agesilaos assembled his army on the island of Euboea, but he, himself, with a few companions, crossed over into Boeotia (the district dominated by Thebes) and he sacrificed at Aulis, the place from which Agamemnon had launched his expedition against Troy. Agesilaos invoked the gods to bless his Asian campaign and to accept him as the successor of Agamemnon. In the midst of his sacrifice, however, the Boeotian cavalry arrived—Agesilaos had not sought their permission to sacrifice at Aulis—and they stopped him and pushed the sacrifice off the altar. Agesilaos was furious, and he remained furious with the Thebans (the Boeotian leaders) for the rest of his life.

Nonetheless, and with the gloomy prediction that his operations in Asia would begin well but come to nothing, Agesilaos joined Lysander in Ionia and immediately set about disabusing him of any idea that the king was his puppet. Agesilaos granted requests that Lysander refused and refused requests Lysander had approved. Lysander got the message, asked for an independent command, no matter how insignificant, and left Ionia. Once Agesilaos had established his authority, he assembled his army in Ephesus, announced that he was ready to march, and ordered markets to be prepared on the route to Caria. Then, when his opponent, the satrap Tissaphernes, moved his army to block the way into Caria, Agesilaos invaded and plundered Phrygia.

In the next year, the king announced that he would march immediately by the shortest route on Sardis, the capital of Lydia. Tissaphernes thought that this announcement was another ruse—which it was!—and so again the Persian moved his infantry to Caria, while Agesilaos marched on Sardis. For three days Agesilaos marched unopposed and then the Persian cavalry caught up to him, attacked and killed the Greeks scattered in the plain, and forced the king to form a square to protect his army as it advanced. During the night Agesilaos set a mixed force of hoplites and peltasts in ambush and at dawn he resumed his march.

When Agesilaos saw that he had drawn the pursuing Persian cavalry and light-armed forces past the ambush site, he wheeled, formed a battle line, and charged the Persians, while, at the same time, the ambushers charged out from concealment. He caught the Persians between his two forces, broke them, and pursued them with his small force of cavalry and his light-armed troops. The combined attacks killed about 600 of the enemy and, more importantly, scattered the rest and eliminated them as an effective threat. Agesilaos captured the enemy camp and enough plunder to fill up his campaign chest, satisfy his soldiers, and amaze Greeks back home with their first sight of camels.

After his victory Agesilaos allowed his soldiers to range through the countryside and to ravage and plunder the enemy as far as they wanted. He marched across the plain of Lydia, through the mountains and into Phrygia and to the banks of the Maeander River, where bad omens—a sheep's liver without a lobe—convinced him to turn back.

As for Tissaphernes, the Persian king had him beheaded and he instructed his replacement to offer Agesilaos terms: the cities would be free and autonomous, but they would pay tribute to the Persian king, and the Spartans would go home. Agesilaos sent the offer to Sparta, but, in the meantime, he demanded a large sum of money from the new satrap which he used to pay for a campaign against the other satrap, Pharnabazus.

Agesilaos, so far, had been successful, but his plundering and destruction of Persian territory made an implacable enemy of the Persian king and, furthermore, convinced the king that the Spartans were determined to continue the war, unless he found some way to stop them. Therefore, the Persian king dispatched a Greek envoy with an enormous sum (fifty talents) of gold coin to distribute to the leading men of Greece, to influence them, and to fund a war on Sparta. The envoy visited Corinth, Argos, and Thebes. In Thebes he had the most success: the Thebans sent representatives throughout the Greek world to seek allies for a war against Sparta. In Athens the Thebans addressed the assembly.

"Can you think of anyone who still likes the Spartans? Certainly not the Argives, who have been their enemies from the beginning of time. Nor the Eleans, who have lost so much land and so many cities. And what about the Corinthians, the Arcadians, and the Achaeans? They risked their lives in the war against you, but the Spartans never gave them a share of any of the power or glory or money that was won. Far from it! Now that things have gone well for the Spartans, they think it perfectly proper to set up their own helots as governors, and treat their free allies like slaves.

"And, as for the people they 'liberated,' these people are enslaved twice, to Spartan governors and to Lysander's Boards-of-Ten. And now the Spartans have made an enemy of the Persian king. Always remember, they are few and we are many and we are just as well armed."

The Athenians wanted to restore their empire, they were ready to fight Sparta without the inducement of Persian money, and they voted to join the Theban alliance.

The Spartans reacted swiftly. They sent Lysander with one army and King Pausanias with another to coordinate an offensive against Thebes, but Lysander was impatient, Pausanias was delayed, and their coordination broke down. Lysander fought a battle with the Thebans near the town of Haliartus, just to the west of Thebes. The battle was a draw, but Lysander was killed and his body lay on the battlefield under the enemy walls. King Pausanias arrived soon after the battle. He had the moral advantage, because the Thebans believed that they had gone too far and they would now suffer severe retribution, but Pausanias did not act quickly enough and the arrival of an Athenian army changed the situation.

Pausanias called together his polemarchs and his unit commanders and put to them the situation—Lysander was already dead, Lysander's army felt as though it had been defeated, their allies, the Corinthians, refused to participate and their other allies were far from enthusiastic, they were heavily outnumbered in cavalry, and to recover the bodies, which lay close to the city wall, they would have to advance into a zone where they would come under fire from the towers. Pausanias and his staff agreed to ask for a truce (an admission of defeat) to recover the bodies, but the Thebans refused to grant a truce unless the Spartans agreed to withdraw from Boeotian territory. Pausanias agreed, he recovered the bodies, and he returned to Sparta.

Back in Sparta, however, the ephors judged that Pausanias had made a dishonorable truce, despite the agreement of his subordinates and advisers, and they decided to try the king on a capital charge. Pausanias may have paid for his earlier opposition to Lysander. Maybe he was suspected of intentionally delaying, maybe he was suspected of opposing the whole campaign, of being hesitant to fight, or of not being sorry that Lysander was dead. In any case, Pausanias did not wait for the verdict. He fled to Tegea and was condemned to death in his absence. His young son Agesipolis ("Leader of the City") became king. As Agesipolis was still a minor, a regent was appointed for him.

Pausanias lived an uneasy life as an exile in Tegea. He could never be sure but what the Spartans might send assassins to carry out the sentence of death. He believed that he had been exiled illegally and as part of the ephors' assumption of power and their subversion of law and custom. While Pausanias was in exile he wrote an essay on Sparta in which he advocated a return to the Lycurgan constitution, attention to the law, an increase of the power of the kings and gerousia, and a diminution of the power of the ephors. He wrote, "The laws should be the masters of men, not men of the laws."

Pausanias had a mordant wit. He praised Sparta while he was in exile, and a citizen of Tegea asked him, if Sparta was so great, why was he was in Tegea, an exile from Sparta.

"Because," he said, "it is the custom of doctors not to spend time with the healthy but with the sick."

Pausanias had a peculiar aversion to doctors (peculiar not in the sentiments but that a king of Sparta had so much to say about them). When a doctor told him, "There's nothing wrong with you," he said, "Because I do not employ you as my doctor."

When another doctor said to him, "You have become an old man," he replied, "Yes, because I never employed you as a doctor."

When one of his friends criticized him for having spoken disparagingly of a doctor, and unjustly, because he had never gone to him, he said, "If I had gone to him, I would not be sitting here."

He said that the best doctor is one who buries his patients before they decompose.

And, finally, when he was asked how Greeks could eliminate the Thracians, he said, "By sending them our doctors instead of our generals,"

Certainly for the Agiad royal family the century after the battle of Sepeia (494 BCE) was not a happy time—Cleomenes committed suicide, Leonidas died at Thermopylae, Pausanias (the regent) was bricked up and starved to death, Pleistarchos, the son of Leonidas, died shortly after he reached adulthood, and his successor Pleistoanax, the son of the regent Pausanias, was exiled for not being aggressive enough in an invasion of Attica (446 BCE)—he lived in exile nineteen years before being recalled to Sparta shortly after the death of King Archidamos. His son Pausanias served as king until his father returned and then again after his father died in 408/7. Pausanias, in turn, was exiled for the truce he negotiated, and lived in exile for about ten years (from 395 to sometime after 385).

The house of the Eurypontids was more stable, but the kings were known for their ability to get along with the citizens and the ephors. Archidamos had an enormous reputation because he had saved the city during the Great Earthquake. Nonetheless, his advice about the Athenian war was ignored, his son Agis was punished for making a treaty instead of fighting, and, furthermore, was subjected to the ignominy of having official advisers accompany him on his future campaigns. Agesilaos went far out of his way to placate the ephors and, as a battle leader, he became indispensable.

During the fifth century the ephors had gained the preponderance of power and, since they served for only one year, unlike the kings, they tended to make decisions without considering the long-term consequences.

— 25 —

"Free and Autonomous"

In 394 BCE delegates from Corinth, Argos, Athens, and Thebes were meeting at Corinth to discuss the war with Sparta—they agreed that the Spartans had to be fought close to home, because Sparta was like a "river or a wasp's nest," best dealt with at the source. And then the delegates debated the questions of contributions, the supreme command, and the division of spoils. While they were still debating these issues, they learned that a Spartan army had arrived at Sicyon, twenty miles away. The allies hurriedly assembled their army at Nemea (about ten to fifteen miles southwest of Corinth) and awaited the Spartan army. The Spartan army was commanded by Aristodamos, a member of the royal family and the regent for Agesipolis.

The allies drew up their phalanx with the Thebans and Boeotians on the left opposite the Spartans, and all seemed ready for battle, but the Theban leaders refused to give the orders to advance because, they said, they had observed that the omens were unpropitious. Day by day, they continued to observe unpropitious omens, until the Athenians agreed to take their place. Then the generals declared that the omens were now propitious and the allied army should join battle immediately. The Thebans and Boeotians drew up their ranks twice as deep as normal, moved to their right (away from the Spartans), and pulled the whole phalanx with them. As they were moving, the Spartans charged.

The Athenians were completely outflanked and in disarray because of the Theban movement and they suffered heavy casualties. The Thebans, however, broke the phalanx of the Spartans' allies and pursued them off the battlefield. The Thebans, and the other contingents with them, were convinced that they had won a complete victory. They formed up in columns, polis by polis, and marched back. Meanwhile, the Spartans halted their pursuit of the Athenians, reformed their phalanx, and advanced to their left.

The Spartan commander, Aristodamos, intended to push his phalanx in front of the enemy columns, cut them off, and force them to fight, but someone in the Spartan ranks called out, "Let the first go by." Aristodamos accepted the advice and held the Spartan phalanx back, drawn up parallel to the enemy's line of march, and then charged the columns, one at a time, first the Argives, then the Corinthians, and finally the Thebans and Boeotians. They put each column to flight.

Meanwhile, Agesilaos was en route to Boeotia. The Spartan ephors, because of the threat posed by the alliance of Thebes, Argos, Corinth, and Athens, had recalled Agesilaos before he could implement his plans to break up the Persian empire in Asia Minor. Later, when Agesilaos was asked why he had left Persia, he said, "Ten thousand archers drove me out." (An archer appears on the Persian gold coin.)

Agesilaos had to move his army by land because the Spartans had lost command of the sea—they had held it for only ten years. Agesilaos marched his army north through Asia Minor, across the straits, west through Thrace—where he heard of the Spartan victory at Nemea—and west and south through Macedonia and Thessaly. As Agesilaos was about to cross into Boeotia from Thessaly, there was a partial eclipse of the sun (August 14, 394) and he learned that the Spartan fleet had been destroyed, and the Spartan admiral killed, in a battle with Conon and the Persian fleet at Cnidus in Asia Minor. Agesilaos, wily commander that he was, told his troops that the Spartans had won a great victory at Cnidus. The army rejoiced and prepared to do their part by winning a great victory on land.

Agesilaos led the army to the city of Coronea, where the Theban army was waiting with its Boeotian allies and its contingents of Argives, Athenians, and Corinthians. Agesilaos had been joined by two units of Spartans and he had his neodamodeis, the mercenaries, the Greeks from Ionia, and some additional troops recruited on the march and in Boeotia. As at the battle of Nemea, so at the battle of Coronea, the Thebans held the far right of their phalanx—it was the point of honor—and routed the troops opposite them (their Boeotian enemies), while Agesilaos and the Spartans broke the troops opposite them (their old enemies the Argives), and then, as at Nemea, the victorious Thebans attempted to march past the Spartans.

Agesilaos now could have waited, as the Spartans had waited at Nemea, and charged the Thebans as they passed in column before him. If he had done so, he would have killed some of them and humiliated and humbled the rest when they threw down their shields and ran, but he hated them so much, he wanted to confront them, fight them, and defeat them, phalanx to phalanx. Consequently, he blocked their line of retreat with his phalanx and forced them to reform and fight. The fighting was vicious and sustained. The Spartans killed many Thebans, but the Theban center forced its way through the Spartan line and the bulk of the Thebans escaped and ran for their lives. The Spartans held the battlefield and Agesilaos had the satisfaction of receiving Theban heralds, come to ask for a truce to bury their dead.

Agesilaos had won a critical victory, but he was so badly wounded that he had to be taken to Delphi to be healed by Apollo himself. He was told bluntly by a friend that he deserved his wound, because he had acted rashly and emotionally. Perhaps he did deserve the criticism, and perhaps he had acted, as he had, only because of his hatred for the Thebans, but he also recognized that he could inflict real damage on the Theban army only if he fought them phalanx to phalanx. The Thebans were Sparta's most formidable enemy. If he knocked them out of the war, no one comparable would remain. And he did inflict real damage—the Thebans would not dare to face the Spartans again in a set battle for twenty years.

With Thebes humbled, the Spartans now decided to knock Corinth out of the war. Corinthian traitors admitted the Spartan army within the long walls between Corinth and its port Lechaeum, and the Spartans caught the Corinthian military forces and their Argive allies completely by surprise. The Argives fled towards the sea and were intercepted by Spartan cavalrymen who dismounted and picked up shields which had been discarded by some Sicyonians. The shields had sigmas on them and the Argives thought they were only facing Sicyonians and they could beat them. The Spartan commander remarked,

"By the twin gods, Argives, you will find these sigmas have deceived you."

Meanwhile the Spartan infantry routed the Corinthians. The Corinthians fled and ran headlong into the Argives who were fleeing from the Spartan cavalry—they had learned their mistake—and the Corinthians turned back, only to meet the Spartan infantry again. All discipline evaporated. Some of the panic-stricken soldiers tried to climb the walls and were struck down, others were trampled and suffocated, none of them made any effort to defend themselves, and the Spartans killed at will. The dead bodies were heaped together "like stacks of wheat or piles of wood or stones." The Spartans also killed the Boeotian garrison.

With this victory, the Spartans gained complete moral ascendancy over their enemies, but their enemies, although they were too afraid to face the Spartans, phalanx to phalanx, sought other ways to fight. An Athenian named Iphicrates retrained light-armed soldiers—the *peltasts*—and used them almost as foot-cavalry, to rush in, launch their javelins at the hoplites, and then rush back out of danger. They could be effective in the right circumstances, but the Spartans dismissed them and mocked their allies for being afraid of them until Iphicrates won a spectacular victory.

Agesilaos released a detachment of 250 Spartan hoplites to return to Sparta to take part in the religious festival of the Hyacinthia in Amyclae. Once the detachment was on its own—seemingly out of range of the enemy—Iphicrates' peltasts attacked it. They ran at the Spartans, launched their javelins, and fled when the Spartans charged them, but, when the Spartans resumed their march, the peltasts reformed and attacked them again and again. In each attack they wounded or killed a few of the Spartans and, as the Spartans became tired and demoralized, the peltasts became bolder, more of them joined in the attack, and, eventually, they killed all but a few of the Spartans.

The Spartans could not continue to sustain such losses nor were they faring well in a war where their enemies avoided a clash of phalanxes. They lost Ionia to the Persians, could not prevent Conon from seizing Cythera and raiding Laconia, were unable to stop the Athenians from rebuilding the long walls and recovering control of Byzantium and the Hellespont (through which their grain and ship-building timber came), and lost Aegina and the commander there because they did not have the money to pay his mercenaries.

This vicious war with its small skirmishes and ambushes, naval battles of forty ships (instead of the hundreds of the Peloponnesian War), civil wars within cities, and financial ruin had demoralized everyone.

26

Sparta's Empire

In the beginning of the summer of 388 BCE, after six years of war in Greece, the Spartan ephors issued orders to their young king, Agesipolis (then in his early twenties), to invade the Argolid. In the recent past their campaigns had been thwarted by their own religious scruples and an Argive subterfuge—the Argives never stopped celebrating a festival sacred both to themselves and to the Spartans; so long as the festival continued, so did a sacred truce, which prohibited the Spartans from taking military action against Argos.

Agesipolis led his army to the border of Laconia and there, having conducted the religious ceremonies to determine that, as far as the gods were concerned, the army could cross the border, he traveled on his own to Olympia, where he visited the oracle of Zeus and asked if he could invade Argive territory despite a sacred truce, when the truce was only a subterfuge. "Zeus" responded that Agesipolis could, indeed, ignore the truce. From Olympia Agesipolis traveled to Delphi (the more prestigious oracle) and there asked Apollo,

"Regarding the truce, do you have the same opinion as your father?"

"Apollo" responded that he did agree with his father and Agesipolis returned to his army and led it out of Laconia, through Arcadia, and to the edge of the Argolid where he was met by two heralds, wearing wreaths. They proclaimed that a holy truce was in effect. Agesipolis replied that the gods had rejected this truce and he advanced into their territory, but that very night, as the Spartans were pouring out the first libations before dinner, the earth shook. A more conservative king—Agis, for instance—would have declared the earthquake an adverse omen and would have withdrawn, but Agesipolis ordered the Spartans to sing a paean to propitiate Poseidon, the god of earthquakes, and then he addressed the army: the earthquake was a favorable omen, he said, because it happened when they were in Argive territory, and so confirmed their action and, furthermore, forebode ill for the Argives.

Agesipolis had studied previous campaigns, and, in particular, the campaign of Agesilaos, and he had decided that he would outdo whatever Agesilaos had done. Agesilaos had gone close to the walls of Argos, so Agesipolis went closer, and he advanced so quickly and boldly that the Argives fled into the city, slammed the gates shut, and abandoned their Boeotian allies to their fate. The Boeotians hugged the walls "like bats" to escape the Spartans—but Agesipolis had dispatched his Cretan archers to plunder another part of the Argolid and so he did not have them to shoot the Boeotians down. He left the city of Argos and proceeded through the Argolid and plundered it systematically, until a day arrived on which he received irrefutable signs that the gods wanted him to leave—a lightning bolt killed some men in his camp and the subsequent sacrifice revealed a liver without lobes. He withdrew from the Argolid and disbanded his army.

After a Spartan commander raided the Piraeus, the Athenians approached King Agesipolis with the suggestion that they settle their differences through arbitration and they suggested that appropriate arbiters might be the Megarians. Agesipolis said to them,

"Athenians, aren't you ashamed to admit that the Megarians know more about right and wrong than you and us, the leaders of the Greek world?"

Greeks everywhere were so sick of war that they agreed to meet at Sparta in the winter of 387/6 and consider—reluctantly—the peace terms which had been dictated by the Persian king and set forth as a royal fiat:

King Artaxerxes considers the following terms just—

(1) The cities of Asia and, of the islands, Clazomenae and Cyprus, should belong to me.
(2) The other Greek cities, big and small, shall be autonomous, except for Lemnos, Imbros, and Scyros, which, as of old, should belong to Athens.

And if either of two parties refuses to accept peace on these terms, I, together with those who accept this peace, will make war on that party, both by land and sea, with ships and with money.

None of the Greeks was happy with the king's fiat. The Thebans were forbidden—by Agesilaos—to sign on behalf of all Boeotians, Argos was isolated, the Athenians' ambitions at sea were curtailed, and the Spartans had to publicly abandon the Ionian Greeks. Greek philosophers lamented the fallen state of Greece and an influential Athenian, the great rhetorician Isocrates, proposed that Greeks unite under the leadership of Athens and Sparta to fight "the only war that is better than peace," a war against Persia.

Isocrates's plan was hopelessly idealistic and impractical, since Agesilaos intended to use the terms of the peace treaty as a pretext to break up all leagues, alliances, and associations, to make everyone weak and vulnerable, and, consequently, to advance Sparta's domination of Greece. Agesilaos's plan, however, had one—ultimately fatal—flaw: it depended entirely upon the superiority of the Spartan army which, in turn, depended upon a core of fully trained Spartiates, who would be opposed by poorly trained opponents. The core, however, of fully trained Spartiates was diminishing even as the constant fighting trained their opponents almost to a Spartan standard.

The Spartans' first victim—in 385—was the Arcadian city of Mantinea. The Mantineans had created one city from four villages, established a democracy, refused to send their contingent of troops for the campaign against Argos, and celebrated the news of Iphicrates's destruction of the 250-man unit of Spartiates. In reaction, the ephors issued an order to the Mantineans to tear down their fortifications, and, when the Mantineans refused, the Spartans voted to dispatch an army under the command of a king. They offered the command to Agesilaos, but he demurred, because of an old friendship between the Mantineans and his father Archidamos—the Mantineans had helped Archidamos at the time of the Great Earthquake—and the command was given to Agesipolis.

Agesipolis accepted the command—despite the friendship that his father, in exile, had with the democratic leaders of Mantinea; he crossed the Laconian border with due ceremonies, collected his allies, and marched into Mantinean territory. He tried to force the Mantineans to come to terms by ravaging their land and threatening more destruction, but he failed to convince them, so he decided to put them under siege. He set half his army to digging a trench and constructing a wall around the city, while the other half stood guard. The king soon learned, however, that the Mantineans were well prepared to withstand a siege—they had gathered in their harvest before the invasion, and, by all reports, the harvest had been bountiful, they had abundant water, because a river flowed through their city, and they were determined to hold out, if need be, for a long time.

Agesipolis was concerned that neither his own Spartans, nor his allies, would be willing to maintain a siege for the length of time required to compel the Mantineans to accept his terms, but, after considering all the circumstances, he came up with a brilliant, yet simple, solution—he had the river dammed just downstream from Mantinea. The river overflowed its banks inside the city, flooded the town, overtopped the houses, and lapped against the city walls; cracks appeared in the walls and the Mantineans became afraid that it would collapse, that the Spartans would break into the city, capture everyone and sell them all into slavery, so they capitulated and agreed to the Spartan terms: to reject democracy, to tear down the walls, and to split up into the four original villages. They asked—and Agesipolis's father, Pausanias, asked with them—and Agesipolis agreed to allow the democratic leaders to leave under a safe conduct.

In 382 BCE envoys from two northern cities, and from the king of Macedonia, appealed to the Spartans to help them against the city of Olynthus and the new Chalcidian League. Olynthus was trying to force all free and independent Greek cities in that region to join the league and, in the process, was also encroaching on Macedonian territory. The envoys also reported that the Boeotians and Athenians were attempting to form an alliance with the Olynthians and so the situation presented a danger to Sparta. The Spartans agreed to break up the

Chalcidian League. They sent an advance force of about 2000 freed helots, Laconian neighbors, and Sciritai to begin operations in Chalcidice. Soon after, they sent a second force under the command of a Spartan named Phoebidas to join the first.

As Phoebidas was leading his troops past Thebes, a faction of Theban politicians, feuding with another faction, met with him and offered to let the Spartans into Thebes. Phoebidas, who was known as passionate for renown but not a deep thinker, agreed, even though Sparta and Thebes were at peace and both had sworn to keep the peace. Phoebidas and the Spartans slipped into Thebes, while the Theban people, suspecting nothing, were celebrating a festival. The Spartans seized the acropolis. About 300 Theban patriots escaped to Athens and raised an outcry over this illegal and outrageous act of the Spartans. Greeks everywhere waited to see what the Spartans would do next, as envoys from Thebes, including the primary instigator of the coup, came to Sparta. The Spartans did not welcome the coup leader and for a time they seemed ready to renounce the seizure of Thebes by Phoebidas (as they should have), but King Agesilaos, driven still by his hatred of the Thebans, asked the Spartans a simple question,

"Did Phoebidas's act help, or hurt, Sparta?"

The Spartans fined Phoebidas, an acknowledgement that he had done wrong, but they voted, nevertheless, to accept the situation, garrison the Theban acropolis, and send another expedition to Chalcidice. They appointed Teleutias, a popular commander and the brother of King Agesilaos, to command an allied army with a Spartan contingent. Once Teleutias arrived in the region, he requested extra troops from the states around Chalcidice and he put together a sizeable army, with which he marched on the city of Olynthus. The Olynthians were ready to fight, their cavalry routed the cavalry of Teleutias and turned his flank, but a special force Teleutias had organized rushed the gates of Olynthus and forced the Olynthians to retreat to the safety of their city.

Throughout the summer Teleutias ravaged the land of the Chalcidians, the Chalcidians raided the territory of his allies, and then Teleutias made another attempt on Olynthus. This time Teleutias's cavalry forced the Olynthian cavalry to retreat and Teleutias pushed the pursuit of the Olynthians right up to their walls, where a rain of missiles caused Teleutias to lose control of his army. It fell back in disorder. Seeing their enemy's confusion, the Olynthians charged from their city and routed the Spartan forces, Teleutias was killed, and his army broke and fled in panic.

When the news reached Sparta, the Spartans decided to send out another expeditionary force, this time under the command of King Agesipolis with a staff of thirty Spartiates. When the news went out that the expedition would be commanded by Agesipolis, such was his reputation, both as a person and as a commander, that he attracted a large number of volunteers from the Laconian neighbors, from foreigners educated in Sparta, and from the illegitimate sons of Spartiates; in addition, he attracted volunteer infantry from allied states and some cavalry detachments from Thessaly.

After Agesipolis had departed, Phlius, a city in the Peloponnesus near Corinth, rejected a Spartan order to accept back some exiles and the Spartans dispatched Agesilaos to compel them to change their minds. IIe put the city under siege, and he was still conducting the siege when Agesipolis arrived in Chalcidice. Agesipolis attacked and captured Torone, one of the allies of Olynthus, and then he fell ill with a high fever. He was carried to a shady grove dedicated to the god Dionysus and there he died. His body was packed in honey and transported back to Sparta for royal burial.

Agesilaos, in particular, was stricken by his death. As kings they had dined together and Agesilaos remarked on what good company the young king had been, on the pleasant conversations the two had had about their youth, hunting, horses, and love affairs, and how courteous the young king had been, treating Agesilaos with the deference due an older man, even though the two were both kings and, by tradition, rivals.

Agesipolis was succeeded by his younger brother Cleombrotos ("Famous Mortal").

After a twenty-month siege Phlius capitulated to Agesilaos, Olynthus sued for peace and agreed to all of Sparta's terms, the Corinthians concluded that they could not fight the Spartans and they withdrew from the war, the Argives were chastened, Thebes was under Spartan control, the Athenians were isolated, and the Peloponnesian League was completely subservient to Sparta.

The ambitions of Lysander and Agesilaos seemed to have been fulfilled, but, as a friend of Agesilaos wrote,

"The gods are not indifferent to evil actions."

27

The Battle of Leuctra

"The Spartans [Agesilaos's friend wrote] had sworn to leave the cities independent and then they had seized the acropolis of Thebes. Now they were punished by the action of these men, and these men alone, whom they had wronged, although before that time they had never been defeated by any nation on earth; and as for the Thebans who had brought them into the acropolis with the aim of enslaving their city to Sparta so that they might act as tyrants, it took only seven men from the exiled party to put an end to their government."

On an evening in 379 BCE seven young men—exiles from Thebes—slipped into the city with the crowd of laborers who returned to their homes inside the wall at the end of every day. That night these heroes, disguised as young ladies, were brought into a banquet hall by an accomplice who had promised the tyrants, now ruling the city, that he would bring them a group of "respectable ladies" to participate in their drunken celebration of the feast of Aphrodite. The "ladies" entered, drew their swords, and struck down the tyrants.

With bloody swords in their hands they ran out into the street and called on the citizens to take up arms. They released all political prisoners and they admitted into the city an Athenian army which had come to help them. They surrounded, and terrified, the Spartan governor on the acropolis—he thought he and his men were going to be massacred—and they offered him safe conduct, if he agreed to leave. He accepted the offer, and the Thebans kept the letter of the agreement, but, as the Spartans marched out, a mob overwhelmed them, dragged out the Thebans who were trying to escape with the Spartans, and killed them.

When the news reached Sparta, the ephors mobilized the army and offered the command to Agesilaos, but he refused because he had reached the age of sixty at which Spartans were excused from service outside Laconia, and so they gave it to the other king, Cleombrotos—it was his first command. He led the army on a raid-in-force into Theban territory—the Theban army did not oppose him—and he put heart into Sparta's allies, but he accomplished nothing else and, on his return he encountered a terrific windstorm, which was so strong that it blew the shields off the arms of his men and filled everyone with the dread of a bad omen.

In 378 BCE the Spartan commander of the forces near Thebes, Sphodrias, a man whose own friends had to admit was not very bright, decided on his own to seize the Piraeus, the port of Athens. He intended to surprise the Piraeus at dawn, but the sun came up while he was in the middle of Attica and he had to withdraw; to add injury to insult, as he withdrew, he plundered the countryside. Some Spartan ambassadors were visiting Athens and the enraged Athenians wanted to lynch them, but the ambassadors, sensibly enough, said that they had had no idea that this would happen, it was not an act of the Spartan state, and the Spartans certainly would punish the commander. Indeed, Sphodrias was ordered to return and stand trial—he decided instead to await the results of the trial at a safe distance—but, as it happened, Sphodrias had a son, Cleonymos, who was reputed to be the nicest and the handsomest boy in Sparta and Agesilaos's son, Archidamos, loved him. Archidamos begged his father to intercede for Sphodrias. King Cleombrotos—the son was his tent mate—also supported Sphodrias, and Sphodrias was acquitted.

The Athenians were furious at the acquittal and they sent their fleet to attack Laconia. They defeated the Spartan fleet, gained control of the sea, sailed around the Peloponnesus, regained everything they had lost to the Spartans, and founded the Second Delian League. The Spartans retaliated by sending Agesilaos twice to raid Boeotia. In general, the Thebans avoided battle, but in one rearguard action their peltasts killed Phoebidas, the instigator of the war, and, in a small unit action at a place called Tegyra, the Theban Sacred Band outfought two regiments of Spartans.

The Theban Sacred Band consisted of three hundred men sworn to die rather than desert each other. Previously the Sacred Band had been dispersed in the Theban phalanx to encourage the rank and file by their example, but their present commander, Pelopidas, had convinced the Thebans that the Sacred Band could be better used as an independent tactical unit. The Spartans forced Pelopidas to fight and the Sacred Band fought furiously and routed the Spartans. After this battle the Theban army was reformed to include the Sacred Band as a unit on the flank of the phalanx. The Theban Sacred Band was as good as any unit in the Spartan army.

In 376 BCE Agesilaos was sick and his doctor prescribed an elaborate and complicated course of treatment and told him to follow it. Agesilaos said,

"By Castor and Pollux, I know, if I do everything you advise, I won't survive."

(Another doctor, who had been so successful in treating the sick that he thought he was Zeus, sent a letter to Agesilaus and in the very beginning wrote,

"May you be healthy."

Agesilaus replied, "May you be sane!")

Because Agesilaos was sick, Cleombrotos commanded the army. He had no heart for the campaign—perhaps because of the omen of the lost shields or the brutal fighting for little gain or the shaky moral ground the Spartans were on—

and he failed to carry the passes into Boeotia and returned home. His failure tainted him with a suspicion of incompetence or worse—that he was somehow soft on Thebes.

The Thebans secured the passes into Boeotia and then, under the leadership of two extraordinary men, Epaminondas and Pelopidas, organized the cities of Boeotia into a league—the citizens, that is, the hoplites, of each city voted for representatives (called Boeotarchs, eleven for all of Boeotia), to meet and make decisions binding on all members. The formation of the Boeotian League, and the reorganization of the Boeotian army, under the direction of Epaminondas and Pelopidas, made the Boeotian League potentially as powerful as Sparta.

Cleombrotos was sent to Boeotia's neighbor Phocis, where he remained poised to invade Boeotia, should the opportunity present itself. The Thebans were influenced by the threat to accept the invitation of the Athenians to attend a peace conference in Sparta (371 BCE), again under the aegis of the Persian king. The Athenians had achieved some of their objectives at sea, but they were running out of money and their fury at the Spartans had burned itself out and been replaced by the fear that the Boeotian League would be a dangerous neighbor.

At the conference the Athenian representatives set out the problem clearly— the enmity between Athens and Sparta was a disaster for Greece (as well as for Athens and Sparta). The two powers should accept the situation—Athens was the sea power, Sparta was the land power—and they should be content with that and become partners in preserving the peace under the new rules. Moreover, they should recognize that there were new factors to consider: Dionysius the tyrant of Syracuse was building an empire in the west, Amyntas the king of Macedonia was resurrecting the power of his kingdom in the north, and Jason of Pherai was uniting Thessaly under his control. The Athenians proposed that all should accept the terms set forth by the Persian king.

1. Spartan commanders would be withdrawn from all cities.
2. All military forces would be disbanded.
3. All cities would be autonomous.
4. In the case of a violation of the treaty, any city might help the injured party, but no one was compelled to do so.

All the representatives agreed to the Persian king's terms and signed the treaty. The Spartans took the oath for themselves and their allies. The Athenians and their allies took the oath separately. The Thebans signed as "Thebans," but the next day they requested that their signature be changed from "Thebans" to "Boeotians," in effect, requesting that the conference—and particularly the Spartans—recognize the legitimacy of the Boeotian League. Agesilaos had already had one exchange with Epaminondas when, earlier, Epaminondas had said that he would sign for all Boeotians. Agesilaos had demanded of him whether he thought it was just that the Thebans should sign for the whole of Boeotia and Epaminondas had retorted,

"Do you think it is just for the Spartans to sign for the whole of Laconia?"

Agesilaos leaped to his feet to reply, but he was so furious that he choked on his words.

Now, on this fateful day in 371 BCE, Agesilaos refused to allow the Thebans to change their signature and the Thebans withdrew, leaving the situation unclear: were the Thebans excluded from the treaty and therefore at war, not only with the Spartans, but with all the signatories of the treaty—if any of them were willing to fight Thebes? King Cleombrotos dispatched a runner from Phocis back to Sparta to ask for advice—were Sparta and Thebes at war, or not? The Spartan assembly at the urging of Agesilaos voted that Cleombrotos should keep his army together, lead it into Boeotia, and break up the Boeotian League. The Spartans also decided to send another army to join Cleombrotos.

Cleomhrotus forced the passes into Boeotia and camped at Leuctra (a small Boeotian town). There he faced the full muster of the citizen army of the Boeotian League under the command of Epaminondas and Pelopidas. Now would have been the time for Cleombrotos to show real moral leadership and to wait for the arrival of the second army, but he was persuaded by his friends and advisers who urged him to engage in immediate battle, so that he would prove, once and for all, that he was neither afraid of, nor partial to, the Thebans.

Phalanx would meet phalanx. The Spartans had not lost such a battle in living memory and the Thebans had never defeated the Spartans in such a battle, but Epaminondas and Pelopidas, the Theban leaders, were confident they could win. They had introduced two tactical innovations: first, the Thebans, would guide to their left and charge directly at the Spartans, and, second, their phalanx would be fifty men deep. (This second innovation influenced Philip to reorganize the Macedonian phalanx when he became king.) The Spartans just did not have enough men to form such a deep phalanx—the Spartan phalanx was twelve men deep.

Illustration 13.   Battle of Leuctra (Alfred S. Bradford)

Epaminondas ordered his weaker, right wing to hold back, and he led the Thebans directly at the Spartan phalanx, where the battle would be won or lost. The Spartans were unsettled by the sight of a phalanx moving at them from the left—like, a contemporary writer said, a trireme skidding sideways—opposite to the usual practice. In every battle in which they had ever fought they had moved to their right and the enemy had moved to his right. And in every battle the enemy had shown some reluctance to close with the Spartans, but now the Thebans smashed into them and the two sides fought with all the fury and hatred they felt for each other.

Cleombrotos and Epaminondas both tried to inspire their men by their personal courage. In the first crush of the battle Cleombrotos was wounded and then wounded again and again until he collapsed. At this moment his bodyguard—and the Spartan line, twelve men deep—pushed back the Thebans and Boeotians, fifty men deep. One of his bodyguards, Cleonymos—the son of the man, Sphodrias, who, as much as any Spartan, had brought them to this day—fell three times and died deep in the ranks of the enemy, fighting for his king. He was the first to die. The Spartans by their heroic efforts recovered the body of their king and removed him to the rear where he died. Both sides fought to the point of exhaustion and the battle hung in the balance. Then, at the moment of crisis, the Theban leader Pelopidas called out to his men, "One more push!" and they broke the Spartan phalanx.

In the immediate aftermath of the battle the survivors debated whether to attack again, but their allies were discouraged (and perhaps not so displeased with the result), so the Spartans asked for a truce to recover their dead (an admission that they had been defeated). The Spartans had not lacked courage. Four hundred of the seven hundred Spartiates at this battle were killed and among the 400 were probably the 300 men of the king's bodyguard who died on the field with their king. If the Spartans could have fielded an army, such as they fielded during the Persian Wars, with five thousand citizens and five thousand Laconian neighbors, they would have won the battle of Leuctra, but their refusal to recognize the problem of the diminishing number of citizens, their short-sighted foreign policy, and their failure to adapt to changed circumstances, all contributed to their defeat.

28

Sparta at Bay

It was on the last day of the Festival of the Naked Boys (the Gymnopaedia) and the men's chorus was in the theater when the messenger arrived in Sparta and brought the ephors the news of the defeat. When the ephors heard what had happened, they were shocked, but they let the chorus continue, while they gave the names of the dead to the relatives concerned and ordered the women to avoid any cries of lamentation. On the following day those Spartans whose relatives had been killed went out in public looking bright and happy, while those whose relatives had survived stayed home or, if they went out, looked gloomy and sorry for themselves. Indeed, some Spartans advocated that the survivors of the battle suffer the penalty reserved for "tremblers."

The dead king had two sons, Agesipolis and Cleomenes. Agesipolis became king, probably as a boy with a guardian, and he died in 370 BCE. His younger brother, Cleomenes (II) became king, also as a boy with a guardian, and he lived, and reigned, until almost the end of the fourth century, 309/8 BCE. Neither king was old enough to lead the Spartans in this crisis and the ephors appointed Agesilaos *nomothetes* (law-giver) with absolute power to reform the state, or take any necessary action, in any way he thought fit. On what should be done about the survivors he said,

"The law is the law but today it must sleep."

On the possibility of reform he said,

"The old ways are good enough."

And he acted swiftly and decisively against his opponents. Many Spartans blamed Agesilaos for the policies that had brought them to this crisis. They remembered the oracle about the "lame king," they believed that Sparta, because of him, had angered the gods, they denounced his private hatred of the Thebans that had made peace impossible, and they were prepared to use force to compel him to step aside. Agesilaos had them—some of them were women—seized and executed in secret, he concealed the number of Laconian neighbors who went over to the enemy, and he called to duty all men up to sixty years of age.

Agesilaos's son Archidamos led the Spartans and the allies who would join them to meet the defeated army near Megara. There he dismissed the allies and escorted the survivors back to Sparta where the Spartans were preparing for the unthinkable, the invasion of their territory. The existence of Sparta itself was on the line. There were only a few Spartiates and Sparta did not have walls. There was a very real chance that the helots, Laconian neighbors, and neodamodeis would join the enemy—and many helots and Laconian neighbors did. Agesilaos hired mercenaries, brought in the few allies remaining to them, and freed 6000 helots for military service.

Epaminondas, the Thebans, and their allies from the Peloponnesus entered Laconia, which had not been invaded since the time of the Dorians, and marched past the city on the opposite bank of the Eurotas River. By chance the Eurotas was swollen and Agesilaos was able to prevent the Thebans from crossing. He refused to let his army engage the Thebans (if it lost, Sparta would fall), and the Spartans had to watch helplessly while the Thebans, and all their allies, plundered and burned Laconia from one end to the other. Agesilaos and the Spartans managed to hold the river line and save Sparta, but the Thebans were able to withdraw safely from Laconia with their loot and their prisoners. The Thebans tried to induce the freed helots to sing the old Spartan songs. They refused. They said the masters wouldn't like it.

The battle of Leuctra put an end to the Peloponnesian League (in its place the Arcadians founded their own league) and thus ended Spartan domination of Greece. Some of the cities of the Laconian neighbors began to break away from Sparta. In the next year the Thebans returned to plunder Laconia again, they freed Messenia, and they founded the "Big City," Megalopolis, on the northern border of Laconia to be a watchdog over Sparta and a staging area for future invasions. The Thebans, as they were now the foremost military power in Greece, received the support of the Persian king as his chief guarantor of peace in a new "king's peace," but Epaminondas had made his intentions all too clear: he intended that the Thebans would be the new masters of Greece.

The Athenians were more afraid of the Thebans then they had been of the Spartans, they believed they were the Thebans' next target, and they, and many other Greek cities, refused to sign the peace accord. In 369 Corinth, Athens, and Sparta formed an alliance to defend the Isthmus against the Thebans, while, within the Peloponnesus, the Arcadian League began independent operations against Sparta and the Spartans had to respond. In 368 BCE Archidamos and the Spartan army met the Arcadian army. Before the battle Archidamos addressed his troops:

"Fellow-citizens, we must now show what we can do and so be able to look people in the eye. Let us leave to those who come after us the Sparta which we received from our fathers. Let there now be an end to our feeling ashamed of ourselves before our wives and our children and the older men and the foreigners—we who were once the admiration of the whole of Greece!"

They routed the Arcadians without the loss of a single Spartiate. When news of the victory reached Sparta, the Spartans became hysterical with joy. They called the battle the "tearless victory" and they believed that, as the gods had turned against them at Leuctra (and, as far as they knew, might never support them again), now the gods again looked upon them favorably.

As hated as the Spartans had been, as agents of the loss of Greek freedom, so now the Thebans were becoming equally hated. The Thebans sent governors to oversee Achaea and they got involved in a civil war which resulted in their being expelled. The Theban machinations created a complete mess. Achaea was hostile to Thebes and to the Arcadians. Thebes and the Arcadians were allies. Sparta and Athens were allies. Athens and the Arcadians were allies. Athens, Sparta, and Corinth were allies, but Corinth was not at war with Thebes (except in blocking the Isthmus). Elis and the Arcadians, both enemies of Sparta, were at war with each other and Elis asked Sparta for help.

In 362 BCE some Arcadians seized the temple of Zeus at Olympia and appropriated the money. The Mantineans voted not to take part in this sacrilege. Other states were worried about the implication and they also refused and the mercenaries abandoned the army. The appropriators of the money then asked the Thebans for help, while the majority of Arcadians decided to make peace with Elis. The Thebans arrested the members of the peace party and, subsequently, were forced to release them. Epaminondas decided to march into Arcadia and the Arcadians asked their enemy Sparta for help. So on one side were Thebes, the Messenians, Argos, and some Arcadians; on the other side were Sparta, Athens, Mantinea, some other Arcadians, Elis, and Achaea. Epaminondas tried and failed to take Mantinea, then he tried a surprise attack on Sparta, which was thwarted by the quick action of Agesilaos and a valiant defense led by Archidamos, and, finally, he resolved to fight a battle which would reestablish Theban dominance in the Peloponnesus.

Epaminondas marched his army out and formed them into a line so that he appeared to be ready to fight, but, when his army was drawn up as he wished, instead of advancing immediately, he led his men away, and, when he reached high ground, with his line fully extended, he grounded arms and so appeared ready to camp and not to fight. Thus he lulled the Spartans and their allies into a careless disposition of their forces and he dulled their mental edge. Epaminondas posted a force of cavalry and infantry on some hills opposite the Athenians on the left wing in order to prevent them from coming to the help of the men on their right and then he massed his army around himself in a wedge formation and he ordered them to take up their arms and follow him.

When the Spartans and their allies saw Epaminondas advancing so unexpectedly, they were completely nonplussed—some ran to take up their positions, others formed into line, others bridled their horses, others put on their breastplates, and all thought that they were caught at a disadvantage and would be defeated. All this time Epaminondas was leading his army forward, "prow on, as it were, like the ram of a trireme." He aimed directly at the elite guard of the Spartans, drawn up in a line six deep, because he believed, if he broke through the Spartiates, the rest of the army would break, and he would have defeated the whole army opposed to him.

"When the Boeotians and Spartans joined battle, they struck at each other with their spears, and when the spears broke, they fought with their swords, and they seemed not to care whether they lived or died. Their bodies were tangled together, many were wounded, and many of the wounded were wounded more than once, but they continued to strike, wound, and kill each other. For a long time the battle hung poised until Epaminondas realized that it was up to him; he selected his best men and led them into the middle of the enemy. He cast his javelin, struck the Spartan commander, fought hand to hand, killed some and terrified others, and he broke the phalanx of his enemies. The Spartans gave way, and the Boeotians pursued, killed the slowest, and piled up heaps of corpses."

Then, in the moment of victory, Epaminondas looked behind him to check on his men and a Spartan thrust his spear into Epaminondas's chest, Epaminondas fell, and the Boeotians instantly halted. They carried Epaminondas to the rear and summoned physicians; the physicians told him that when the spear was removed from his chest, he would die.

"Then it is my time to die," he said, and he gave the order to draw out the spear.

The historian Xenophon summed up the situation in Greece at this time.

"Nearly the whole of Greece had been engaged on one side or the other, and everyone imagined that, if a battle was fought, the winner would become the dominant power and the losers would be their subjects. But God so ordered things that both sides put up trophies, as if for victory, and neither side tried to prevent the other from doing so; both sides gave back the dead under a truce as though they had won and both sides received their dead under a truce, as though they had lost. Both sides claimed the victory, but it cannot be said that either side was any better off after the battle than before it.

"In fact, there was even more uncertainty and confusion in Greece after the battle than there had been before."

PART VII
THE MACEDONIAN WARS

Table 7. The Kings of the Macedonian Wars

Eurypontid Royal House

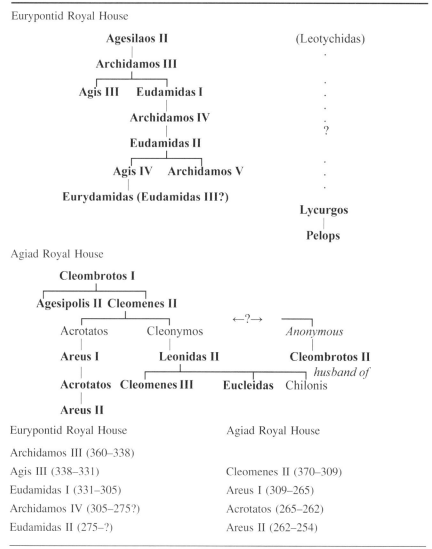

Agiad Royal House

Eurypontid Royal House	Agiad Royal House
Archidamos III (360–338)	
Agis III (338–331)	Cleomenes II (370–309)
Eudamidas I (331–305)	Areus I (309–265)
Archidamos IV (305–275?)	Acrotatos (265–262)
Eudamidas II (275–?)	Areus II (262–254)

(*continued*)

Agis IV (244–241)

"Eudamidas III" (241–228?)

Archidamos V (228–227)

(Eucleidas 227–222)

Lycurgos (219–211?)

Pelops (211–205)

Leonidas II (254–243)

Cleombrotos II (243–241)

Leonidas II (241–235)

Cleomenes III (235–219)

Agesipolis III (219–215)

Kings highlighted in bold.

Illustration 14. Cleomenes III (from a Spartan coin) (Pamela M. Bradford)

— 29 —

The Struggle to Survive

The Spartans survived the battle of Mantinea, but their continued survival was by no means assured. They were shut up in Laconia, blocked to the north by Megalopolis, to the west by the newly independent Messenia, surrounded by hostile powers, and limited by their own allies' independence. In addition, those Spartiates who depended upon their land in Messenia to supply their monthly ration to the mess lost their land and their citizenship. They could have been reassigned new lots in Laconia—Laconia was fertile enough to support 1500 cavalry and 30,000 hoplites—but the land had passed into just a few hands and the Spartiates, rather than reapportioning the land to create new allotments for the disenfranchised citizens and the enrollment of new citizens, decided to fill their ranks by hiring mercenaries. For that they needed money, and, consequently, King Agesilaos, at the age of eighty, went to Egypt as a mercenary general to earn money for Sparta. There, once again, he proved what an extraordinary tactician he was, earned his pay, received a bonus, and was released. He died on the way home (in 360 BCE). His son, Archidamos, became king.

Archidamos was an active and well-known figure in Greece. He was the foremost, and most formidable, spokesman for Spartan policy and plans. In a speech written by Isocrates, Archidamos set forth his views on the Messenian question. He had been advised that the Spartans should accept the situation that Messenia was now free and should, in justice, be free. He said,

"We have the right to hold Messenia. In the many peace treaties we negotiated in the recent past, never did the Persian king or the Athenians suggest that we held Messenia unjustly. The Delphic oracle clearly proclaimed that Messenia was ours as a gift when the sons of Cresphontes asked us to come save them and to receive that land. Apollo, himself, upholds our claim to this land.

"I am told to do what is expedient, but what is more expedient, than to do justice? Is not a man destroyed by injustice, but saved by justice? Do not nations,

in the end, win wars because their cause is just? Did we not establish our system
of law to make us just? We must be strong now and have courage in the future.
There is no other city as experienced in war as we are and our way of life is the
best in Greece."

As the Spartans were struggling to formulate a plan to defend themselves, to recover Messenia, and to regain their former position in the Peloponnesus, far away
in the north beyond Mt. Olympus the Macedonians hailed a new king—Philip.
Philip faced formidable challenges—his brother had been killed in a battle against
the Illyrians, the Macedonian army had been all but annihilated, the Illyrians were
planning to occupy the land of Macedonia, the Thracians and the Athenians
were promoting pretenders to the throne, the Athenians were poised to invade,
and the treasury was empty.

Philip, however, was an extraordinary man—he had lived in Thebes, he had
known Epaminondas, and he had learned what the Theban had to teach him. Philip
reformed the army of the Macedonians into a deep phalanx armed with a long
spear (the *sarissa*, 16–26 feet long). When the first five ranks of the Macedonian
phalanx lowered their sarissas, they formed a five-fold hedge of spear points in
front of the fifty-man-deep phalanx. Philip's phalanx became an immoveable
barrier on the battlefield; coordinated with his shock arm, the heavy cavalry, he
was almost unbeatable.

In the first three years of his reign, Philip thwarted an Athenian invasion,
defeated the Illyrians, defeated the ring of enemies on his northern and eastern
borders, eliminated the rivals to the throne, became the hegemon of Thessaly,
and expanded Macedonian control across the Balkan peninsula to the Adriatic
Sea. He did all this while Greeks concentrated on their own affairs—the Athenians
were fighting a losing war to hold on to the new Delian League, the Spartans were
concerned with the Peloponnesus, and the Thebans were involved in a devastating
war with their western neighbor, Phocis.

Phocis—the object of Theban aggression—was just a tiny district, and no threat
to the Thebans, but the Thebans convinced the Council of Neighbors (the *Amphic-
tyony*), which administered Delphi, that the Phocians had committed sacrilege and
needed to be punished. The Phocians refused to accept the verdict and the Council
declared a Sacred War—"sacred," because it involved Delphi and sacrilege. The
Phocians seemed to have no chance whatsoever against the Theban army, and the
Thebans thought that they would win an easy victory, but the Phocians asked
Archidamos for help. Rumor had it that the Phocians bribed his wife to convince
the king to help the Phocians, but, given the threat the Thebans posed for the
Spartans—to lead their Peloponnesian allies in another invasion of Laconia—
he needed little persuading.

Archidamos gave them fifteen talents. With that money they were able to hire
mercenaries and hold off the Thebans. When that money ran out, the Phocians
took the next step, seized Delphi, and used Delphi's treasuries to fund their war
and hire more mercenaries. They fought the Thebans to a draw. The result
worked to the Spartans' advantage: the Sacred War dragged on for almost ten

years, it completely occupied the attentions of the Thebans, wore down their army, and concluded only when Philip and the Macedonians intervened.

When it became obvious that Philip intended to bring his army into Greece, the Spartans and the Athenians joined together once again to guard the pass at Thermopylae and prevent Philip, the new "barbarian" threat, from entering Greece. They held the pass for one year, but the next year, when the Phocians' mercenaries were on guard, Philip bribed them to let him through. Philip advanced on Athens, but the Athenians convinced the Thebans that Philip threatened them, too, and the Thebans and the Athenians joined together to resist Philip; the Athenians invited the Spartans to join the war against Philip.

Some Spartans believed that they should join the fight and they were debating where would be the best place to fight Philip, when Archidamos told them,

"What we should be considering is, will we be stronger in battle than he is?"

The Spartans refused to join the alliance.

Archidamos, meanwhile, had responded to a request from the Tarentines that he come to Italy to help them in the name of their colonial ties with Sparta against a native Italic tribe, the Lucanians, who were pressing on the territory of the Tarentines. (He may also have seen an opportunity to earn some money for Sparta.) He fought bravely but died in battle near Mandorion in Italy, slain by the Lucanians. His body was not recovered. (Greek historians believed that the battle in which Archidamos was killed coincided with the battle of Chaeronea.) When word reached Sparta of the death of Archidamos, his son, Agis (III), became king.

In 338 BCE at the battle of Chaeronea in Boeotia Philip defeated the combined armies of Athens and Thebes. Philip used his victory to establish a new League of Corinth, the purpose of which was to coordinate all Greek poleis under one command—his—to invade the Persian empire and free the Ionian Greeks. He sent a blunt demand to the Spartans that they cease their actions against his allies in the Peloponnesus and join the League. Philip had made numerous friends—some called them "traitors"—throughout the Greek world, but not in Sparta. Sparta, though isolated, was still the most powerful city in the Peloponnesus and still an object of fear to the Peloponnesians. The Spartans did not conceal their ambition to reconquer Messenia and reestablish the Peloponnesian League. The Spartan attitude towards a free Messenia was provocative: a Messenian insisted to a Spartan ephor that Philip had proclaimed that Messenia would be free. The ephor said,

"And has he also given you the power to win battles?"

Philip wanted Sparta to join his new league, but failing that, to acquiesce and to keep quiet.

The Spartans replied in Laconic fashion to his demands,

"To Philip. Regarding your message, no."

When he asked them whether they wanted him to come as a friend or an enemy, they replied,

"Neither."

The leaders of Messenia, Arcadia, and Argos urged Philip to come into the Peloponnesus and to humble the Spartans and he acquiesced. With his powerful army and numerous allies he could have occupied Sparta, but he feared the repercussions if he destroyed one of the oldest and most famous cities in Greece.

Philip camped near Mantinea before he invaded Laconia. Agis went, as ambassador, to talk with Philip. Philip said,

"What's this? You've come alone?"

He said, "Indeed, one man to one man."

Philip camped in Laconia with his allies, the Messenians, Megalopolitans, Tegeans, Argives, and the Eleans. He sent threats, both numerous and onerous, if the Spartans did not do what he demanded, and all thought they would be destroyed. Nonetheless, they made a number of noble statements. Philip demanded of one of the Spartiates, "What will you do now, Laconians?" The Spartan replied, "What else but die courageously? For we alone of the Greeks are free and we have not learned how to give in to others."

Philip and his allies ravaged the land and burned villages. The Spartans defended the city of Sparta, fought back where they could, and had some minor successes. They defeated a detachment of Macedonians looting the coastal territory of their harbor, Gytheion and they paid thanks to the god Asclepius for (somehow) preserving them.

Philip detached numerous border regions of Laconia and gave them to the Spartans' neighbors, the Argives, the Tegeans and Megalopolitans, and the Messenians. His intention was to weaken and limit the influence and power of the Spartans, and, in general, he did, but he did not convince the Spartans to alter their policy and objectives.

A year later, Philip was dead at the hands of an assassin. His son Alexander became king and within two years had established his authority on all his borders and among his allies. The Greeks mostly waited to see what would develop, but the Thebans rebelled and Alexander razed their city. The Thebans had been the dominant power in Greece for thirty-six years. Some of the Spartan survivors of the battle of Leuctra may still have been alive to hear of this destruction and perhaps find grim satisfaction in the final denouement of Theban hubris.

30

In the Shadow of Great Powers

In 334 BCE Alexander invaded the Persian empire. Some Spartans joined the Persian king (as was their right—they were not allies of Alexander) and King Agis competed with the Macedonians in Crete to win over cities and allies and he attempted to win allies in Greece against a time when he could use the diversion of Macedonian resources to Asia to reestablish the Peloponnesian League and create a new alliance of Greeks which could hold its own against the Macedonians.

In 333 after the battle of Issus, when Alexander defeated Darius and Darius abandoned 8000 Greek mercenaries, Agis organized the rescue of the Greeks and enrolled them for a war with Antipater, regent of Macedonia. Agis could not afford to pay a large force of mercenaries for any length of time and he gambled everything on one decisive battle. The regent of the Macedonian kingdom, Antipater, led the Macedonia army down into the Peloponnesus, collected his allies, and confronted Agis at the city of Megalopolis in 331 BCE.

King Agis III and his Spartans were fighting for the leadership of the Peloponnesus, the mercenaries were fighting for revenge against their hated enemies, the Macedonians, and, also, of course, for their pay. The Macedonians were fighting for their distant king and their reputation. Agis, even with the addition of the mercenaries to his army, was outnumbered, so he tried to compensate for his inferior numbers by choosing a constricted battlefield, where the Macedonians could not employ their full strength. Consequently, many soldiers on each side were forced to watch rather than fight, and could only cheer on their own side.

Both sides fought ferociously: the Macedonians with their deep formation and massed sarissas tried to push the Spartan phalanx from the narrow space, while the Spartans and the mercenaries struggled to hold their ground. King Agis, surrounded by his guard, fought in the front of the phalanx. In the intense fighting, he was badly wounded and had to be carried out of the line by his bodyguard. They removed his breastplate to assess his wound and they remained with him, as they were sworn to do. The Spartan army, however, without its king to inspire them, and under the relentless pressure of the Macedonian phalanx, grew tired— the Spartans could scarcely hold their spears, now slick with sweat—and they were pressed back, foot by foot. When the king's bodyguards saw the phalanx giving way, they decided to carry him away from the battlefield.

The king, however, ordered his guard to put him down, to leave him, and to save themselves for the future of Sparta. They did what he commanded (and later were accused of cowardice). Agis, now by himself, attempted to stand, but he was too weak, so he supported himself on his knees, put on his helmet, held out his shield with all his remaining strength, and challenged the enemy, "Come rob this fallen man of his arms."

No one dared come to close quarters to fight. They threw spears from a distance and he threw them back, until a javelin got past his shield and pierced his bare chest. Weakened by this wound he leaned forward and rested his head for a little while on his shield and then, finally, as his life drained out with his blood, he died and fell amid his armor and weapons.

In the battle 5300 men in the Spartan army were killed; in the Macedonian army not more than 1000 men were killed, but many more returned to camp wounded. This battle was a catastrophe not only for Sparta and its immediate allies, but it also dashed the hopes of all the Greeks who anticipated that the Spartans might defeat the Macedonians and free Greece.

Antipater let the council of the League of Corinth decide what should be done with Sparta. The council directed the Spartans to send envoys to Alexander, and he, in his turn, directed the Spartans to join the League of Corinth, but he did not punish them otherwise. Nonetheless, the shock of the defeat deeply demoralized the Spartans. While Eudamidas, the younger brother of Agis, was king, the Spartans discontinued many of their Lycurgan customs, including the common messes and the common life of the barracks.

Both kings, Eudamidas and Cleomenes, recognized that the Spartans needed peace above all else—Cleomenes had not shared the ambitions of Agis—and the two kings worked together to promote and maintain peace. Eudamidas reigned for over thirty years, down into the beginning of the third century. Cleomenes II reigned for over sixty years, down to 309 BCE. While they were kings, the Spartans enjoyed a generation of peace, but, in the third century, their successors adopted a more aggressive foreign policy.

Cleomenes II had two sons, the elder Acrotatos, the younger Cleonymos. Acrotatos proposed, after the battle of Megalopolis in which Agis had died, that the survivors be deprived of their citizenship, because they deserted their king. It was not a popular proposal and the survivors ganged together and beat him up. Some time later in about 314 BCE a delegation came from Acragas in Sicily, looking for a general to command their forces against the new tyrant of Syracuse, Agathocles.

Acrotatos left Sparta without the permission of the ephors, and on his way to Acragas had several successes—he freed a Greek city on the Adriatic from an

Illyrian siege and he convinced the Tarentines to send twenty ships to help him in Sicily. When he arrived in Acragas, he was appointed general. He was supposed to expel Agathocles from Syracuse, but, instead, he adopted a luxurious lifestyle, acted just as he pleased, made a number of enemies with his abrasive character, and murdered a rival (who appeared to be no better than Acrotatos). The people, who had invited him, stripped him of his command and sent him back to Sparta. (He barely escaped a stoning.)

Acrotatos died before his father, Cleomenes II, and so, when Cleomenes died, the younger son, Cleonymos expected that he would be chosen king, but he was passed over in favor of his brother's young son Areus. Cleonymos was appointed regent and given command of the armies. Cleonymos, apparently, was a general of considerable ability. He aided Tarentum against the Lucanians in 309/8 BCE, he annexed Metapontum, and he seized Corcyra, (ca. 303 BCE). He may have been extending Spartan power, trying to stabilize the region in the interests of Tarentum, or simply working for himself—we just do not have enough information to judge.

While Cleonymos was busy elsewhere, Archidamos IV, the son of Eudamidas, commanded the army in Sparta. Sparta attracted the attention of one of the Successors of Alexander the Great, Demetrius "the Besieger." Whether the Spartans had become involved in the struggle between the Successors or Demetrius just wanted to add the illustrious city of Sparta to his collection of illustrious cities (including Athens), is just not known, but Demetrius invaded the Peloponnesus and Archidamos fought a battle with him near Mantinea in 294 BCE. Archidamos was defeated (and does not appear in our sources again). Demetrius invaded Laconia, fought a battle with the Spartans near Sparta, defeated them, killed two hundred Spartans, and appeared poised to capture the city, when he received word of turmoil in Macedonia and a chance to become king there. He immediately withdrew his army from Sparta.

Archidamos died—we do not know in what year—his son, Eudamidas, became king. (We do not know much about him.) Eudamidas was the father of Agis IV (who was born about 265 BCE).

In retaliation for Demetrius's invasion of Laconia, Cleonymos aided Boeotia against Demetrius, (ca. 293 BCE), but was outmatched by Demetrius (and gave him reason to return to the Peloponnesus and invade Laconia, but again other opportunities drew him away). Cleonymos and the Spartans were active after that in the Peloponnesus. He seized Troezen, (ca. 279 BCE); he was engaged in operations against Messene and he mediated a truce in Crete between two warring cities, but his ward, Areus (I), had long before come of age and was asserting his rights, and, moreover, Areus's son, rumor had it, was having an affair with Cleonymos's young wife, Chilonis. Cleonymos in his old age, between seventy and eighty, married Chilonis, a beautiful woman of royal blood, the daughter of Leotychidas, but she fell in love with Acrotatos, the son of Areus, a young man in the prime of youth, and this was a grief to Cleonymos (who loved her) although and technically within the customs of Sparta; as these affairs always do, it made the elderly husband look like a fool.

Cleonymos, because of his inclination to force and his monarchical character, had lost the good will and trust of the Spartans. He left Sparta and in 272 BCE joined Pyrrhus, the king of Epirus. (His son Leonidas had already left Sparta and joined Seleucus to help him create an empire.) Cleonymos in his own head at least, should have been king, and he could have imagined that by bringing Pyrrhus down on Sparta, he was righting both a public and a private wrong.

Pyrrhus had twenty-five thousand foot, two thousand horse, and twenty-four elephants. The size of his force made it immediately clear that he had not come just to restore Cleonymos to Sparta, but to conquer the whole of the Peloponnesus, starting with Sparta. The Spartans sent an embassy to him at Megalopolis. He said that he intended to free the cities taken by the Macedonian king, Antigonus, and, "by Zeus," to send his younger sons to Sparta, if nothing prevented it, to be trained in Laconian habits.

After he had said this, and reassured the Spartans, he invaded and plundered Laconia. His invasion took the Spartans by surprise. As he was advancing into Laconia, he met some Spartiates, who complained about his sneak attack, and he said,

"But you Spartiates, we know, did not announce to others what you were going to do."

One of those present replied,

"If you are a god, no harm will come to us, for we have done nothing wrong, but if you are a man, there will be something stronger than you."

King Areus was in Crete with the army at this time. A messenger had been sent to him, to recall him, and Cleonymos urged Pyrrhus to attack the city of Sparta immediately when they arrived in the evening, but Pyrrhus had Gallic mercenaries and he feared that if they broke in under the cover of darkness they would loot and ravage the city, so he decided, since he knew there were few soldiers in Sparta and the city was poorly fortified and defended, to wait for the morning.

During the evening the Spartan men decided to send the women away to Crete, but Archidamia, the foremost of the women and their spokesperson came into the gerousia with a sword and asked them if they thought that the women would want to live if Sparta were lost? No, they would stay. Chilonis, the wife of Cleonymos, said that she would not be taken alive. All night the women, the older men, and, of course, the helots labored to dig a trench opposite the camp of the enemy, the direction from which they expected the attack. They dug a trench 800 feet long by nine feet wide and six feet deep with wagons dug into the earth on each side to hinder the elephants. Before dawn they woke the younger men and gave them their weapons and called upon them to fight to the death for their fatherland—it would be a noble death, indeed, to die in the arms of their wives and mothers.

Pyrrhus took command of his hoplites and charged the trench and barricade, but he could not break through the line of shields and his men lost their footing in the soft earth of the newly dug trench. His son led two thousand Gauls around the flank and attacked the line of wagons. The Gauls had pulled some out of the earth, when Acrotatos with three hundred Spartans—he had slipped around behind the enemy—attacked the Gauls from their rear and the Gauls had to fight front and back from within the trench and were slaughtered. The struggle was visible to all and the Spartans cheered Acrotatos, as he returned, covered in blood, and the men yelled to him to go visit Chilonis right then and beget brave sons for Sparta. The Spartans in the shield wall also fought bravely and, for some, to the death.

During that day Pyrrhus was unable to break into Sparta. That night he had an omen-filled dream and the next morning he dismissed the omens and declared to his men (in a parody of the *Iliad*) that . . .

The best omens are clearest
To fight on for Pyrrhus.

He advanced at dawn and his men tried to fill up the trench with rocks and dirt thrown on top of the corpses and the abandoned and broken weapons lying in the trench. The Spartan women brought the men weapons to replace those that had been broken and they brought them food and drink. Pyrrhus, however, on horseback, forced his way through the barrier and the women fled, thinking the city was falling, but Pyrrhus's horse was struck in the belly with a javelin; it reared up and threw Pyrrhus. His men stopped their attack and rushed to help the king. The Spartans formed up, charged, and drove the attackers back. Pyrrhus was unhurt, but he ordered the assault to stop to give the Spartans, many of whom had been killed and many more wounded, a chance to surrender.

At this moment of crisis, however, mercenaries sent by the king of Macedonia, Antigonus (who was at Corinth), arrived at Sparta, were admitted to the city and took up defensive positions. Not much later King Areus returned from Crete with 2000 soldiers and they replaced the old men (the men past the age of service) in the defensive line. The women went back to their houses. Pyrrhus, nonetheless, decided to remain camped in Laconia and to continue to try to take Sparta. He changed his plans when he heard that a civil war had broken out in Argos and that he might take Argos if he moved quickly. On his retreat out of Laconia King Areus occupied the passes and attacked Pyrrhus's rearguard. Pyrrhus's son was killed.

Pyrrhus succeeded in entering Argos, but, once inside, his troops were attacked by the Macedonians of King Antigonus and by the troops of King Areus (1000 Cretans and some light-armed Spartans). He was struck in the head by a roof tile and killed by a Gaul.

For a brief time the Spartans and the Macedonians joined together as allies to fight Pyrrhus, but after their victory, Areus resumed his attempts to drive the Macedonians out of the Peloponnesus and to unite Peloponnesians under Spartan leadership. King Areus fell in a battle near Corinth, and his son Acrotatos became king. Acrotatos and the Spartans continued their efforts to put together an alliance of the Peloponnesians and Acrotatos died in a battle near Megalopolis against the tyrant Aristodemus.

Acrotatos left behind a pregnant wife. She gave birth to a boy and Leonidas, the son of Cleonymos, who had returned to Sparta when the situation there seemed to offer him an opportunity, became regent, and, when the boy died, though Leonidas was not entirely pleasing to his fellow citizens, he became king.

While in the east the successor kingdoms fought each other for parcels of land, and in Greece the successor kingdoms contended for possessions and allies, in the west the Romans and the Carthaginians were locked in a struggle which would determine the fate of the whole of the Mediterranean world. A Spartan mercenary general led the Carthaginians to a critical victory over a Roman consul and his army. (This Spartan—Xanthippos—was the only Greek ever to defeat a Roman consular army.)

31

The Gentle Reformer

Over a hundred years had passed since the Spartan defeat at Leuctra and in that time the kings had led a small Spartiate army augmented by a larger force of mercenaries in futile attempts to form a new Peloponnesian alliance and eject the Macedonians.

Agis became king while still a boy and his mother's brother, Agesilaos, became regent. Although his mother, Agesistrata, and his grandmother, Archidamia, were the wealthiest persons in Sparta and Agis had access to every luxury possible, he preferred to follow the old, Lycurgan way of life with its simple clothes and simple habits.

Agis came to realize that the Spartan kingship meant little, that not more than seven hundred Spartiates remained and of these perhaps a hundred possessed land and lot, and that the ephors and the wealthy ran Sparta. His Sparta, like so many poleis in Greece, had become two cities: a city of the rich and a city of the poor, and the poor hated the rich.

Agis wanted to return to the "ancestral constitution" with its daily regimen of exercise and simple communal meals in the evening. He appealed to the young men to emulate his own life style and to "practice to be free." His idealism and zeal unsettled the older, wealthy men, who "feared Lycurgos."

He recruited three advisers, his uncle Agesilaos, Lysander, and Mandrocleidas, and they encouraged him. Lysander had a great reputation among the citizen body; Mandrocleidas was known as the cleverest planner in Greece; Agesilaos was a powerful speaker, but, otherwise, he was soft and avaricious and not enthusiastic about real change, but his son encouraged him. With this group eager to change things, Agis persuaded his mother—with her friends and connections and her money she had real power in the city—and his grandmother to support his attempts to restore the honor of the Spartan kings.

Other women, however—they owned a large percentage of the land—and wealthy men appealed to the other king, Leonidas, to save them from this idealistic young king. Leonidas surreptitiously undercut Agis; he would fall into casual conversation with the ephors about Agis's intentions: to confiscate the property of the wealthy and divide it up among the poor, to create spear bearers for himself, not citizens for the state, and, in short, to become tyrant.

With the support of Agis, Lysander was chosen ephor and introduced a rhetra to the gerousians, of which the main parts were, first, to cancel debts, and, second, to divide Lacedaemon into 4,500 lots, to be divided among the same number of Spartiates, whose ranks would be filled by Laconian neighbors and foreigners, whoever had the "desire for freedom" and was fit and young—and they were to be arranged into fifteen syssitia of four hundred and two hundred and they were to observe the way of life their ancestors had observed. The land outside Lacedaemon would be divided into 15,000 lots and distributed among the Laconian neighbors capable of bearing arms.

The rhetra was published and the gerousians could not come to a consensus, so Lysander summoned the assembly and he himself spoke to the citizens, and so did Mandrocleidas and Agesilaos, that they should not let the machinations of a few men turn their eyes from the good of Sparta, and they repeated an earlier prophecy that love of possessions would be the ruin of Sparta. Agis came and spoke briefly and then he said that he himself, first, would contribute his wealth to the state, land and property, good for farming and grazing, and 600 talents in coin, and then his mother and grandmother did the same, and their friends and relatives, being the wealthiest of the Spartiates. The people were captivated by the young man's generous spirit and his charm and they believed that, after more than a hundred years, Sparta finally had a king worthy of itself.

Leonidas led the debate for the opposition, for he reckoned that if he were compelled to contribute his property, he would not receive any gratitude from the citizens—honor would only go to the first to do it—and so he asked Agis,

"Do you think that Lycurgos was a just and honorable man?"

When Agis agreed that he had been, he asked,

"Where had Lycurgos granted cancellation of debts or invited foreigners into the citizen body—Lycurgos, the man who didn't consider the city to be healthy until he had driven out all foreigners?"

Agis replied that he was not surprised if Leonidas, who had been raised in a foreign land and had had children from a marriage in a satrap's family, did not understand Lycurgos; Lycurgos had cleansed the city of debt, interest, and coinage, too, and he had been opposed to those foreigners in the city whose way of life and daily habits were alien. He drove them out, not because he was opposed to them personally, but because he feared their way of life, that their daily habits might accustom the citizens to softness and luxury and might instill in them a love of gain.

"You," he said, "praise the ephors who chopped out the two extra strings some foreign musicians added to their lyre, but us you blame, we who would remove luxury and lack of direction and fakery from Sparta. Those ephors were not concerned about the technical aspects of musical instruments, but that the arrhythmic and false might make the city herself inharmonious and discordant."

After this debate the majority followed Agis, but the wealthy called on Leonidas not to desert them, and they used strong measures and pleas to persuade the gerousians (who had the power to set the agenda for the popular assembly), so that by a majority of one the rhetra was voted down.

Lysander, who was still ephor, began proceedings to prosecute Leonidas according to an ancient law which prescribed the death penalty for any Heraclid who had children by a foreign woman or settled among foreigners. Lysander and his fellow ephors watched the heavens for a sign that the king was guilty. (In every ninth year the ephors choose a clear and moonless night and sit in silence watching the heavens. If a shooting star passes from one region of the sky to another, they judge the kings have committed a violation against the divine and they suspend their rule until an oracular response comes from Delphi or Olympia clearing the suspected kings.) Lysander said that he saw this sign and he set forth a judgment on Leonidas, and he provided witnesses, that from an Asian woman, whom he had cohabited with, getting her from one of the subordinates of Seleucus, he had had two children, and then he had abandoned her and had come back to Sparta.

Lysander persuaded Cleombrotos to assume the kingship—he was the son-in-law of Leonidas and a Heraclid. Leonidas sought sanctuary and, later, with his daughter, went into exile. Agesilaos wanted him killed, but Agis sent an escort to protect Leonidas on his way to Tegea. The year ended, Lysander left office, and the new ephors began proceedings against him. Lysander and Mandrocleidas convinced the two kings that the ephors drew their power only from the disagreements of the kings, and, when both kings were in agreement, their power was uncontestable, and it was illegal to resist them.

So the kings together forced the ephors from their chairs of state and they appointed others in their place, one of whom was Agesilaos. The kings had plenty of supporters and many of them were armed. The wealthy feared for their lives, but Agis reassured them and controlled his followers. Agesilaos, however, never intended to let the reforms go through in their entirety. He owned a good quantity of fine land, but he was heavily in debt and he did not want to sell any of his land, so he persuaded Agis that they should proceed in stages, first to cancel debt and then to redistribute the land. Agesilaos convinced Agis and Lysander and their followers and so they gathered up all the tablets of indebtedness and heaped them in one pile in the agora and burned them.

As the flames shot up, the wealthy and the money-lenders went away, visibly unhappy, but Agesilaos exulted over them and said that he had never seen a brighter light or a purer flame. The majority expected that the land would be divided up right away and the kings gave the orders that this be done. Agesilaos, however, as ephor, always had an excuse to put off the division, until the Spartans' allies, the Achaeans, asked for their help against an expected invasion of the Peloponnesus through the Isthmus, and he could send Agis and his army of supporters away from Sparta on a campaign.

Agis was moved by the love of glory and enthusiasm of those campaigning with him. Most of them were young men and poor; having already had their debts cancelled, now they were looking forward to a division of the farmland when they returned from the campaign, and they showed themselves off splendidly to Agis. They were a sight to behold, as they marched through the Peloponnesus without plundering and practically without any commotion, so that Greeks marveled at them, discussed how the Spartan army was as disciplined as that of Agesilaos or Lysander or even the ancient army led by Leonidas, how the army revered that young man, their king, the youngest man in the whole army, and how he outshone them all in his frugality and willingness to work and in his pride in his arms and armor. He was a worthy sight and many came to see him, although the wealthy were not pleased because they feared he would set an example for the poor in their own cities.

Agis joined Aratus, the leader of the Achaeans, near Corinth, where Aratus was debating whether to fight. Agis said that he thought they should fight and not give up the gates to the Peloponnesus and allow the enemy to enter inside, which Aratus seemed about to do. Agis considered himself free to speak his mind, even though Aratus was older and the general of the Achaeans, because the Spartans were not part of his army, nor under his command, but they had come to campaign with him and to give assistance. When Aratus decided not to fight and dismissed his allies with praise, Agis was amazed, but already the situation in Sparta was demanding his return.

When Agesilaos became ephor, he revealed his true nature. He proved to be greedy and unscrupulous, he stated that he would insert a thirteenth month in the year (to allow himself to remain in office), and he assembled a bodyguard who accompanied him wherever he went. He openly showed contempt for Cleombrotos and only less for Agis, because Agis was his nephew, and he announced that he would remain ephor for another year.

The moment of crisis had come. Agis needed to use the army to dislodge his uncle and force through the reforms, but he would have had to fight Agesilaos and shed the blood of fellow Spartiates, even, perhaps, the blood of his own uncle. He drew back from that step, failed his supporters, and gave his enemies their opportunity. They brought Leonidas back and Agis was able to do nothing, because his followers were angry that he had cheated them and had not redistributed the land.

Agesilaos would have been killed, if his son had not interceded. He went into exile. Agis took refuge in the temple of Athena of the Brazen House, Cleombrotos in the temple of Poseidon. Leonidas let Agis be, but he took troops and went after Cleombrotos. He castigated him, that he, a son-in-law, plotted against his own father-in-law, took away the kingship, and cast him out of his fatherland. Cleombrotos had nothing to say, but he sat there at a loss and remained silent. Chilonis, the daughter of Leonidas, pleaded for her husband's life and Leonidas, after conferring with his friends, ordered Cleombrotos to stand up and to go into exile. (Chilonis went with him, as she had gone into exile with her father.)

With Cleombrotos out of the way, Leonidas expelled the former ephors from their office and appointed others, and then he tried to persuade Agis to come out of sanctuary and be king with him, as the citizens agreed with the view that he had been fooled by Agesilaos, because he was young and loved glory, but he refused and remained in his asylum. Leonidas had him watched and Agis continued to live in the sanctuary, supported by his friends—one of whom was an ephor—and accompanied by them, to protect him, when he went to bathe.

His supposed friend, the ephor, however, saw a chance to plunder the estate of Agis, his mother, and his grandmother. He caught Agis off guard one night and with his henchmen dragged him before the other ephors to stand trial. The ephors voted that he be executed and they commanded their subordinates to take him into the adjoining chamber where they executed condemned criminals, but their subordinates refused to lay their hands on Agis, and neither would the mercenaries who were present, so the ephors, themselves, dragged Agis to his execution.

Already many Spartans had learned of the arrest and they were gathering at the doors with torches and Agis's mother had come and his grandmother, and they were shouting and demanding that the judgment of a king of the Spartiates belonged to the citizens. The ephors were afraid of what might happen, as more citizens arrived, and they rushed the trial and execution.

One of the bystanders inside was crying and Agis said to him,

"Don't cry for me, for I, whom they intend to murder, are better than they."

The ephors also ordered that the grandmother and then the mother be hanged. Agis's mother, before she was hanged, kissed the face of her dead son and said,

"My son, your piety and your gentleness and your generosity have destroyed you and us with you."

When the tragedy was announced through the city and the three bodies displayed, the fear was not so great that the citizens concealed their grief at what had been done. They hated Leonidas and the ephors, and they thought that nothing more dreadful or unholy had been done in Sparta since the time the Dorians settled in the Peloponnesus.

Leonidas, however, had his mercenaries to protect him and he remained king.

— 32 —

The Revolutionary

Agis was survived by a brother, who immediately fled to Messene, and also by an infant son and by his wife, Agiatis. Agiatis was a wealthy woman, and as—potentially—the mother of a king, an infant under her control, with access to an immense inheritance of royal, as well as personal, property, she was a powerful figure and a real threat to Leonidas, so he forced her to marry his underage son, Cleomenes. In the end this forced marriage served her very well—she and her son were safe and she could influence Cleomenes, eventually, to complete the plans of Agis and punish his murderers. In addition, the infant—his name may have been Eudamidas—probably became king with no regent and no power. His appointment would have maintained the form of the dual kingship without diminishing Leonidas's power, given something to the adherents of Agis, and eliminated any rival claims to the kingship.

No one could doubt the lessons of the reign of Agis IV: the wealthy would not voluntarily divide up their land for the benefit of the landless and they were prepared to use force to prevent any reform which would cost them any part of their property. The ephors were instruments of the status quo and they were all too conscious of the dangers presented by an ambitious king. When Leonidas died in 235 BCE, Cleomenes became king, and, although the ephors tried to limit his power, the king was still the commander of the army, and the ephors found themselves caught up in events in the Peloponnesus beyond their control.

Aratus, the brilliant, if flawed, leader of the Achaean League, wanted to unite the whole of the Peloponnesus into one league, his Achaean League. He had driven the Macedonians out of the Peloponnesus, he had convinced some tyrants to lay down their tyrannies and join the league, and he was prepared to use force against those who resisted: the Spartans, the Eleans, and as many Arcadians as were allies of the Spartans. When he learned of the death of Leonidas, Aratus set out to harass the independent Arcadians, the Tegeans and Orchomenians, and to gauge how weak the Spartans might be, with their new, young, and inexperienced king.

The majority of Spartans—the disenfranchised—did not have the will to fight, the wealthy were not prepared to pay for a mercenary army, and the kings were powerless, but the ephors could not ignore the threat. They dispatched Cleomenes with the limited objective of securing the northern pass into Arcadia. Cleomenes seized the pass and fortified it, before Aratus could, and Aratus turned away, as though he accepted the situation, but he marched that night to Tegea where some traitors had offered to open a gate for him. When he arrived, however, he found the gate closed, and he marched away. Cleomenes wrote to him and asked him, like one friend to another, why he had gone out for an evening stroll. Aratus replied that his only purpose had been to prevent Cleomenes from fortifying the pass. Cleomenes replied that, personally, he believed him, "but, tell me, don't those lamps and ladders of yours tell a different story?"

Aratus laughed when he read the letter, but a Spartan exile told him, "You'd better do something about this fighting cock before he grows his spurs."

The ephors recalled Cleomenes, because he had completed the mission they had assigned him, but Aratus decided to test the Spartans again by advancing on Laconia with a large army, and the ephors again had to send the king out. Cleomenes was eager to fight, even though he was outnumbered four to one, but Aratus did not want to provoke a battle, he had only wanted to test the Spartans' defenses, and he withdrew. Cleomenes, however, was determined to fight and he followed the Achaean army into Elis, forced them into a battle, and routed them. Cleomenes had won a signal and startling victory, and, to cap it all off, he was informed that Aratus had been killed in the fighting. Unfortunately for Cleomenes, the report was wrong and Aratus used the confusion to make a surprise attack and capture the city of Mantinea. The ephors were discouraged and they ordered Cleomenes to return to Sparta.

By this time the young son of Agis had died and the Eurypontid kingship was vacant. Cleomenes invited Agis's brother, Archidamos, to return to Sparta to be king with him; he thought that two kings together might persuade the ephors to act. Archidamos agreed, but, on his way back to Sparta, he was waylaid and murdered. Some Spartans blamed Cleomenes, but most believed that Archidamos had been murdered by Agis's murderers, because they feared retribution. In any case, Cleomenes now decided that his only recourse was to answer violence with violence and to force through the reforms of Agis. He turned to his mother, Cratesicleia, for help and she, to further her son's ambitions, married the most influential Spartan of that time (a man named Megistonous).

As Sparta was still under pressure from the Achaeans, and Cleomenes had conducted himself so that he did not seem to be a threat to the established order in Sparta, he was able to persuade the ephors to give him money to hire mercenaries for a campaign. Cleomenes seized a village belonging to the Megalopolitans and the Achaeans reacted quickly, Aratus moved to defend Megalopolis, fought a battle with the Spartans, and drove back part of Cleomenes' army, but Aratus ordered the pursuit to halt. A Megalopolitan general ignored the order and led his cavalry in a wild charge which became entangled in fields of vines, ditches, and fences. Cleomenes counterattacked with his light-armed soldiers, defeated the cavalry, and killed the general. He then led the rest of the Spartan army, which had regained its confidence, in an attack and routed the Achaean army.

Cleomenes was elated by his victory and he was convinced, if only he could build a legitimate Spartan army, he could lead Sparta once again to the domination of the Peloponnesus. He was determined to carry out the necessary reforms. Moreover, as he was laying his plans, he was given a sign that he had divine sanction—an ephor told him that he had had a dream in which the ephors' chairs had been removed and a divine voice told him that this was best for Sparta. Cleomenes accepted the dream as an omen and, when he had command of the whole Spartan army, citizens and mercenaries both, he seized the opportunity. He marched it up and down and back and forth, until the citizens were worn out and ready to remain in camp while he made another foray. He took his mercenaries and some trusted accomplices and made a forced march towards Sparta with the intention of falling upon the ephors at dinner.

When he was near the city, he sent his brother to the mess hall of the ephors, as though he had come from the army with a message for them; four of Cleomenes' closest companions accompanied him, and a few soldiers. While his brother held the ephors' attention, the companions rushed in and struck them down with their swords. The first ephor, Agylaios, fell and feigned dead, and then crawled from the room into the little temple of Fear, which, by sheer chance, happened to be unlocked, and he locked the door. The conspirators killed the other four ephors and ten other men who came to their aid. They did not harm anyone else, nor did they prevent anyone from leaving the city, and they even spared Agylaios when he came out of the temple the next day.

When day came, Cleomenes proscribed eighty of the wealthiest citizens and he removed the official seats of the ephors, except for one, in which he sat to announce state business. He defended his actions before the assembly—he said that the kings and the gerousians had been made partners by Lycurgos, and, for a long time, had governed the city, needing no other magistracy, but, later, during the long war with the Messenians, the kings, because of their extended absences, appointed some of their friends to be judges and to act for them in Sparta, and they were called *ephors*, but the ephors gradually assumed the power of the kings. He accused the ephors of subverting the Lycurgan constitution which forced him, in turn, to use strong measures to restore the constitution, measures which he regretted, but which had been necessary.

He promised to act with restraint: those who were opposed to "the salvation of Sparta" he would eliminate, but, for the rest, he said, each would have a share in the land, all their debts would be cancelled, and he would scrutinize and judge the outsiders (the Laconian neighbors and the mercenaries) so that the strongest might become Spartiates, save the city with their arms, and then,

"We will stop looking on as Laconia, because of a lack of men to defend her, is made the booty of invaders."

Then he contributed his own wealth, and so did Megistonous, his father-in-law, and each of his other friends, followed by all the other citizens, and the land was divided up among both old and new citizens, including a land lot for each of the exiled citizens with a guarantee that they all could return when affairs had settled down. He appointed his brother Eucleidas as his fellow king (even though they came from the same house) to preserve the form of the dual kingship. He created four thousand citizen hoplites and he trained them to use the sarissa—the Macedonian spear which was about twenty feet long—holding it in both hands and bearing the shield on a strap, instead of a handle. He reinstituted the agoge, the syssitia, and the Lycurgan way of life.

As soon as he believed his reformed army was ready, and before Aratus thought he could act, he invaded the territory of Megalopolis, pillaged and ravaged it, and, while he was in their territory, watched a performance by a group of actors he had captured, to demonstrate to his enemies how at home he was in their territory.

The Mantineans were the first to call upon him; he fell upon the city at night, drove out the garrisons of the Achaeans, restored their laws and constitution, and brought them into his alliance. The next day he marched into the territory of Tegea, made a circuit through Arcadia and into Achaea to the north, where he pursued the Achaean army, as Aratus retreated, until he cornered them and forced them to fight. He turned their phalanx, he killed many in the battle, and he took many prisoners. Then he marched west and drove out the Achaean garrisons on the borders of Elis.

He wore down the Achaeans and made them ready to listen to his terms, which were, in effect, that they would join a new Peloponnesian League, but as he was traveling to speak to the Achaean envoys, on a very hot day, he drank cold water and had a throat spasm, coughed up blood, and lost his voice. He thought that he had reached an agreement with them and he could afford to wait until he had recovered his voice, so he sent back the most distinguished of the prisoners-of-war to the Achaeans, but postponed the meeting and returned to Sparta.

Aratus now refused office and announced that he would retire from public life. At the same time, in secret, he negotiated with the king of Macedonia, Antigonus, to return to the Peloponnesus. Aratus had spent his whole life driving the Macedonians out and now, for personal reasons, he was inviting them back.

The Achaeans came to Argos again to a parley, and Cleomenes came from Tegea, and the Greeks of the Peloponnesus all hoped that they would reach an agreement to end the war, but Aratus had already made his deal with Antigonus and he convinced the Achaean envoys to delay. Cleomenes said that he had been wronged, he marched away quickly, and he sent a herald with a declaration of war to the Achaeans in Achaea, not the Achaeans at Argos, so that he might act before they were prepared.

The renewed war caused an uprising among the Achaeans, and the cities bordered on revolution, because the people hoped for a cancellation of debt and a division of land, and the leading citizens everywhere blamed Aratus, and some were furious that he was bringing the Macedonians into the Peloponnesus. Wherefore Cleomenes, to incite these, invaded Achaea. He took three cities and expelled the Achaean garrisons. The Achaean leadership became afraid that someone might betray even their chief cities, Corinth and Sicyon, and so they brought their cavalry home from Argos and sent other troops back to replace the cavalry, but, before the troops could arrive, Cleomenes appeared unexpectedly at Argos. He threw the city into turmoil—it was filled with a throng of festival participants and spectators. He seized a strong point and overawed the Argives. They agreed to receive a garrison, to give as hostages twenty citizens, and to become allies of the Spartans, with Cleomenes as leader.

Cleomenes was the first Spartan king ever, after centuries of warfare between the two cities, to gain possession of Argos.

── 33 ──

The Betrayal of Greece

More cities came over to Cleomenes and Aratus felt his control slipping. He was in Corinth, and he feared that the Corinthians might arrest him, so he fled to his home town of Sicyon. With him gone, the Corinthians allied themselves with Cleomenes, but their citadel, the Acrocorinthus, was held by Achaean troops loyal to Aratus. Cleomenes sent Megistonous to ask Aratus to give over the Acrocorinthus in exchange for a great deal of money. Aratus replied that he was no longer in control of events, but events were controlling him.

Cleomenes continued, as more and more cities came over to him, to try to win Aratus over or, at least, dissuade him from bringing in the Macedonians, but Aratus was determined to carry out his own plans, he sent his son as hostage, and he persuaded the Achaeans to vote to hand over the Acrocorinthus to Antigonus. Cleomenes ravaged the territory of Sicyon, confiscated Aratus's possessions in Corinth, and then returned to the Isthmus to try to prevent Antigonus and the Macedonians entering the Peloponnesus.

Cleomenes intended to avoid a battle and to guard the approaches and wear down the Macedonians, who had not collected rations for a long campaign. Cleomenes intercepted the Macedonians, when they attempted to slip through at night, and drove them back with some casualties. He was elated with the victory and believed now that he could guard the Isthmus. Antigonus was so discouraged that he entertained the idea of trying to cross into the Peloponnesus by sea, but the idea appeared impractical because of the time it would take to organize the fleet.

Then, in this moment of discouragement, an Argive friend of Aratus came to see him with the news that the Argives were dissatisfied with Cleomenes and were prepared to rebel. The majority of citizens had believed that Cleomenes would carry out his program of cancellation of debt and redistribution of land in Argos, not just in Sparta, and they were angry with him. Aratus took fifteen hundred soldiers from Antigonus, sailed to Epidaurus, and from there advanced on Argos, while inside the city his allies attacked the garrison on the acropolis.

Cleomenes learned of this that night and he was enraged at Megistonous, because he had assured Cleomenes that they did not have to exile anyone and that the Argives would be loyal. He sent Megistonous with two thousand soldiers to hold Argos, but Megistonous was killed in the fighting, and Cleomenes knew that he had to take the army to Argos—because if Argos fell, the enemy could close off his routes past Argos and then plunder Laconia and lay siege to Sparta—but when he marched away, Antigonus entered Corinth and installed a garrison. Before Cleomenes could take Argos, Antigonus brought his army from Corinth into the Argive plain and Cleomenes had to withdraw. Argos went over to Antigonus.

Cleomenes led his force homeward; in the evening at Tegea some individuals arrived from Sparta to deliver more bad news: his wife had died. When he heard the news, he rushed to Sparta. He loved his wife and put her almost before everything, but, nonetheless, on the same day that he went to Sparta and shared the grief with his mother at home and with the children, he issued orders concerning the security of Tegea.

Cleomenes needed money and Ptolemy the king of Egypt had offered to help him, but he had asked Cleomenes to give him his mother and children as hostages. Cleomenes was ashamed to reveal this condition to his mother, and, although he visited her often and wanted to tell her, he could not. She inquired from his friends whether something was bothering him that he wanted to tell her. Finally, when he found the courage to speak, she laughed.

"Is this," she said, "what you were going to talk about so often but were afraid to?"

She went willingly with her grandchildren to Egypt and Ptolemy sent money to support Cleomenes. Cleomenes used the winter season to prepare for the coming summer campaign. He freed those helots who could pay five Attic minas, he collected five hundred talents, he armed two thousand men in hoplite fashion like the Macedonians, and he created a unit which corresponded to the "White Shields" of Antigonus. Once he had completed his preparations, he conceived a great, and totally unexpected, action—to take Megalopolis. Megalopolis was then no smaller or weaker than Sparta, it had Achaean and Macedonian troops, and its own citizens, too, eagerly opposed the Spartans. Cleomenes ordered his forces to take five-days rations and he led them into Megalopolitan territory, as though he were just passing through.

He camped, had dinner (as though he were going to spend the night), and then, straightaway, after it grew dark, marched towards the city. When he was not far away he detached two units of Spartans and ordered them to advance quickly and seize a middle tower, for he had learned that this tower was the least defended part of the walls. He followed at a more leisurely pace with the rest of the army. The Spartan detachment found not just the tower, but a large stretch of the wall, was unguarded. The Spartans seized the tower, demolished a part of the wall, and killed members of the garrison. Cleomenes joined the detachment and got into the town with his forces before the Megalopolitans knew he was there.

As soon as the catastrophe was apparent to the Megalopolitans, some grabbed as much of their money as they could and fled, some rallied with their arms, and resisted and even attacked their enemies, and though they were not strong enough to drive them away, they did give those of their fellow citizens who were fleeing an opportunity to escape, so that not more than a thousand persons were captured, all the others along with their wives and children slipped away and escaped to Messene. Two prominent Megalopolitan leaders, however, who stayed to defend their city, were captured and brought to Cleomenes. As soon as one of them saw Cleomenes, he called out,

"Now it is possible," he said, "O King of the Spartans for your accomplishment to become even more beautiful and brilliant and you to gain greater glory."

Cleomenes suspected what he wanted and said,

"What do you mean? You're not saying that you want me to give the city back, are you?"

And the leader said,

"I do say that very thing and I give you the advice, not to destroy such a city, but to fill it with friends and allies, who will be faithful allies forever to the one who gives them back Megalopolis, their fatherland, and is the savior of such a people."

Cleomenes was silent for a short time.

"It is hard," he said, "to trust in this, but let the urge towards our reputation conquer the risk."

He dispatched the men to Messene and heralds with them, that he would give the Megalopolitans back their city, if they would become his friends and allies and defect from the Achaeans. Thus Cleomenes extended his good will and generosity, but an Achaean leader in Messene would not allow the Megalopolitans to desert the accord with the Achaeans; he accused Cleomenes of not seeking to give back the city, but to catch the citizens too, and he had the Megalopolitan leaders thrown out of Messene.

When the reply was brought back to Cleomenes, although he had kept the city untouched and undamaged, so that no one could secretly take even the least item, then everywhere he plundered and looted and confiscated the treasury, he sent the statues and paintings to Sparta, and he tore down the major and largest part of the city and destroyed it and then returned home, for he feared that Antigonus and the Achaeans would act. In fact, they did nothing.

They happened, at that time, to be holding a council and Aratus climbed the rostrum, placed his cloak before his face, and wept. The councilors were amazed and they kept calling on him to speak, until he announced that Megalopolis had been destroyed by Cleomenes. The meeting of the Achaeans broke up immediately and they all lamented the suddenness and the magnitude of the disaster. Antigonus tried to help, but his forces came from winter quarters so slowly, that he ordered them to remain in place, and he himself came to Argos with only a few soldiers.

Cleomenes decided to take advantage of the situation—the Macedonian army was scattered in their winter quarters and Antigonus was wintering in Argos with his friends—and he invaded the Argolid, as he figured that either Antigonus would be aroused through shame to come out and fight, in which case he could be defeated, or, if he remained inside the walls, Cleomenes would diminish his reputation among the Argives. He devastated the land and carried off everything portable or drivable, and the Argives mobbed the doors of the headquarters, where Antigonus was staying, and they shouted that he should either fight or cede the leadership to someone who would. Antigonus remained inside his headquarters, even when Cleomenes took his army up to the walls and shouted insults at him.

After the winter passed and Antigonus collected his army and advanced on Tegea, from which he might invade Laconia, Cleomenes quickly gathered his forces, bypassed Tegea and Antigonus's army, and appeared at daybreak before the city of the Argives. He plundered their land and destroyed their grain crops, not with sickles and swords, as usual, but by cutting down trees and fashioning wooden broadswords, with which, in the way children play, his troops could go along, knock the ears off the stalks, and destroy the crops.

Antigonus moved back towards Argos and secured the heights and the passes, but Cleomenes showed his lack of concern by sending heralds to ask to receive the key to the Heraeon, so that he might sacrifice to the goddess inside her temple. So he joked, and he did sacrifice by the locked temple, and then he marched his army away. He campaigned through the Peloponnesus, he took towns and expelled their garrisons, and he demonstrated his skill and daring and his ability to his own citizens, and also to his enemies. He, setting out from one city, was able to make war on the Macedonian forces and all the Peloponnesians and not only keep Laconia unharmed, but also ravage his enemies' territory and seize cities of substance, so that he seemed to be an extraordinary leader.

But Cleomenes was running out of money to pay his mercenaries and the necessity of provoking a battle while he still had them in his employ forced the issue. If he could have delayed, events in the north would have compelled Antigonus to withdraw and Cleomenes could have been reconciled with the Achaeans on his own terms. A new Peloponnesian League under the leadership of Spartan kings might have been able to keep the Macedonians out, might have been powerful enough to avoid entanglement in the big power politics of the next century, and could have avoided the incessant and futile bloodshed between the factions in the Peloponnesus. Aratus killed that possibility.

Cleomenes had to fight a force of 30,000 men with a force of 20,000. He used the rolling hills at Sellasia (north of Sparta) as a barrier to protect his flanks and force the Macedonians to fight on a limited front. Both Cleomenes and Antigonus drew the same conclusions—that the key to the battle was the Spartan right flank. Cleomenes put this key position under the command of his brother, Eucleidas, while Antigonus dispatched the Illyrians and Acarnanians in secret to circle around and to outflank him.

Cleomenes examined the Macedonian army from an observation point. He could not see the Illyrians and Acarnanians, and he suspected that Antigonus was using them in such a maneuver. He questioned the commander of his scouts (the krypteia) about the security of the flank, the scout reassured him—erroneously—that all was well, and Cleomenes launched his charge. The force of the charge of the Spartiates with him drove the Macedonian phalanx back almost five hundred yards, but he did not break it, and, at the very moment when he thought he had won the victory, he learned that his brother had been surrounded and overwhelmed, his own force was trapped and doomed, and he had no choice except to fight to the death or to escape immediately before the trap closed.

"Alas my dear brother," he said, "alas, you were a noble man and an example to the sons of the Spartiates and sung of by women."

Cleomenes returned to Sparta, advised the Spartans to receive Antigonus without fighting, gathered a small group of friends, caught a ship at Gytheion (which had already been prepared just in case), and sailed to Egypt.

Of the army he left behind, many of the mercenaries died in the fighting, and, as for the Spartans, who had been 6,000 in number, our sources report that all but 200 perished. (It is likely that the report of the number of Spartan survivors is really a report of the number who, out of 6,000, retained their citizenship after Antigonus's restoration of the old constitution.) Antigonus wasted no time in occupying Sparta. He treated the Spartans kindly and he restored their laws and constitution—that is, he restored the ephors and the dual kingship, disenfranchised the new citizens and returned the land to its former owners—and then he sacrificed to the gods, and on the third day withdrew, for he learned that Macedonia had been invaded and ravaged by Illyrians.

—— 34 ——

The Last Kings of Sparta

Cleomenes traveled to the court of King Ptolemy in Alexandria, but, soon after he arrived, Ptolemy died and Cleomenes became embroiled in the politics of the court. When he learned that Antigonus had died and that the Achaeans were fighting a war with the Aetolians, he wanted to return to Sparta—the Spartans still considered him their king—but the new Egyptian king would not give him permission, or the means, to leave. He tried to break out by force, his attempt failed, and he committed suicide.

Cleomenes had been king of Sparta for sixteen years.

Sparta reclaimed its independence when Antigonus died, but the city was divided between Cleomenes's supporters and his opponents and each faction was ready to resort to violence: Cleomenes's supporters wanted to make an alliance with the Aetolians against the new Macedonian king, Philip V, but the ephors opposed them and convinced a majority in the assembly that the Aetolians were the real enemy. During a religious festival while the ephors were sacrificing inside the temple of Athena of the Brazen House, Cleomenes's supporters surprised them, murdered them, and appointed their own ephors. Shortly after that, they learned that Cleomenes, and his children, had died in Egypt and they chose new kings.

As the successor of Cleomenes in the Agiad line, they turned to the descendants of Cleombrotos (the dead king's sister's husband who was king when Leonidas was deposed). He had two sons, Agesipolis and Cleomenes, but Agesipolis had died and so they chose his young son of the same name, Agesipolis (i.e., Agesipolis III) as king and they appointed his uncle, Cleomenes, as regent.

In the Eurypontid house the succession was not so clear. Agis IV had had a son who died without issue, Agis's brother, Archidamos, had two sons, and Agis's uncle, Agesilaos, also of the Eurypontid royal family, had a son Hippomedon (who had served as a commander of one of the regions of the Ptolemaic empire and who was famous enough that a poet had composed an epic about him). These men, however, were probably not living in Sparta (given that Archidamos had been murdered there, Agesilaos had barely escaped execution and been driven into exile, and Hippomedon was in the service of Ptolemy). Therefore, the ephors chose a man with the promising name of Lycurgos to be the Eurypontid king.

Our ancient source—one hostile to Sparta—claims that Lycurgos "had no ancestor who had enjoyed that name [i.e., *king*]," but he won the kingship by paying the ephors a huge bribe to appoint him. A modern theory is that he was a descendant of that Leotychidas, who lost his claim to the kingship because Spartans were convinced that he was, in reality, not the son of Agis II, but the son of the Athenian exile, Alcibiades. (If so, than Alcibiades's ambition to have his descendants become kings in Sparta came true!) He seems to have been connected somehow with two obscure figures, Machanidas and Nabis.

Cleomenes the regent (in the name of King Agesipolis) and King Lycurgos supported an alliance with the Aetolians against the Macedonians. They were able to attract allies in the Peloponnesus, because the Achaean League and its leader Aratus had been discredited by their alliance with Macedonia. They enrolled Elis and convinced the Messenians to remain neutral. Lycurgos led a successful invasion of Argive territory and, buoyed by this success, forced Agesipolis and his uncle to go into exile. (For whatever reason, the two appear to have alienated their fellow Spartans; despite many changes of fortune and circumstance in Sparta, no one ever seemed to want them back.)

In the year 219 BCE, Lycurgos was laying siege to Megalopolis, the Achaeans were trying to raise a mercenary army (and having trouble because they had defaulted on their debt to the mercenaries in the Cleomenic Wars), and Philip V was preparing to enter the Peloponnesus with an army. Lycurgos pushed the siege of Megalopolis, the Eleans forced three cities to leave the Achaean League, and the Achaean League seemed unable to respond effectively.

In the winter of 218 Philip finally arrived in the Peloponnesus. Lycurgos had returned to Sparta and was at home when a Spartan named Chilon (a Heraclid) tried to seize power.

Poor Sparta was treated to the unedifying spectacle of a "Chilon" trying to murder a "Lycurgos" for his own personal gain. [These men were born in the time of Agis IV. If their names mean anything, the father of Lycurgos supported Agis and advocated a return to a strong dyarchy and the Lycurgan system with its revolutionary slogan, "cancel debts and divide the land," and the father of Chilon opposed Agis and advocated the primacy of the ephors and the people, and compromise by the kings.] Chilon and his fellow conspirators killed the ephors as they were dining together and then broke into the house of Lycurgos to kill him, but Lycurgos escaped, a crowd overpowered the conspirators, and Chilon fled from Sparta.

With Chilon gone, Lycurgos and the Spartans continued their efforts to split the Achaean League and to secure their borders. Lycurgos conducted operations in Messenia, pressed the siege of Megalopolis, and captured the city of Tegea, although he failed to capture its citadel; then Philip V arrived in the Peloponnesus and Lycurgos withdrew from Tegea, abandoned the camp at Megalopolis, and retreated to Sparta. He thought by abandoning all military operations he could satisfy Philip, but Philip collected allies at Tegea, marched past Megalopolis, and invaded Laconia.

Philip caught the Spartans by surprise, bypassed their city, and camped at Amyclae. He ravaged this area and then proceeded slowly through Laconia down to Taenarum, plundering and destroying as he went. From Taenarum he advanced on Gytheion and from Gytheion he continued to devastate Laconia. As Philip plundered southern Laconia, Lycurgos heard that the Messenians had sent a force of 2,000 men to join the Macedonians. Lycurgos took his mercenaries and some citizens and with a quick march caught the Messenians by surprise. After a short engagement, he captured all their baggage and expelled them from Laconia.

As Philip was returning to Amyclae, preparatory to withdrawing from Laconia, Lycurgos made plans to attack him as he marched between Sparta and the Menelaion, where his troops would be drawn out in column. Lycurgos had the Eurotas River dammed so that the stretch of land between Sparta and the Menelaion would be wet and slick and he took up a position on the Menelaion. Philip, however, deduced the plan, attacked Lycurgos, and dislodged him. Nonetheless, Lycurgos and the Spartans drew up a battle line outside the city. Philip intended to march past Sparta, not to attack it, and Lycurgos let him pass and then attacked his rearguard. Philip repulsed the attack, camped to the north on the old battlefield of Sellasia, and then withdrew to Tegea with his plunder.

Philip's invasion did not change Sparta's policy towards the Achaean League, but it did discredit Lycurgos and his policy of an alliance with the Aetolians—the Aetolians had done nothing to help Sparta. Therefore, when, in 218 BCE, an informant told the ephors that Lycurgos intended to become tyrant, they moved against him and Lycurgos fled to Aetolia. In 217, however, the ephors decided that the charge against Lycurgos had been false and they recalled him.

Lycurgos made a plan with the Aetolian commander in Elis for a coordinated invasion of Messenia, but, after Lycurgos entered Messenia and achieved some success, the Aetolian commander turned back without effecting a conjunction with him and Lycurgos returned to Sparta; the Achaean League set about strengthening their defensive line around Laconia.

The Peloponnesus was in turmoil. The Spartans wanted to refound the Peloponnesian League, their army was the equal of the Achaean army, and they considered the Achaeans their principle, and most hated, enemies, but they did not stand a chance against the Macedonians and they knew it. Therefore, they had to find allies who could stand up to the Macedonians or they needed to separate the Macedonians from the Achaeans. They tried the Aetolians, but the Aetolians had their own agenda, were not reliable allies, and, anyway, were having the worst of it in their war with the Macedonians.

The warring parties in the Peloponnesus settled into what appeared to be an unbreakable stalemate, but then Philip signed a treaty with Hannibal and got himself involved in the war between Rome and Carthage (the Second Punic War).

The Romans made an alliance with the Aetolians; and Sparta, as an ally of the Aetolians, became an ally of Rome in its war against Philip. By the time the Spartans signed the treaty in 211 BCE Lycurgos was dead and his son Pelops was king. The name "Pelops" was a statement—made by his father Lycurgos—of the Spartan claim to primacy in the Peloponnesus. Pelops, then, became the "friend and ally" (*socius and amicus*) of Rome. He was still a boy and his first regent, Machanidas, commanded the army in his name. (Machanidas was remembered in Sparta with enough fondness that he had a gymnasium named after him.)

In 208 BCE Machanidas, in his position as ally of the Aetolians and the Romans, conducted operations against the Achaean League and was encamped near Argos, but retreated when he learned that Philip was advancing on him. In the next year, in the absence of Philip, Machanidas determined to fight the Achaeans, who were led by their foremost and most experienced warrior, Philopoemen. The two armies met at Mantinea with Philopoemen's mercenaries drawn up opposite Machanidas on the Spartan right, Machanidas deployed catapults in front of his phalanx with the intention of breaking the enemy phalanx, but Philopoemen immediately launched his cavalry and then his light-armed troops and the skirmish developed into a phalanx battle too quickly for Machanidas to use his catapults.

Machanidas's mercenaries fought fiercely and broke Philopoeman's mercenaries, but then Machanidas lost control of the pursuit, Philopoemen maneuvered his phalanx to split the Spartan army, forced the Spartan phalanx to retreat, and then turned Machanidas's retreat into a rout. Philopoemen spotted Machanidas in the turmoil, engaged him in single combat, killed him, and cut off his head. He then led the Achaean army in an invasion of Laconia.

Spartan affairs once more were in crisis. Spartans could not count on the Aetolians, who were busy with the Macedonians, and they could only hope that the new power on the scene, the Romans, would swing the balance in their favor.

—— PART VIII ——
THE ROMAN WAR

Table 8. The Kings of the Roman War

Eurypontid Royal House

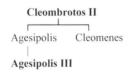

The ancestry of *Laconicus* is unknown, but the name is similar to "Pelops."

Agiad Royal House

              Cleombrotos II
          ┌——————┴——————┐
       Agesipolis   Cleomenes
         │
       Agesipolis III

Eurypontid Royal House	Agiad Royal House
Pelops (211–205)	Agesipolis III (in exile)
Nabis (205–192)	
(Laconicus, 192–?)	

Kings highlighted in bold.

Illustration 15.   Nabis (from a Spartan coin) (Pamela M. Bradford)

35

The Tyrant Who Was a King

After the death of Machanidas in 207 BCE, Pelops was assigned a new regent, a man named Nabis. (Lycurgos, the father, and the regents, Machanidas and Nabis, were likely to be related somehow, but how we do not know.) Nabis was—it seems—a descendant of that King Damaratos who was exiled in the time of the Persian wars. Nabis became regent for Pelops, and, not so much later, Pelops died under suspicious circumstances (some said), and Nabis became king.

Nabis moved quickly to consolidate his position in Sparta and end internal squabbling. He exiled all potential opponents, that is, mainly the men of wealth, and redistributed their property and wives (who, in Sparta, owned property of their own). When Nabis learned that the exiles in the various Achaean towns were working against him, he sent assassins to eliminate them. In Sparta he carried out a social revolution; he claimed, of course, that he was restoring the constitution of Lycurgos and following the example of Cleomenes, but, in fact, he went far beyond them. He enfranchised the helots to enlarge his army and he granted citizenship and property to his mercenaries regardless of their past or their origin. He minted coins with the name "king" in Spartan dialect and with a portrait which shows him with a full beard and no mustache in the most orthodox Spartan fashion.

Nabis continued the struggle with the Achaean League. In 202–201 BCE Nabis was allied with Elis, the Aetolians, and Messenia, and he was engaged in a war with the Achaeans. By the next year he had shaken the Achaeans with his effective and aggressive campaigns. The Achaeans appealed to Philip V, the king of Macedonia, and, at a League meeting in 200 BCE, Philip offered to invade Laconia, if, in return, the Achaeans would reciprocate by giving him what he wanted. They refused. By then Philip was at war with the Romans (the Second Macedonian War) and the Achaeans wanted no part of it,

In 198 BCE the Romans asked the Achaean assembly to renounce their alliance with Philip and become allies of the Romans. The Achaeans did, partly in the hope that the Romans would help them against Nabis, and, thereby, help them become masters of the Peloponnesus, but the Romans had their own agenda. Philip V, betrayed by his former friends, the Achaeans, turned to his enemy, Nabis, and attempted to bribe him to remain neutral by offering him the city of Argos. Nabis agreed: he would occupy Argos and give it back if Philip won the war, but keep it if Philip lost.

Once he had his hands on Argos, however, Nabis confiscated the wealth of the richest men, divided up the land among the poor, cancelled debt, imposed military service, and then asked the Romans for an alliance and treaty. Nabis met with the Roman commander and procured an alliance with two conditions: he would furnish 600 Cretan auxiliaries to the Romans for use against Philip and he would observe a truce of four months with the Achaeans.

Although Nabis had helped the Romans, once they had concluded peace with Philip, they were easily convinced by the Achaeans that Nabis was little better than a pirate. Had he not armed ships, engaged with the Cretans, and made naval raids from Gytheion? And did he not hold Argos in violation of Greek liberty? At the Isthmian games of 196 BCE the Roman commander, Quinctius Flamininus, agreed to act, if the Achaeans could convince the Roman Senate to authorize the campaign.

Achaean envoys traveled to Rome and described Nabis to the Roman Senate as the most evil tyrant who ever lived, a threat to the whole of the Peloponnesus, and, in particular, to the Achaean League. They described his fabulous torture machine, fashioned to look exactly like his wife, Apega, seated in a chair. When an unsuspecting victim offered her a hand to help her rise, she would draw him into her embrace, crushing him, and piercing him with spikes which sprang out of the breasts. The Roman Senate declared war on Nabis.

Quinctius Flamininus moved first on Argos, but, when the uprising he instigated there failed—Nabis really had won the Argives over—he turned south and invaded Laconia. Quinctius had many Spartan exiles with him including Agesipolis, the exiled king of the Agiad house. Nabis, in the face of the Roman invasion, eliminated all potential opponents and prepared to defend Sparta with a force of 1000 Cretans, 3000 mercenaries, and a citizen army of 10,000. Twice he attacked the Romans as they negotiated the narrow way between the Eurotas, the hills, and Sparta, but the Romans fought their way through and camped at Amyclae. From Amyclae they ravaged all the land around Sparta.

Meanwhile, the Roman fleet detached the coastal towns of Laconia and attacked Gytheion. After a fierce fight to which Quinctius had to send reinforcements from his army at Sparta, the Spartan commander of Gytheion surrendered on condition that he be allowed to march out with his troops. He joined Nabis in Sparta. At the same time, the commander of the troops in Argos, Pythagoras, the brother of Nabis's wife and husband of Nabis's daughter, arrived in Sparta with 1000 mercenaries and 2000 Argives. At this point Nabis asked for a conference with the Roman commander.

"Titus Quinctius," Nabis said, "and you others here, I would just await my fate in silence, if I could figure out why you have declared war on me and why you have brought war here, I really want to know, before I die, why I must die. By Heracles! If you were the sort of people the Carthaginians are supposed to be, faithless for-swearers who hold nothing sacred, then I would not be surprised at what you are doing.

"But I see Romans, men who hold not only the divine as most sacred, but alliances and treaties, too. I thought that, as a Spartan, privately and publicly, I was covered by the most ancient treaty, and, in my own name, by friendship and alliance, renewed recently in the war against Philip. Have I violated it or overturned it? Is it because I hold the city of the Argives? Shall I defend myself with the facts or with the timing? The facts offer me a double defense. First, I received the city at the request of the citizens themselves, and I didn't take it by force, and then, too, I received it when it was Philip's and not your ally. As for the timing, that acquits me as well, because I already held Argos when I made the alliance with you. And I sent auxiliaries to help you in the war and you did not then demand that I withdraw from Argos.

"By Heracles! In this disagreement over Argos, the facts are on my side, but the Achaeans paint me with the name and acts of a tyrant, because I freed slaves and gave land to poor people. On the face of it, I could reply that I am the same person I was when you made the treaty with me, Titus Quinctius. Then, I remem-ber, you called me 'king.' Now I see that l am called 'tyrant.' If I had changed my title, I could be accused of inconsistency, but, when you change it, you should explain the reason for it.

"I can defend my freeing a large number of slaves and dividing up the land for the poor again by the timing. I had done this already when you made me an ally and accepted my help in the war against Philip, but, even if I did it now, might I not ask, 'How does this injure you or violate our friendship?' I acted in accor-dance with our ancestral customs and constitution.

"Under your laws and customs you do not want what the Spartans want. You have a few men who are extremely wealthy, you call them a Senate, and you wish the people to be subject to them, but, by our law, we do not want the state to be in the hands of the few, but we believe equality of fortune and status will provide many men to bear arms for the state.

"I confess that I have spoken at length contrary to my county's normal brevity. My conclusion is brief. Since we became allies I have done nothing that deserves your punishment."

Quinctius replied,

"Our treaty of friendship and alliance was not with you, but with Pelops, the rightful king of Sparta. You seized your position by force.

"Do you really think that after we have fought so many wars, just now against Philip, for liberty that we would leave a tyrant in those two ancient and famous cities, Sparta and Argos?"

The Romans, he continued, had freed even the closest allies of Philip and, of course, the Romans favored the property classes: the abolition of debt and the redistribution of land was patently criminal. Moreover, Nabis promoted piracy and was a pirate himself.

The Roman position was not logically consistent, but it was consistent with their policy, beliefs, and prejudices.

Nabis agreed to withdraw from Argos and return all prisoners and deserters. He asked that the other demands be put in writing so he could consult about them with his advisers. Quinctius wanted to negotiate a peace treaty, but his Greek allies wanted him to expel the tyrant. Quinctius, after the Achaeans told him how much the Spartans hated Nabis, had expected his mere arrival would cause the Spartans to rise up, but he had to consider how difficult Sparta would be to take and how long a siege would last, now that the Romans were being threatened by Antiochus (the king of the Seleucid empire). When Quinctius saw that his allies were not convinced, he agreed to a siege, but he explained to them that it would last the whole winter, that it would be expensive—all supplies would have to be imported—and, finally, that they would have to pay for everything. Once they realized that they would be stuck with the bill, they changed their minds.

Nabis was willing to accept the dozen conditions placed on him for peace—he knew he could not defeat the Romans—although three of the conditions particularly galled him: he would have to get rid of his fleet, give up control of the coastal cities, and renounce his possessions in Crete. He summoned an assembly to explain the conditions. The assembly became angry and unruly. The freed helots feared they would be enslaved, the newly propertied thought they would lose their land, and the mercenaries thought they would be expelled and homeless. They demanded that he resist and he agreed.

The Spartans skirmished against the Romans and were driven back. Quinctius rode around Sparta and inspected it carefully. Nabis and his immediate predecessors had walled the open approaches to the city, but they had not walled several rugged, inaccessible spots. Quinctius had, all in all, about 50,000 troops and he decided to encircle the city, divide his forces into three divisions and make three simultaneous assaults. He had siege ladders brought forward and all the siege engines which would be required for the attack—he hoped to terrify the Spartan population into surrendering. The Romans appeared by their shouts and their activity to be everywhere and the frightened Spartans did not know where the attack would come.

Quinctius ordered three divisions to attack three of the unwalled areas. Fear spread through the city, but Nabis kept his head and rushed from place to place with reinforcements. At first the Spartans held the Romans in the narrow ways as they fought three battles simultaneously, but, as the struggle grew, the Romans gained the advantage. The Spartans were fighting with missiles, from which— even though there were a lot of them—the Romans easily defended themselves with their large shields. Many casts missed and others struck lightly because in the narrow way and the thick crowd the Spartans had no room to run and throw and they hardly had a steady place to stand. For that reason no missiles stuck in flesh and few in the shields.

Still, as the Romans advanced, they encountered an unexpected danger from javelins and roof tiles, cast at them from above, and some Romans were wounded. Consequently, the Romans lifted their shields over their heads and held them so close together that missiles could not penetrate their roof of shields. Step by step, they pushed the Spartans back through the narrow way and, when they broke out into the open, they drove the Spartans before them.

The Spartans broke and ran. Panic spread. Nabis was certain the city had fallen. He went into shock, and he did not know what to do, but his commander, Pythagoras, immediately saw the one way to save the city. He ordered the buildings next to the wall near the fighting to be set on fire, the fire blazed up and the Spartans fed the flames. Roofs and roof beams collapsed on the Romans and smoke obscured the scene and confused and frightened the soldiers more than the flame. The Romans outside the city stopped and retreated from the fire and those in the city were afraid that they would be cut off so they also retreated. Quinctius ordered everyone to pull back.

The Roman commander rather thought the terror he had induced would be enough to force Nabis to capitulate and he was right. Spartan envoys came as suppliants and the two parties made peace on the stated terms. The coasts of Laconia were detached from the control of Sparta. (In time the cities would form a "League of Free Laconians.") Armenas, the son of Nabis—accompanied by other Spartans—was sent to Rome as a hostage, marched in Quinctius's triumph, and, eventually, died in Rome.

So Quinctius concluded the war to his own satisfaction, but not the way the Achaeans had wanted because, although he gave them general oversight over Sparta, Nabis was still the ruler and he was a dangerous man. Quinctius may have concluded from the ferocious resistance of the Spartans that Nabis was, indeed, their legitimate ruler and, for that reason, perhaps, Quinctius did not insist that Nabis take back the exiles. Agesipolis had to withdraw with the Romans.

When, in 193 BCE, the Romans were preparing for a war against Antiochus, Nabis saw his chance to win back the coastal towns (the source of many of his troops) and he attacked Gytheion. The Achaeans warned him to cease operations and sent envoys to Rome, but, the next year, before anyone could take action, Nabis was murdered in Sparta by a band of Aetolians who expected to be able to gain control of Sparta in the confusion. Instead, a crowd of Spartans rallied around "Laconicus"—who had been raised with the children of Nabis and was a member of one of the royal families—put him on a horse, proclaimed him king, and hunted down and killed the Aetolians.

With both Nabis and Armenas dead, the Roman Senate released all the Spartan hostages. The many exiles from Sparta collected in the towns of Laconia, as the towns, with no Spartan king to hold their loyalty, coalesced into a League. The Spartans tried to drive the exiles out and to regain access to the sea. After their first attempt was beaten back, the League of Free Laconians asked the Achaeans and the Achaean leader, Philopoemen, for help, and Philopoemen, against the express wishes of the Roman Senate, entered Spartan territory, occupied Sparta, forced it to join the Achaean League, and executed almost a hundred men, named by him as hostile to the Achaeans. He, then, ordered the Spartans to tear down their walls, dismiss all mercenary soldiers (including those who had been given citizenship), and expel all freed helots. Finally, he ordered them to give up the Lycurgan code and accept the Achaean constitution and way of life. Philopoemen ended Sparta's history as an independent polis. He boasted that he had "cut the sinews from the city." After this year, 189 BCE, Sparta was never ruled by kings again.

"Laconicus," then, was the last king of Sparta. Was he murdered by Philopoemen or did he escape into exile? We do not know. Perhaps he is to be identified with the "Leonidas," an exile, known to have been of royal descent, who led a unit of 500 Greeks from different poleis in the army of the Macedonian king Perseus in 171 BCE.

The Achaean League now, for a brief time, encompassed the whole of the Peloponnesus, but Rome observed without pleasure the development of its power and acquiesced in the request by the Spartans to free themselves from the League and put themselves directly under the control of Rome. As a sort of sad distinction, Sparta was the first city in Greece to take this step.

Agesipolis, the exiled king, was an envoy to Rome in about 184 BCE, but he was killed by pirates on the way. His companion on the journey was Areus, who was also supposed to be a Heraclid, although not king. Meanwhile, with the consent of Rome the city was allowed to return to its antique form of government but without its kings. This restoration led to a conflict within the Peloponnesus which eventually led to the return of the Roman legions, when the Senate decided to punish the Achaean League for its lack of servility to Rome. The Achaeans foolishly proceeded to war with Rome and the Romans easily defeated them and, as an object lesson, sacked and razed Corinth (in 146 BCE). The Spartans disassociated themselves from the war.

The Achaean League was disbanded, but the Spartan state also disappeared to be replaced by the city of Sparta, a free city, free of tribute and under the protection of, and beholden to, Rome. The cities of the coasts of Laconia, now freed from the control of the Achaean League, were able to establish the independence of the League of Free Laconians, with a central religious shrine at the sanctuary of Poseidon on Cape Taenarum.

— 36 —

Sparta under the Romans

After the brutal sack and destruction of Corinth and the defeat of the Achaean League, the Romans organized the Peloponnesus (excluding Sparta) into the province of Achaea and declared Sparta a free city, partly as a reward for its hostility to the Achaean League, partly out of respect for its history. Greeks acquiesced in the conquest—what choice did they have?—but, in general, they were dissatisfied with Roman rule. The Romans did as they pleased, had no respect for Greek rights, disdained the Greek people, and exhibited an insatiable appetite for their possessions—their art, their money, and even, as Roman armies crisscrossed Greece to fight each other, their food.

Many Greeks, therefore, supported the self-proclaimed savior and defender of Greek liberty, the hellenophile king of Pontus and descendant of Persian royalty, Mithridates (120–63 BCE). Some Laconians, if not some Spartans, declared for him, but, fortunately for them, they did not become involved in his war against Rome. The Athenians, who did, underwent appalling suffering at the hands of the Romans, as the Laconians might have—the Romans had a much better memory for grievances than for benefactions—but those Romans who might have taken revenge on Laconia became involved in a civil war in Italy.

Theoretically, Sparta, as a free city, owed nothing to the Romans, neither taxes nor troops. In reality, Sparta was just one more place to be exploited as individual Roman commanders saw fit. Marcus Creticus, for example, extorted a loan before his ill-fated war against the pirates of Crete. Pompey recruited troops from the whole of Greece for his war with Caesar. His forces at the fatal battle of Pharsalus included, as a Greek historian wrote, "Laconians drawn up by their own kings." (This Greek historian was certainly overly romantic and mistaken, at least as far as "kings" go.) What happened to those Laconians, we do not know, but they did fight for the losing side.

In the subsequent civil wars the Spartans suffered as much for choosing the victor, Octavian, as they had for choosing Pompey: their 5000-man contingent, sent to aid Octavian, arrived in camp just as Brutus raided it. One of Brutus's troops scratched on a rock, "Here we slaughtered the Laconians," and Brutus promised to lead his troops to Sparta to loot at their pleasure.

Finally, however, in the midst of so many disasters a Spartan named Eurycles rescued his fellow citizens by choosing Octavian in the ensuing civil war between Octavian and Mark Antony. Mark Antony had executed Eurycles's father for piracy. Eurycles, himself, had taken to the sea, perhaps as a pirate, and he brought his ship to the battle of Actium, where he pursued the fleeing Antony and drew close enough to taunt him, before he turned aside to capture a supply ship (a more profitable, and safer, endeavor).

The victorious Octavian granted Eurycles the hegemony of Sparta, the island of Cythera as a personal possession, and Roman citizenship for himself, his wife, and all his descendants. Eurycles claimed to be a descendant of the Dioscuri (and thus of Zeus), and, therefore, while not a Heraclid, still kingly. Eurycles was, for a time, the sole ruler of Sparta. He became an influential figure in Greece, as anyone with the support of Octavian (soon to be "Augustus") was bound to be—he spent money on building projects wherever they would do him some good, in the province of Achaea, in Laconia, and in Sparta (where he built a rather nice theater, still to be seen today), but, benefactions aside, he appears to have been a rather shabby character with ambitions far beyond his circumstances.

He made a considerable sum of money by exploiting the passions and suspicions in the court of Herod, he acted as though Sparta was his personal property, he pursued a plan to reincorporate Laconia under Spartan, that is, his own, control, and he had ambitions in the Peloponnesus, too. Augustus supported him for a long time, but, at last, his patience ran out and he ordered Eurycles to go into exile. Eurycles's son and then his grandson were hegemons in Sparta, each promoted and then exiled by subsequent emperors. Eurycles's great-grandson became a Roman senator and commanded a Roman legion.

Sparta prospered during the early empire, partly because of the reputation of ancient Sparta, although the sad truth was that the Spartans of the early empire had fallen far from the ways of their ancestors and their modern ways brought them—according to the story—the rebuke of one of the most revered men of the first century.

Apollonius of Tyana was a philosopher, a miracle worker, and a sort of pagan saint. When he was on his way to Olympia (during the reign of Nero, CE 54–68), Spartan envoys met him and asked him to visit their city. He examined their smooth legs, sleek hair, beardless faces, and luxuriant clothes and then fired off a hot letter to the ephors. In response, the ephors issued a public proclamation that forbade the use of pitch plasters in the baths, expelled the women who professed "to rejuvenate men with their sexual expertise," and restored the Lycurgan system in every respect. The consequence was that the wrestling grounds were filled with youths, the common messes were restored, and "Sparta became once more like itself."

The Spartans were not alone in their yearning for the past. Greeks, and many Romans, including the emperor Nero, felt a nostalgia for the distant Greek past, the days of Achilles, Hector, Leonidas, and Socrates. Peace and prosperity in the Roman empire allowed Greeks, and Roman philhellenes, to give concrete form to their feelings of nostalgia. The Spartans just went farther than others: they attempted to reintroduce the Lycurgan system.

"Even today [writes an author of the first century BCE] the Spartans are whipped according to the precepts of Lycurgos, live under the open sky, go about only lightly clothed, and cling to many disciplines, which others find too severe."

The custom that is perhaps most frequently mentioned by contemporaries as an example of the old Spartan discipline, is the beating of boys at the Altar of Artemis Orthia. In Roman times this contest was a simple endurance of pain and such a tourist attraction that the Spartans built a theater for the spectators. The boy who could stand the most pain was the victor, honored by the state. For the rest of his life he bore the title, "altar-victor for endurance."

Two other contests, both team sports, attracted tourists. In one, a team of naked boys tried to push the other team off an island into the water. In the other, two teams played some sort of a ball game. Lucian (second century CE) describes the contests.

"We ourselves in Sparta have seen teams of young men struggle with unbeliev- able competitiveness; they used their fists, feet, fingernails, and even their teeth, and they would as soon die as let themselves be beaten."

The ballgame took place in the theater. Each obe, or tribe, had its own team of fourteen players. The rules, as far as we know, were uncomplicated: the ball was thrown between two teams and the team that came up with it, won. Spartans loved the game so much that a Spartan official noted in an inscription that his team had won a tournament for the first time in forty years.

After the suicide of Nero, the Roman civil wars caused a deep depression in the Greek world, but the victory of Vespasian (CE 69–79) and his careful administration of the finances of the empire led to a revival. In the year 78 or 79 the emperor pro- vided imperial money for the building of a colonnade next to the theater in Sparta to protect the spectators from the weather.

By the reign of Nerva (CE 96–98) some Spartan citizens had amassed enough money to finance two major festivals, one in honor of the imperial house, the other in honor of the ancient Spartan hero Leonidas. (At a time when a Roman soldier earned not quite one denarius per day, the two benefactors financed the Leonidian festival with a capital investment large enough to provide first prizes of 100 to 500 denarii.) In the same year the same two men introduced the Uranian games in honor of the Roman emperors.

The Spartans were anxious to prove that in their veins the blood of the heroes of bygone days still flowed. Romans were skeptical, but some Spartans traced their ancestry back to Lycurgos, Heracles, and the Dioscuri, to the kings Eudamidas and Archidamos, to Poseidon, Perseus, and Rhadamanthys, to Crios (a seer during the time of the Dorian invasions), to Megatas, and Scopelos (probably titans or pre-dorian gods), to the Elean seer, who in the fifth century before Christ was given full Spartan citizenship. Fathers gave their sons names from the heroic past—Agesilaos, Agis, Brasidas, Cleomenes, and Leonidas, among others. One Spartan was honored as a descendant of the man who had killed Epaminondas in 362 BCE. Some Spartans traced their ancestry by the number of generations they were removed from Heracles, providing proof that they were Heraclids.

An official, a "Lycurgan interpreter and guide," was chosen to protect the Lycurgan way of life. Of course, the Spartan attempt to recreate their concept of the Lycurgan state was impossible, because that state existed only in the minds of philosophers and rhetoricians. And even in so far as they did comprehend some of the truth of the Lycurgan system, still it had no purpose anymore, except to attract tourists.

During the reign of Marcus Aurelius (CE 161–180), the picture of prosperity and old-fashioned virtue began to crack. The strain of foreign wars was beginning to tell on the Roman economy, Spartan citizens no longer had the money to spend in office, and the wars began to find their way into the city. Spartans participated, and died, in the campaigns of Lucius Verus (CE 162–163) against the Parthians.

By the beginning of the third century the emperor sent consular correctors to Sparta because of Sparta's financial difficulties. These officials reported that bridges and buildings were in disrepair.

In CE 211 the Roman emperor Caracalla proclaimed that all free inhabitants of the Roman empire would be Roman citizens. Roman citizens could be taxed and drafted. In 214 Caracalla led an expedition to the east to prosecute a war against the Parthians. Caracalla wanted to emulate Alexander the Great and, because he imagined that he was fighting "Persians," he enrolled a Spartan unit. He called this unit the *pitanatan lochos*. (Thucydides tells us that there was no such unit.) In 215 the Spartans again met the Persians. We know almost nothing about this campaign; there were no big battles and nothing more is heard of the Spartan unit, except that gravestones survive of some of those Spartans who "fell in the war against the Persians."

In the 260s the Germanic tribe, the Heruli, sacked Sparta, but, with the help of imperial funds, the state raised itself again. The festivals, particularly the whipping at the altar of Artemis Orthia, were still being held in the fourth century. But in CE 396 Alaric, the king of the Goths, plundered Sparta, the inhabitants fled, and those who returned, returned to a much diminished Sparta.

Conclusion

When a king died, horsemen rode throughout the whole of Laconia to spread the news. The women in Sparta walked around the city and beat bronze pots. Two free persons from each household, men and women, were enjoined to make public lamentation. The Laconian neighbors were required to come from all over Laconia and attend the funeral, and helots, too, and all the Spartiates. The crowd numbered in the thousands. They struck themselves on the forehead, men and women, and they wailed without ceasing and cried, "Woe is me," and they said of the departed king, "He was the best king we ever had." A prominent individual would deliver a eulogy. (In the case of Agesilaos, that person was Xenophon the Athenian writer and historian.)

When Leonidas was killed and the Spartans did not have his body to bury, they made an image of him, and carried the image on a gorgeously decorated bier to the burial site. When a king died abroad, the body was packed in honey (to preserve it) and brought back to Sparta for the funeral.

After the burial the market was closed for ten days, public business was prohibited, and the Spartans continued to mourn. During the period of mourning the Spartans would remember and memorialize their king, so let us, at the end of this book, do the same.

We could recall their personal lives: the king whose friend walked in on him at home while he was playing horsey with his children. The friend laughed and the king said, "I have only one request—wait until you have children before you tell anyone."

We remember the king with two wives and the king who stole his best friend's wife. We could remember all the duties they performed in Sparta, their presence at the festivals, at every public sacrifice, and performance, or their hunting, their travels—visiting oracles and the Olympic games—inviting prominent and interesting Greeks to visit Sparta and to dine with them. They invited the first natural philosophers to visit. They opened Sparta to the wider, intellectual world.

We could remember their consistent leadership under which the Greeks came as close to national unity and collective security as they ever did . . . in the Peloponnesian League.

Most of all, however, we remember individual kings: Theopompos, "loved by Zeus," who led Sparta to the conquest of Messenia; to the kings involved in the great political compromise which introduced the Lycurgan constitution; Cleomenes I, who prepared Greece to fight the Persians; and, of course, the most famous of all the kings, Leonidas, who fought the Persians at Thermopylae and willingly gave his life for Sparta and Greece. We remember the kings like Archidamos, whose quick thinking saved Sparta during the earthquake and whose sensible advice might have saved the Spartans from that most devastating of Greek wars, the Peloponnesian War, and his successors who promoted peace even though they became unpopular because of it. We remember the later Cleomenes, who, for a time, raised Sparta to power again, and, finally, I think of the last Agis, who preferred the ruin of his reforms to the bloodshed of his fellow Spartans.

Always the kings fulfilled their primary role—to lead the army in battle and to be willing to fight to the death. Let Homer speak their epitaph:

"Courage is the greatest power."

Notes

I have organized the notes in a particular way, giving complete ancient sources for the kings, king by king, and for other notables, such as Lycurgos and Chilon. The reader will see that, for the most part, the sources are bits and pieces. I have done this for the simple reason that this is a book about the kings.

INTRODUCTION

Leotychidas and the serpent. Plutarch. *Moralia (Apophthegmata Laconica).* 224E Leotychidas 2.

Battle ritual. W. Kendrick Pritchett. *Ancient Greek Military Practices*, Part I, Berkeley, 1971; Xenophon. *Constitution of the Spartans* 13.2–3.

PART ONE: THE DORIAN WARS

1. By Bus to the "Hollow"

The Isthmus—Plutarch *Theseus* 25.4.
Eat all they wanted—Herodotus I 71.2 (about the Persians)
First Map—Aristophanes *Clouds* ll. 215–216.
Spartan song—Alcman frag 20. Denys L. Page. *Alcman: The Partheneion*. Oxford, 1951, p. 38 (Athenaeus X 416D).
Description of ancient Sparta—Thucydides I 10.2.

2. "Tell the Spartans ..."

Go Tell the Spartans—Herodotus VII 228.2.
Hyacinthos—Ovid *Metamorphoses* X 162–214.
No wide plain—Homer *Odyssey* II 602.

Good to plow—Tyrtaeus Fragment 3 (Prato). Carlo Prato *Tyrtaeus*. Rome, 1968.
Kalamata earthquake—Jelle Zeilinga de Boer and Donald Theodore Sanders. *Earthquakes in Human History*. Princeton, 2005, p. 57n.
Menelaus, you are the master—Homer *Odyssey* II 602.
Die under the lashing—Cicero *Tusculanean Disputations* II 14.34.

3. The Sons of Heracles

"Through that no word."—Plutarch *Moralia (Apophthegmata Laconica)* 236F.
The black broth—Plutarch *Lycurgus* 11.
"Hair is cheap"—Plutarch *Moralia (Apophthegmata Laconica)* 232C.
"Crapper"—*Iliad* XV 639–640.

4. The First Kings of Sparta

Other invasions, for instance, the Gallic conquest of Europe, the destruction of the Roman empire in the West, the Viking onslaught on Europe, continued over several generations—first a raid by a small party of fifty or a hundred men—to test the resistance—then more raids by larger parties, and occupation by the whole tribe; the legends of the Dorians' return—that the Dorians invaded en masse—could conceal a long history of testing raids.
Procles (930–)—Herodotus IV 147, VI 52, VIII 131; Plutarch *Lycurgus* 1; Pausanias IV 3.4; Nepos *Agesilaus* 1; Athenaeus XI 463ʙ.
Eurysthenes—Diodorus Siculus XII 45.1 (Eurystheus); Herodotus VI 52, VII 204; Nepos. *Agesilaus* 1, 7; Eusebius (Schoene) I 223.
[Soos] (–895)—Pausanias III 7.1; Plutarch *Lycurgus* 1; Plato *Cratylos* 412b (knows Soos only as a Spartiate).
Agis I (930–900)—Herodotus I 65, VII 204; Strabo VIII 365; Pausanias III 16.9.
Eurypon (895–865)—Herodotus VIII 131 (Euryphon); Strabo VIII 366; Plutarch *Lycurgus* 1; Polyaenus II 13.
Echestratos (900–870)—Herodotus I 65, VII 204; Pausanias III 2.2.
Prytanis (865–835)—Herodotus VIII 131.
Labotas (870–840)—Herodotus I 65, VII 204 (Lewbwvth"); Eusebius I 223; Pausanias III 2.3–4.
Polydectes (835–805)—Pausanias II 36.4; Plutarch *Lycurgus* 1; Herodotus VIII 131; Justin III 2.5.
Doryssos (840–815)—Diodorus VII 8 (Dorysthos); Herodotus VII 204; Pausanias III 2.4.
Eunomos (805–775)—Plutarch *Lycurgus* 1; Pausanias III 7.2; Diodorus Siculus VII 8; Dionysius Halicarnassus II 49.4.
Agesilaos I (815–785)—Herodotus VII 204; Pausanias III 2.4.
Charillos (775–750)—Herodotus VIII 131 (Carilaos); Diodorus VII 8 (Chariclus); Pausanias II 36.4, III 2.5, VIII 5.9; Heraclides Ponticus in Müller, *Fragmenta Historicorum Graecorum*, Paris, 1878, II p. 210; Plutarch *Cleomenes* 10, *Lycurgus* 1. 3. 5; Sosibius fr 2 in Müller FHG II 625; Justin III 2.5.
Archelaos (785–760)—Herodotus VII 204, Pausanias III 2.5–6, Eusebius I 225.
Nicandros (750–720)—Diodorus VII 8; Herodotus VIII 131; Pausanias II 36.4, III 7.4–5.

Teleclos (760–740)—Herodotus VII 204; Eusebius (Schoene) I 225; Pausanias III 2.6–7, 7.4, IV 4.2–3, 31.3; Strabo VI 279.

The diver—*Iliad* XVI 745–750.

The water oath—Plutarch *Moralia (Apophthegmata Laconica)* 232A.

Armed gods—Plutarch *Moralia (Apophthegmata Laconica)* 232C.

War with Amyclae—Pausanias III 2.6.

Oeolycos—Herodotus IV 149.

They honor their own fathers—Plutarch *Moralia (Apophthegmata Laconica)* 232B 3.

If it wasn't something—Plutarch *Moralia (Apophthegmata Laconica)* 232AB 1.

PART TWO: THE MESSENIAN WARS

5. Over the Mountains

Theopompos (720–675)—Herodotus VIII 131; Polyaenus VIII 34; Quintilian *Instutiones oratoriae* II 17.20; Pausanias III 7.5, 31–2, IV 7.7–9, 8.8–9, 15.3; Tyrtaeus 5, fragment 2 (Prato); Plutarch *Agis* 21, *Lycurgus* 6; Diodorus VII fr 8; Aristotle *politica* V p 1313a26; Valerius Maximus IV 1.8.

Alcamenes (740–700)—Herodotus VII 204; Pausanias III 2.7, IV 4.4; FGrH (Apollodorus *Chronika*) II 244 (86/7).

Anaxandridas (675–660)—Herodotus VIII 131.

Polydoros (700–665)—Herodotus VII 204; Pausanias III 3.1–4, 11.10, IV 7.7; Plutarch *Moralia (apophthegmata Laconica* s. v.) 231DEF, *Lycurgus* 8.

Stone Age—McDonald, William A. (1913) and George Robert Rapp (1930), eds., *The Minnesota Messenia expedition: reconstructing a bronze age regional environment*, Minneapolis, 1913, 1930.

The account of the First Messenian War is based on two fourth–century epics. No historian believes that a fourth century epic could have much historical value and yet we do not know what sources the poet had available. And some of the elements of the story are hard to dismiss—the importance of tripods, oracles, the general conduct of war in that period. (Pausanias IV).

"Are you really."—Plutarch *Moralia (Apophthegmata Laconica)* 231D2.

The gory details are taken from the following passages in the *Iliad*: XII 160–161, XIII 408–410, IV 446, IV 517–531, V 290–293, XIV 493–496, XII 383–385, XVI 345–350, XIII 567–569, XI 145–147, XVII 125–127.

A Spartan told—Plutarch *Moralia (Apophthegmata Laconica)* 232C.

6. Shoulder to Shoulder

"Men who stand their ground."—Thucydides IV 126.

7. "Never Retreat"

Archidamos I (660–645)—Herodotus VIII 131.

Eurycrates (665–640)—Herodotus VII 204; Pausanias III 3.4–5, IV 15.3.

Anaxilas (645–625)—Pausanias III 7.6, IV 15.3; Herodotus VIII 131.

Anaxandros (640–615)—Herodotus VII 204; Pausanias III 3.4–5, 14.4, IV 15ff.

Beginning of the war—Pausanias IV 15.1–3.

Pigs and Donkeys—Herodotus 5.65.

Tyrtaeos—Athenaeus XIV 630F; Diodorus XV 66.3; Pausanias IV 15.6; Plato *Laws* I 188–191; Stephanus Byzantius s. v. [Afidna; Strabo VIII 362; *Suidas* s. v. Tyrtaios; *Tirteo*, ed. Carlo Prato, Rome, 1968 (fragments and testimonia collected). Prato testimonia (with Prato's abbreviations) not found in Poralla: Aelian *de natura animalium* VI 1, *varia historia* XII 50; L. Ampelius *Liber memorialis* 14 (p. 27 Assmann); Aristides *Orationes* XXXIII 425 (I p. 639 Dind.); Aristotle *Politica* V 1306B; Dio Chrysostum *Orationes* II 29, XXXVI 10; Diodorus VIII 27. 1–2; Diogenes Laertius II 43 (I p. 74f Long); Eusebius Praep. ev. V 28, I p. 274, 15ff Mras (= Oenom. fr. 10 Mull.); Eustathius in Il. III 76, p. 386, 1ff; Galen de Hippoc. et Plat. plac. III 4 p. 281 Mue.; Harpocration *Lexicon* s. v. (p. 295 Dind.); Hieronymus Chron. 96b, 17 ad annum 633, 96b Helm; Horace *ars poetica* 401f; Insc. Acarn. saec. III–II a. Chr., ed. Klaafenbach, Sitzungber. Preuss. Akad., 1935, pp. 718f; Joannis Sicel. Doxop. Comm. in Hermog. *peri ideon* (VI p. 139 Walz); Justin III 5, 4–15; Lycurgus *In Leocratem* 106f, Maxim. Tyr. XXXVII 5 (p. 432, 15 Hob.); Orosius Adv. pag. I 21, 7 (p. 32 Zang.); Pausanias IV 15.2, 16.2, 16.6, 18.2; Philod. de mus. 28 Kemke (XI 89, fr. 16); Plato *Laws* I 629A–E, 630C, II 666E–667A, IX 858E; Plutarch *Moralia (apophthegmata Laconica)* 230D, 235F, Cleomenes II 3, pro nob. 2 (Mor. VII p. 200 Bern.), terra an aqua anim. sint callidiora 959a; Pollux IV 107 (p. 233 Bethe); Polyaen. Strat. I 17; Porphyrio ad Hor. art. poet. 402 (p. 176 Holder); Procl. in Plat. Remp. comm. 402 (p. 186f Kroll); Ps. Acro ad Hor. art. poet. 402; Quintilian X 1, 56, XII 11, 27 Raderm.; Strabo VIII 5,6; schol. in Aristot. Eth. Nic. III 11, 1116b; Schol. in Dionys. Thrac. Art. gramm. p. 168, 8 Hilgard; Schol. T in Hom. Il. XV 496 (II p. 138 Maas); Scholia to Plato *Laws* I 629A, 630A (p. 301 Chase Greene); Tzetz. Chil. 692ff; Themist. Or. XV 197C–198A (p. 284 Downey), 198C (p. 285 Downey).

8. Deeds of the Wolf

Lycurgos—SEG XI 1064 (ii\iii CE); Heliodorus *Aethiopica* II (Bekker) 27: Aristotle *rhetorica* 1398b18, *Politica* 1270a7, 1271b25, 1273b33, 1274a29, 1296a20; Cicero *epistulae ad Atticum* I 13,3 (or is this a reference to the Attic orator?); Epictetus II xx 26; Plutarch. *Lycurgus passim*—1, 2–3, 31; *Theseus* 1.4, *Numa* 4.7,8, *Lysander* 1.2, 17.6, *Agesilaus* 4.3, 20.9, 26.5, 33.4; *Agis passim, Solon* 16.1, 22.2, *Aristides* 2.1, *Philopoemen* 16.8; *Moralia (de liberis educandis)* 3A, *(quomodo quis suos in virtute sentiat profectus)* 85B, *(apophthegmata Laconica)* 225E–229A, *(de Alexandri magni fortuna aut virtute)* 337D, *(de Iside et Osiride)* 354E, *(de Pythiae oraculis)* 403E, *(de amore prolis)* 493E, *(de garrulitate)* 510E, *(de invidia et odio)* 537D, *(an seni respublica gerenda sit)* 789E, 795E, *(praecepta gerendae reipublicae)* 810D, *(de unius in reipublica dominatione)* 827B, *(de esu cranium orationes)* 997C, *(de Stoicorum repugnantiis)* 1033F, *(adversus Colotem)* 1116F, 1125D, 1127–8; Strabo VIII 366. Herodotus I 65/66; VIII 131; Pausanias III 16,6; Libaniu s*epistulae* 469.2, 1119.4, 1210.3, 1488.3; *orationes* 1.131, 17.8, 25.34, 46.29, 64.6, 7, 10, 81; *declamationes* 24.1 (pro): 2, 24.2 (mel): 14, 15, *(Archidami defensio)* 24. 425; Plato *leges* IX 630d, 632d, 858e, *symposium* 209d, *Phaedrus* 258c, *respublica* 599d, *Minos* 318c, *epistulae* 320d, 354b; SEG XI 810 (statue), 1064; *Anthologia Graeca*16.173; Lucian *de astrologia* 25, *Anacharsis* 38, 39, *macrobii* 28, *verae historiae* 2.17; Cassius Dio (epitome) LXII 14.3; Justin III

2.4–3.12; Athenaeus VI 233A, XI 508A, XIV 635F; Philostratus *Apollonius* VI 21 (end), VIII 6, 7; Philo *quod omnis probus liber sit* 47; Diogenes Laertius II 23.3, 49.4, 61.2; Josephus *contra Apionem* II 154, 225; Isocrates *orationes* XII 152, 153; Grunauer, Gruppe. XVII, Tafel 13 (coin portrait, 43–31 BCE).

Contradictions in every account—Plutarch *Lycurgus*1.

Apollo said to him—Herodotus I 65–66.

Embraced and wept—Diodorus VIII 28.

Eunomia—Plutarch *Moralia (Apophthegmata Laconica)* 232C Lycurgus 4.

a lesser kingdom—Plutarch *Lycurgus* 7.

"They deliberate for many days."—Plutarch *Moralia (Apophthegmata Laconica)* 216F/217B Anaxandridas 6.

"Why do you not."—Plutarch *Moralia (Apophthegmata Laconica)* 216F/217B Anaxandridas 3.

The cowardly man's skin—*Iliad* XIII 278–286.

I ran and left—Archilochus, *The Oxford Book of Greek Verse*, (ed. Gilbert Murray et al.), Oxford, 1966, #104, p. 154.

9. The Spartan Way

Two dogs—Plutarch *Moralia (Apophthegmata Laconica)* 225E/226B Lycurgus 1.

The Age Classes: *Rhobidas, promikkichizomenoi, mikkichizomenoi, pratopampaides, hatropampaides, melleirenes, eirenes* (in other poleis called ephebes).

The boy and the fox—Plutarch *Lycurgus* 17.

Seventy-two medimni—Plutarch *Lycurgus*11.

"Those who say few words."—Plutarch *Moralia (Apophthegmata Laconica)* 232B Charillos 1).

Choruses of old men sang, "We once were brave young men."—Plutarch *Lycurgus* 20.

"Leave for a time the slopes of beautiful Taÿgetus—Aristophanes *Lysistrata* 1296–1311.

Theban poet Pindar wrote—"are the counsels of the older men."—Plutarch *Lycurgus* 20.

"Sweet, clear voiced Muse of many tunes."—Denys L. Page, *Alcman: The Partheneion*, Oxford, 1951.

Taxes—Plutarch *Moralia (Apophthegmata Laconica)* 217B Anaxander the son of Eurykrates.

"Why I had him."—Plutarch *Moralia (Apophthegmata Laconica 241C)* Anonyma 8.

PART THREE: THE ARCADIAN AND ARGIVE WARS

In this part I follow closely the account of Herodotus, the first historian and one of the greatest storytellers of all time.

10. The Spartan Alliance

Leotychidas I (625–600)—Herodotus VIII 131; Pausanias IV 15.2; Plutarch. *Moralia (apophthegmata Laconica* s. v. Leotychidas) 224CD; *Lycurgus* 13.

Eurycratidas (615–590)—Pausanias III 3.5 (Eurykrates); Herodotus VII 204; Plutarch. *Moralia (apophthegmata Laconica)* 221B.

Hippocratidas (600–575)—Herodotus VIII 131.

Leon (590–560)—Herodotus I 65, VII 204.

Agasicles (575–550)—Pausanias III 7.6–7; Herodotus I 65.

Chilon—Diogenes Laertius I 68, 69; *Suidas* s. v.; Iamblichus *de vita Pythagorica* 267, cf. Dam-
agetos"; Plutarch *Moralia* (*de aud. poet* 14) ??; 86c, 96a, 148a, 151–156, 163d, 284c, 385e;
Plato *Protagoras* 343A.; Eusebius (Schoene) II 96/7; FGrH II (Apollodorus *Chronika*)
p 183ff; Pausanias III 16.4, X 24.4; Libanius *declamations* 2.9; *Anthologia* Graeca VII
81, IX 366; SEG XXIX 1123 (represented with Socrates in Ephesus, AD 200–220); Aulus
Gellius I 3.1–8; Diogenes Laertius I 30, 41; Aristotle *rhetorica* 1389b4, 14.

The Spartans are so ready—Plutarch *Moralia (Apophthegmata Laconica)* 216F/217B
(Anaxandridas 5).

You want the whole of Arcadia—Herodotus I 66.

Chains in Tegea—Herodotus I 66f.

Eurypontid philosophy—Plutarch *Moralia (Apophthegmata Laconica)* 208B Agasicles 2.

new temple of Artemis—Herodotus 1.65.1; Cartledge pp. 118–119.

"I will not be the student."—Plutarch *Moralia (Apophthegmata Laconica)* 208B (Agasicles 1).

In the year 556 bc—Diogenes Laertius, *Lives of the Philosophers*, I 68–73. (Ephoros).

Was Chilon—Diogenes Laertius *Lives of the Philosophers*, I 68–73.

A positive spin—Plutarch *Moralia (Apophthegmata Laconica)* 221AB (Eurykrates).

Complained to him—Plutarch *Moralia (Apophthegmata Laconica)* 232B 2.

Utopian society—Plutarch *Moralia (Apophthegmata Laconica)* 224F Leo 1.

Even at the Olympic games—Plutarch *Moralia (Apophthegmata Laconica)* 224F Leo 2.

Exile from justice—Plutarch *Moralia (Apophthegmata Laconica)* 216F/217B Anaxandridas 1.

Temple-robbers should be happy—Plutarch *Moralia (Apophthegmata Laconica)* 216F/
217B Anaxandridas 4.

Tyrants—Aristotle *Politics* II 9.

Did not rise—Xenophon *Lacedaemonion politeia* 15.

This discourtesy—Plutarch *Moralia (Apophthegmata Laconica)* 217C Anaxidamos (Anaxilas).

Oaths—Xenophon *Constitution of the Spartans* 15.

Bones of Orestes—Herodotus I 67.4.

The treaty—F Gschnitzer, *Beiträge zur klassische Philologie* 93 (1978).

11. The "Strangers"

Anaxandridas (560–520)—Plutarch *Moralia* (*apophthegmata Laconica* s. v. Anaxandridas) 216F–217B; Herodotus I 67–8, V 39–41; Pausanias III 3.5–6, 9.

Ariston (550–515)—Herodotus I 67, VI 61–63; Pausanias III 7.7–8; Plutarch *Moralia*
(*apophthegmata Laconica* s.v.) 218AB.

The oracle of Croesus—Herodotus I 47–55.

Battle of Champions—Herodotus I 82.

From its tyrant—*Fragmente der Griechischen Historiker* 105F1.

Samian exiles—Herodotus III 46, 54–56.

Sun to dry—Herodotus III 122–125.

Second wife of Anaxandridas—Herodotus V 39–41.

12. The Accidental King

Cleomenes I—Herodotus V 39–41, 48, 61, 64–66, 70, 72–75, VI 61, 65–66, 73–82, VII
239; Pausanias II 20.8–10, III 3.10, 4.5 (different versions of his death); Plutarch

Moralia (*mulierum virtutes* 4) 245c–f; Aristotle *Athenaion Politeia* 19; *Politica* 1303a7; Aelian *varia historia* XII 8.

13. The King Who Saved Greece

Damaratos (515–491)—Herodotus VI 50–51, 61—66, 70, 75, VII 3, 101–104, 209, 234–235, 239, VIII 65; Plutarch *Moralia* (*mulierum virtutes* 4) 245c–f, (*de Herodoti malignitate* 31. 3) 864f, Themistius 29; Polyaenus VIII 33; Pausanias III 4. 3–5; Diogenes Laertius I 72; Xenophon *Hellenica* I 6; Athenaeus I 29f; *Olymp* 157.
Leotychidas II (491–469)—Herodotus VI 65–66, 71–73, 85–86, 131–32. IX 96–105, 114; Diodorus XI 34–36; Pausanias III 7.9–10.

PART FOUR: THE PERSIAN WARS

15. Defeat and Victory

Leonidas I (490–480)—Herodotus V 41, 48, VII 205–239, IX 10; Pausanias III 14.1; Simonide sfr 4 in Bergk *Poetae Lyrici Graeci* III p. 384; Libanius *orationes* 18.297, 64.10, *declamationes* 17.66, 18.27, 24.2 (mel): 12; Plutarch *Lycurgus* 14.8, 20.1, *Pelopidas* 21.3, *Artaxerxes* 22.3, *Themistocles* 9.1, *Moralia* (*coniugalia praecepta*) 145f, (*apophthegmata Laconica*) 221c, 225a–e, (*parallela Graeca et Romana*) 306d, (*de Herodoti malignitate*) 864–7, (*terrestriane an aquatilia animalia sint callidiora*) 959a; cf. *Cleomenes* 2.3 (anecdote about Tyrtaeus); Lucian *rhetorum praeceptor* 18; Aristophanes *Lysistrata* 1254; Demosthenes LIX 95.5; Pausanias I 13.5, III 3–5.1, VII 6.3, VIII 52.2, X 20.1, 22.8; Aulus Gellius III 7.19; Nepos *Themistocles* II 3; Philostratus *Apollonius* VIII 6, 15.
An Athenian tragic writer: Aeschylus. *The Persians* 353–432.

16. The Battle of Plataea

A veteran of such campaigns wrote—Aeschylus *Oresteia* 555ff.
Various sound the voices—Aeschylus *Oresteia* 324ff.

17. The Treason of Pausanias

Thucydides I 94–95, 128–134.

PART FIVE: THE ATHENIAN WARS

18. The Precarious Entente

Archidamos II (469–427)—Plutarch *Agesilaus* 1, 2.6; Herodotus VI 71; Xenophon *Agesilaus* 9.6, *Hellenica* V 2.3; Pausanias III 7.10, 15.1, VI 1.6; Diodorus XI 63.4–64.1, XII 42.6–8, 47.1–2; Thucydides II 10–12, 18–23, 47, 71–78, III 1; Libanius *declamationes* 20.19; Athenaeus XIII 566a.

Pleistoanax (459–445, 426–409)—Thucydides I 107, II 21, III 26, V 16–19, 24, 33, 75; Pausanias III 5.1; Plutarch *Pericles* 22; Diodorus XI 79.6, XIII 75.1.

Pausanias (445–426, 409–395)—Thucydides III 26; Pausanias III 5.6–7; Diodorus XIII 75, 107, XIV 17, 89; Xenophon *Hellenica* II 2.7ff., 4.29–39, III 5.6–7, 17–25, V 2.6; Plutarch *Lysander* 21, 28–9; Aristotle *Athenaion Politeia* p. 38; *Politica* VII 1301b20, 1333b34, 1301b20, 1307a4; Strabo VIII 366; IG V 1. 1564; Nepos *Thrasybulus* 3; *IDelos* 87; PW XVIII 2.2578–2584 (Schaefer); *Suidas* s. v.; Aelian *varia historia* xii 61.

The Great Earthquake—Plutarch *Cimon* 16.

Jelle Zeilinga de Boer and Donald Theodore Sanders. *Earthquakes in Human History*. Princeton, 2005, p. 57n.

Michael Denis Higgins and Reynold Higgins. *A Geological Companion to Greece and the Aegean*. Ithaca, NY, 1996, p. 54.

He sat down as a suppliant—Aristophanes *Lysistrata* 1138–1144.

The bones of King Leonidas—Pausanias III xiv 1 says that it was the *regent* Pausanias who recovered the bones "forty years after the battle," that is, in 440 BC, but the regent by then was dead and King Pausanias is the logical figure to recover the bones of his ancestor.

19. King Archidamos Gives Sound Advice

Archidamos' speech—Thucydides I 80–85.

20. The Archidamian War

Agis II (427–399)—Thucydides III 89, IV 2. 6, V 19, 24, 54, 57–60 & 63–75, 83, VII 19 & 27, VIII 3, 5–11 & 70–71; Plutarch *Agesilaus* 1. 3; Diodorus XI 48, XII 35.4, 78–79, XIII 107; Xenophon *Hellenica* I 1.33–35, II 2. 7–13, II 3.3, III 2.22–29 & 3.1; Pausanias III 8.3–5, VI 2.3; *IDelos* 87 (IG V 1. 1564); Justin V 2.5; Nepos *Agesilaus* 1; Athenaeus XII 535B, 543B.

Speech of Archidamos at the border—Thucydides II 10–12.

Speech at Plataea—Thucydides II 72–74.

120 were Spartiates—Thucydides IV 38.5.

21. War within Peace

"Take our young men."—Plutarch *Moralia (Apophthegmata Laconica)* 215C Agis 1.

"We have to be willing to fight."—Plutarch *Moralia (Apophthegmata Laconica)* 215D Agis 4.

Description of the Spartan army—Thucydides V 66–68.

"Don't worry."—Plutarch *Moralia (Apophthegmata Laconica)* 215E Agis 8.

22. The Decelean War

"Your scheme is good."—Plutarch. *Moralia (Apophthegmata Laconica)* 216A Agis 13.

"Do you mean, when you aren't talking."—Plutarch *Moralia (Apophthegmata Laconica)* 215E Agis 7.

"Tell them that you spoke at length."—Plutarch *Moralia (Apophthegmata Laconica)* 215E
   Agis 9.
"I don't see that it's such a big thing."—Plutarch *Moralia (Apophthegmata Laconica)*
   215EF Agis 10.

23. The Man Who Would Be King

"Yes, I remember."—Plutarch *Moralia (Apophthegmata Laconica)* 216B Agis 17.
"A suitable place for women."—Plutarch *Moralia (Apophthegmata Laconica)* 215D Agis 6.
"If you want to remain free."—Plutarch *Moralia (Apophthegmata Laconica)* 216C Agis 18.

PART SIX: THE THEBAN WARS

In Part Six Xenophon's *Hellenica* and his minor works are the major sources.
Xenophon has come into some disrepute among modern historians, but he knew
Agesilaos and he is an eyewitness to many of the events.

24. The Common King

Agesilaos II (399–360)—Diodorus 14.8[a], 15.31–34, 82.6–83.5, 92–3; Nepos *Agesilaus*
   (8), *Timotheus* 1.3, *Conon* 2, *Chabrias* 1,2, *de regibus* 1; Pausanias III 8.8ff, 9.1–5,
   IV 17.5, VI 4.9, 15.7, VIII 6.2, IX 13.2, 14.5; Plutarch *Agesilaus* (1, 3, 6, 7–13,
   17–22, 27–8, 31–40), *Lysander* 22, 24, *Lycurgus* 30.5, *Artaxerxes* 22.4–7, *Moralia*
   (*de audiendis poetis*) 31c, (*de adulatore et amico*) 52f, 55d, (*de profectibus in virtute*)
   78d, 81a, 85b, (*regum et imperatorum apophthegmata*) 189e, (*apophthegmata Laconica*) 208b–215a, 229f, (*parallela Graeca et Romana*) 308b, (*de Alexandri fortuna*)
   343a, (*de Pythiae oraculis*) 399b, (*de fraterno amore*) 482d, (*de vitioso pudore*)
   533e–534b, (*de laude ipsius*) 545a, (*de genio Socratis*) 577e, 578f, (*quaestionum con-
   vivalium II 10.2*) 644b, (*an seni sit gerenda res puiblica*) 784ef, 790b, (*praecepta gerendae reipublicae*) 805e, 807e, 809a/b, (*non posse suaviter vivi secundum Epicurum*)
   1099b; *Hellenica Oxyrhyncus* 11.2–5, 12.1–4, 13.1, 21.1–4, 22.2,4; Xenophon *Agesilaus* (1.25–35; 2.17, 21, 26–7, 9.6); *Hellenica* III 3–4 passim; IV–VI passim, VII 5.9,
   10; Aristotle *Politica* 1306b35; SEG XI 457 (father?); Libanius *declamationes* XXIV
   2 (*mel*): 6; Isocrates *epistulae* IX 11–14, *orationes* IV 144, 153, V 62, 86, 87; Athenaeus IV 144b, IX 384a, XII 511c, 550e, XIII 609b, XIV 613c, 616d, 657b; Josephus
   Bellum Judaicum II 359; Diogenes Laertius II 51, 52, 57, VI 39, VIII 87; *Die Inschrif-
   ten von Ephesos* (der Österreichischen Akademie der Wissenschaften) II 133.
"Son, either get stronger."—Plutarch *Moralia (Apophthegmata Laconica)* 218E Archidamos
   8.
"Marched on Sardis."—Xenophon *Hellenica* III 4. 20–25; *Hellenica Oxyrhynchia* XI–XII.
Sayings of Pausanias."—Plutarch *Moralia (Apophthegmata Laconica)* 230F–231A (1).
Plutarch *Moralia (Apophthegmata Laconica)* 230F–231A (2).
Plutarch. *Moralia (Apophthegmata Laconica)* 230F–231A (3–7).

25. "Free and Autonomous"

The louse—Plutarch *Moralia (Apophthegmata Laconica)* 208E Agesilaos 8.

"Athenians, aren't you ashamed to." Plutarch *Moralia (Apophthegmata Laconica)* 215C
    Agesipolis.
"Well, I know, if I do everything you advise."—Plutarch *Moralia (Apophthegmata Lacon-ica)* 208E Agesilaos7 and 213A 59.

26. Sparta's Empire

Agesipolis I (395–380)—Diodorus XIV 89, XV 22,2, 23,2; Pausanias III 5.7, VIII 8.7–9;
    Xenophon *Hellenica* IV 2.9, 7.2–7; V 2.3–7, 3.8–9, 18–9 (Agesipolis and Agesilaus
    have been confused in *Suidas* s. v. Agis and Diodorus XIV 97.5.).
"Regarding the truce." Xenophon. *Hellenica* IV vii 2.

27. The Battle of Leuctra

Cleombrotos I (380–371)—Pausanias I 13.4, III 5.7, IX 13.3–10; Diodorus XV 23.2; Xen-
    ophon *Hellenica* V 4.14–18, 4.59, VI 1.1, 2.1, 4.2–15; Plutarch *Agesilaus* 28, *Pelopi-
    das* 23.

28. Sparta at Bay

Agesipolis II (371–370)—Plutarch *Agis* 3, Diodorus XV 60.4; Pausanias I 13.4, III 6.2.
"When the Boeotians and Spartans joined battle."—Xenophon *Hellenica* VII 5.23ff.

PART SEVEN: THE MACEDONIAN WARS

29. The Struggle to Survive

Archidamos III (360–338)—SEG XI 457 (treaty with [Ach]aeans); Xenophon *Hellenica* V
    4.25, VI 4.18–19, 26, VII 1.28–32, 4.20–25, 5.12–13; Plutarch *Agis* 3, *Agesilaus* 19,
    33, 34, 40; *Camillus* 19.8; Pausanias III 10.3–5, VI 4.9; Arrian *Anabasis* II 13.6; Isoc-
    rates *Epistulae* IX (*Archidamos*); Diodorus XVI 24, 39, 59, 62–63, 88; Aeschines II
    133; Athenaeus VII 289E, XII 536CD, XIII 591B; Libanius *orationes* 64.83; *declama-
    tiones* (*Archidami defensio*) XXIV *passim*.
Laconia was fertile enough—Aristotle *Politics* II 9.
"We have the right."—Isocrates *Epistulae* IX (*Archidamos*).
Asclepius for (somehow) preserving them—*Inscriptiones Graecae* IV^2.1.58f, 57ff,
    68ff, 74ff.

30. In the Shadow of Great Powers

Agis III (338–331)—Plutarch *Agis* 3; Pausanias III 10.5; Arrian *Anabasis* II 13.6; Diodo-
    rus XVI 88.4, XVII 48.1–2, 62.6–63.4; Curtius VI 1.
Cleomenes II (370–309)—Pausanias I 13.4, III 6.2; Plutarch *Agis* 3, *Moralia* (*Lacaenarum
    apophthegmata* s. v. Gyrtias) 240EF; Diodorus XX 29; *FDelph* III 5.9I19 (336/5 BC)
Eudamidas I (331–305)—Plutarch *Agis* 3.3; *Moralia* (*apophthegmata Laconica*) 220D–
    221A, (*regum et imperatorum apophthegmata*) 192A–B; Polybius IV 35.13; Pausanias
    II 8.5; III 10.5; VI 2.4; VII 7.3; VIII 8.11, 10.8, 27.13 confuses Eudamidas I and II,
    Archidamos IV and Agis IV.

Areus I (309–265)—Diodorus Siculus XX 29.1; Justin XXIV 1.5; Pompeius Trogus *prologi* 26; Pausanias I 13.5; III 6.2–6; VI 12.5–6, 15.9; Plutarch *Agis* 3.6–7, *Pyrrhus* 26.17–19, 27.2, 29.11, 30.4, *Moralia* (*apophthegmata Laconica*) 217ᴦ; Josephus *Antiquitates Judaicae* XII 225–27, XIII 167 (AREIOS); 1 *Maccabees* 12.1–23; Athenaeus IV 142ʙ; *ICret* II xxiii 12A; *IOlymp* 308; IG IV 1. 332; SEG XXV 444; SEG XI 668 (Dedication to Athena); [SIG³ 430, see Areus (2) II]; Grunauer, pp. 112–113 (Gr. I–II, Tafel 1: BASILEOS AREOS).

Archidamos IV (305–275?)—Plutarch *Agis* 3.3, *Demetrius* 35.1; [Polyaenus IV 7.9–10]; [Pausanias II 8.5; III 10.5; VII 7.3; VIII 8.11, 10.5–8, 27.13–14, 36.6 confuses Archidamos and Agis (1) IV and perhaps other kings].

Acrotatos (265–262)—Athenaeus IV 142ʙ; Parthenius 23; Plutarch *Agis* 3.7, *Pyrrhus* 26.18, 28.4–7, *Moralia* (*apophthegmata Laconica*) 240ᴇꜰ}; Pausanias III 6.6; {VIII 27.11–13, VIII 30.7}; SIG³ 430.

Eudamidas II (275–?)—Plutarch *Agis* 3.3; {Pausanias II 8.5; III 10.5; VI 2.4; VII 7.3; VIII 8.11, 10.8, 27.13 confuses Eudamidas I and II, Archidamos IV and Agis IV}.

Areus II (262–254)—SIG³ 430; Pausanias III 6.6; Plutarch *Agis* 3.7–8; [*Pyrrhus* 26.17–18].

31. The Gentle Reformer

Agis IV (244–241)—Plutarch *Agis* passim, *Cleomenes* 1–3, *Agesilaus* 40.5; *comparatio Agis Cleomenes Ti. Gracchus C. Gracchus*, *Aratus* 31.1; *Moralia* (*apophthegmata Laconica*) 216ᴅ; *Lamprias catalogue* Number 9; Cicero *de officiis* II 80; Pausanias II 8.5; III 10.5; VI 2.4; VII 7.3; VIII 8.11, 10.5–8, 27.13–14, 36.6 (Pausanias confuses Agis IV and Archidamos IV); *Prometheus* VII 1981, pp. 35–42: Agis became king as a child with Agesilaos as his regent.

Leonidas II (254–243)–Plutarch *Agis* passim; *Cleomenes* 1.1–3, 3.1; Pausanias II 9.1, 5; III 6–8, 10.7; VII 7.3; VIII 27.15; Polybius IV 35.11; [Teles, *reliquiae*, ed. O. Hense, Hildesheim, 1909, page 28]; Th. Lenschau, "Leonidas (3)," RE, XXIV Halbband 2018–19.

Cleombrotos II (243–241)—Plutarch *Agis* 11.7–9, 16.6–18.4; Pausanias III 6.7–8; Polybius IV 35.10–12; Strabo VIII 337; Gerth, "Kleombrotos (4)," RE XXI 679.

32. The Revolutionary

"Eudamidas III" (241–228?)—Pausanias II 9.1, III 10.5 (Pausanias may have derived this name from a confusion with Eudamidas II, in which case the name of the son of Agis IV would not be known); {Plutarch *Cleomenes* 1.1}; B. Niese, "Eurydamidas," RE, XI Halbband (Stuttgart, 1907), 1322.

Archidamos V (228–227)—Polybius IV 35.13; V 37.1–5; VIII 35.3–5; Plutarch *Cleomenes* 1.1; 5.2–4; *comparatio Agis Cleomenes Ti. Gracchus C. Gracchus* 5.2.

Eucleidas 227–222—Plutarch *Cleomenes* 11.5, 28.3–8, *Philopoemen* 6.5, *comparatio Agis Cleomenes Ti. Gracchus C. Gracchus* 5.2; Polybius II 65.9, 68.3; [IG V 1. 458]; Pausanias II 9.1, 3 (Epikleidas); RE XI Eukleidas (19) 999.

Cleomenes III (235–219)—Plutarch *Cleomenes*; *Agis* 2.10; *comparatio Agis Cleomenes Ti. Gracchus C. Gracchus*; *Philopoemen* 5–6; *Aratus* 35–46; *Moralia* (*quomodo adulator ab amico internoscatur*) 53ᴇ, (*de solertia animalium*) 961ʙ; Polybius I 13.5; II 45–71; III 16.3, 32.3; IV 1.8, 5.5, 6.5, 7.7, 9.4, 35.6–9, 37.6, 60.2, 65.5, 76.7, 81.2 & 14; V

9.8, 24.8, 34–39, 93.2; VIII 35.3; IX 18.1, 23.3, 29.8–10; XV 25.2; XVIII 53.1; XX
5.12, 6.8; XXXIX 8.5; Macrobius *Saturnalia* I 11.34; Pompeius Trogus *prologi* 28;
Justin XXVIII 4.7; XXIX 1.6; Livy XXXIV 26.14, 28.1; XL 54.4; Athenaeus IV B–F;
Pausanias II 9.1–3; III 6.9, 7.1, 10.7; IV 29.7, 9, 10; VII 7.3, 4; VIII 8.11, 27.15, 16,
28.7, 49.4–6; *Lamprias Catalogue* number 9; [*Olympia* 309]; [IG V 1. 458(?)]; Por-
phyrius *de abstinentia* (Nauck 213, 23ff) III 21; [Synesius *peri basileias* 28]; Themistius *orationes* VIII 115B; Cicero *de natura deorum* (Ax 146,5) III 65; Grunauer, pp.
113–116 (Gr. III–VII, Tafeln 1–4: portrait of the king); Th. Lenschau, "Kleomenes
(6)," RE, XXI 702–10; F. W. Walbank, *A Historical Commentary on Polybius*, I
(Oxford, 1970 <1957>), 272 on Polybius II 65.

34. The Last Kings of Sparta

Lycurgos (219–211)—Polybius IV 2.9, 35.13–37.7, 60.3, 81; V 5.1, 4, 17–23, 29.8, 91–
    92; Justin XXIX 1.6; Livy XXXIV 26.14; Diodorus 27 fragment 1; U. Kahrstedt,
    "Lykurgos (8)," PW XXVI 2445–46.
Agesipolis III (219–215)—Polybius IV 35.10–12; XXIII 6.1–2; Livy XXXIV 26.14.
Machanidas—Livy XXVII 29.9; XXVIII 5.5, 7.14 & 17, 8.3; [XXXIV 26.14; XXXVIII
    34.8]; Polybius X 41.2; XI 11–18; XIII 6.1; Plutarch *Philopoemen* 10, 12.4; Pausanias
    IV 29.10; VIII 50.2; IG V 1. 236 (dedication); SEG XI 492 ([gymnasium] named after
    him); V. Ehrenberg, "Machanidas," RE, XXVII 142.
Pelops (211–205)—Diodorus Siculus XXVII 1.1; Livy XXXIV 32.1.

PART EIGHT: THE ROMAN WAR

35. The Tyrant Who Was a King

Interview between Nabis and Quinctius—Livy XXXIV 31–32.
Nabis (205–192)—Appian *Macedonica* Fragment 7; Zonaras (Cassius Dio XVIII) 9.16,
    (Cassius Dio XIX) 9.18, 19; Polybius IV 81.13; XIII 6, 7, 8; XVI 13.1–3, 16–17, 37;
    XVIII 17.1; XXI 3.4, 9.1, 11.10; [XXIII 5.2]; XXXIII 16.6; fragment 128; *de viris
    illustribus* 51; Pausanias IV 29.10–11; VII 8.4–5, 9.2; VIII 50.5–10, 51.2; Livy XXIX
    12.14; XXXI 25.3–10; XXXII 19.6, 21.9–13, 38.2–4, 40.10; XXXIII 43.6, 44.7–45.4;
    XXXIV 22–52 passim; XXXV 12–35 (35.18–19) passim; XXXVII 25.6, 11, 12;
    XXXVIII 59.7; *periochae* XXXIV, XXXV; Justin XXX 4.5; XXXI 1.5, 3.1; Pompeius
    Trogus *prologi* XXXI; L. Annaeus Florus I 23.12; Diodorus Siculus XXVII 1; XXVIII
    13.1; Eutropius IV 2.3; Plutarch *Flamininus* 13.1, *Philopoemen* 12.4–15.6, *comparatio
    Flamininus Philopoemen* 3.2; *Moralia* (*praecepta gerendae reipublicae*) 809E, 817E;
    Aelian *de natura animalium* 5.15; *Suidas* s. v. Nabis; IG IV 497; V 1. 885 (Bailei
    Nabi); XI 4. 716 (= Durrbach, Délos I 58); SIG³ 595, 605 (= *Die Inschriften von Perga-
    mum* {in *Altertümer von Pergamon* VIII}, ed. M. Fraenkel, Berlin, 1890–95, Numbers
    60–63); Grunauer, Gruppe VIII 24–XII (IX 4–5, Tafel 6 #17: NABIOS BAILEOS),
    Tafeln 6–7; V. Ehrenberg, "Nabis (1)," RE, XXXII Halbband (Stuttgart 1935), 1471–82.
Laconicus (192–?)—Livy XXXV 36.8.

36. Sparta under the Romans

"Laconians drawn up by their own kings."—Appian *Civil Wars* II 70.
Apollonius of Tyana was a philosopher—Apollonius *Letters* LXII–LXIV.
"Even today."—Cicero *Tusculanean Disputations* II 14.34.
"We ourselves in Sparta."—Cicero *Tusculanean Disputations* V 27 (Lucian *Anacharsis* 38).

CONCLUSION

Burial customs—Herodotus VI 58–59.

"Courage is the greatest power."—Homer *Iliad* IX 39.

Bibliography

MAJOR ANCIENT AUTHORS

Herodotus.
Pausanias. *The Description of Greece*, Book III: *Laconia* and Book IV: *Messenia*.
Plutarch. *Lives*: "Agesilaus," "Lycurgus," "Lysander," "Agis and Cleomenes."
Plutarch. *Moralia Apophthegmata Laconica* ("Sayings of Spartans").
Plutarch. *On Sparta*, Richard J. A. Talbert, (Ed.) Rev. Ed. New York, 2005.
Polybius.
Thucydides.
Xenophon. *Hellenica, Agesilaus Constitution of the Lacedaemonians*.

MAJOR SECONDARY SOURCES

Africa, Thomas W. *Phylarchus and the Spartan Revolution*. Berkeley, 1961.
Badian, E. *From Plataea to Potidaea: Studies in the History and Historiography of the Pentecontaetia*. Baltimore, 1993.
Bommelaer, J. F. *Lysandre de Sparte. Histoire et Traditions*. Paris, 1981.
Bradford, Alfred S. *A. Prosopography of Lacedaemonians from the Death of Alexander the Great, 323 B.C. to the Sack of Sparta by Alaric, A.D. 396, Vestigia*. Munich, 1977.
Cartledge, Paul. *Spartan Reflections*. Berkeley, 2003.
Cartledge, Paul. *Thermopylae: The Battle that Changed the World*. Woodstock, 2006.
Cartledge, Paul, and Spawforth, Antony. *Hellenistic and Roman Sparta*, 2nd ed. London, 2002.
Cartledge, Paul. *Sparta and Lakonia. A Regional History 1300–362 B.C.*, 2nd ed. London/New York, 2002.
Cartledge, Paul. *Agesilaos and the Crisis of Sparta*. Baltimore, 1987.
Cavanagh, W. C., and Walker, S. E. C. (eds.). *Sparta in Laconia*. Proceedings of the 19th British Museum Classical Colloquium, London 1993 [British School at Athens, Studies, 4].

Cavanagh, W. G., Crouwel, J., and Catling, R. W. V. (eds.). *Continuity and Change in a Greek Rural Landscape: The Laconia Survey: Continuity and Change in a Greek Rural Landscape*, Vol. I: Methodology and Interpretation 2002 [British School at Athens: Supplementary Volume 26].

Cavanagh, W. G., Crouwel, J., and Catling, R. W. V. (eds.). *The Laconia Survey: Continuity and Change in a Greek Rural Landscape*, Vol. II: Archaeological Data 1996 [British School at Athens: Supplementary Volume 27].

Chrimes, K. T. *Ancient Sparta*. Manchester, 1949.

Chrimes, K. T. *The Respublica Lacedaimoniorum ascribed to Xenophon*. Manchester, 1948.

Dawkins, R. M., et al. *The Sanctuary of Artemis Orthia at Sparta*. London, 1929.

Den Boer, W. *Laconian Studies*. Amsterdam 1954.

Devoto, John G. *Agesilaos II and the Politics of Sparta: 404–377 B.C.* 1982.

Ducat, Jean. *Spartan Education. Youth and Society in the Classical Period*. Swansea, 2006.

Figueira, Thomas J. (ed.). *Spartan Society*. Swansea, 2004.

Fitzhardinge, L. F. *The Spartans*. New York, 1980.

Forrest, W. George. *A History of Sparta*, 2nd ed. New York, 1968.

Förtsch, Reinhard. *Kunstverwendung und Kunstlegitimation im archaischen und frühklassischen Sparta*. Mainz, 2001.

Hamilton, Charles D. *Sparta's Bitter Victories*. Ithaca, 1979.

Hamilton, Charles D. *Agesilaus and the Failure of Spartan Hegemony*. Ithaca, 1991.

Hooker, J. T. *The Ancient Spartans*. London, 1980.

Huxley, G. L. *Early Sparta*. Cambridge, MA, 1962.

Jones, A. H. M. *Sparta*. Oxford, 1967.

Kagan, Donald. *The Archidamian War*. Ithaca, 1974.

Kagan, Donald. *The Peace of Nicias and the Sicilian Expedition*. Ithaca, 1981.

Kennell, Nigel M. *Spartans: A New History*. West Sussex, UK, 2010.

Kiechle, F. *Lakonien und Sparta*. München, 1963 [Vestigia, 5].

Kourinou, Eleni. *Sparti*. Athens, 2000.

Lazenby, J. F. *The Spartan Army*. Warminster, 1985.

Lewis, D. M. *Sparta and Persia*. Leiden, 1977.

Link, St. *Das frühe Sparta. Untersuchungen zur spartanischen Staatsbildung im 7. und 6. Jahrhundert v. Chr.* St. Katherinen 2000.

Malkin, Irad. *Territory in the Spartan Mediterranean*. Cambridge, 1994.

Meier, M. *Aristokraten und Damoden. Untersuchungen zur inneren Entwicklung Spartas im 7. Jahrhundert v. Chr. und zur politischen Funktion der Dichtung des Tyrtaios*. Stuttgart, 1998.

Michell, H. *Sparta*. Cambridge, 1964.

Ogden, Daniel. *Aristomenes of Messene. Legends of Sparta's Nemesis*. Swansea, 2004.

Oliva, Pavel. *Sparta and Her Social Problems*. Amsterdam, 1971.

Ollier, F. *Le mirage spartiate*. 2 vols. Paris 1933, 1943; reprint 1973.

Petterson, M. *Cults of Apollo at Sparta: The Hyakinthia, the Gymnopaidiai, and the Karneia. Skrifter utgivna av Svenska Institutet i Athen*, 12. Stockholm, 1992.

Piper, Linda J. *Spartan Twilight*. New Rochelle, 1986.

Pomeroy, Sarah B. *Spartan Women*. New York, 2002.

Poralla, Paul. *Prosopographie der Lakedaimonier* 1913, 2nd ed. by A. S. Bradford. Chicago, 1985.

Powell, Anton. *Athens and Sparta: Constructing Greek Political and Social History from 478 B.C.*, 2nd ed. London, 2001.

Powell, Anton. *Classical Sparta*. Oklahoma, 1989.

Powell, Anton, and Stephen Hodkinson. *Sparta beyond the Mirage*. London, 2002.

Shimron, B. *Late Sparta: The Spartan Revolution 243–146 BC*. Buffalo, 1972.

Sommer, Stefan. *Das Ephorat*. St. Katharinen, 2001.

Steinhauer, George. *Museum of Sparta*. Athens, 1976.

Stibbe, Conrad M. *Das andere Sparta* (tr. Herbert Post). Mainz, 1996.

Thommen, Lukas. *Lakedaimonion Politeia. Die Entstehung der spartanischen Verfassung*. Stuttgart, 1996.

Tigerstedt, E. N. *The Legend of Sparta in Classical Antiquity*. 3 vols. Stockholm -Göteborg-Uppsala, 1965, 1974, 1978.

Toynbee, Arnold J. *Some Problems in Greek History*. Oxford, 1969.

Whitby, Michael (ed.). *Sparta*. London, 2001.

Index

About the Author

ALFRED S. BRADFORD holds the John Saxon Chair of Ancient History at the University of Oklahoma. He earned his PhD in Classical Languages and Literature from the University of Chicago. He served with the 1/27th Infantry in Vietnam. He has been a research assistant and a member at the Institute for Advanced Study, Princeton. His books include *Flying the Black Flag: A Brief History of Piracy* (Praeger, 2007) and *Philip II of Macedon: A Life from the Ancient Sources* (Praeger, 1992).